FROM THE GROUND UP

Building and Selling the American Dream

Tony Craver

ISBN: 1466424249
ISBN-13: 9781466424241

TABLE OF CONTENTS

DEDICATION

This book is about my job and my career and the people whose paths I crossed during the journey. The book is dedicated, however, to my family.

To Mom and Dad for the way they got me started.

To my wife Cathy for sticking with me through thick and thin and for not only being a loving wife, but my best friend as well.

To my four children and their spouses, of whom I could not be more proud: my daughter Carrie Evans and her husband Rick; my daughter Ginny Nagy and her husband Steve; my daughter Amy Mofield and her husband Mark; and my son Jeff Craver and his wife Kirsten.

Finally, to our ten grandchildren, the fruits of our labor and with whom the hopes of the future reside.

INTRODUCTION

My Dad wanted me to be a Realtor™ and a builder. My Grandfather wanted my Dad to be a builder. I told my son he needed to go to law school. Three generations of living off of the ups and downs and the ins and outs of the housing business was enough for any family. But it was not without its rewards. For years, many folks, and especially my family, have been urging me to write down the stories and experiences that have accompanied this journey through life in the building and real estate business.

This book is more than just a collection of funny stories. It is also meant to be a resource of helpful hints to home buyers and sellers. Hopefully it can be used as a guide through the home building process as well. And, if you already have a home, maybe you will learn a little more about it and how to take care of it. But more than that, it is the story of "The American Dream" as it has occurred for generations of Americans wanting to own their own homes in small and mid-sized towns and cities throughout our country. Urban living is something I do not proclaim to know much about. These stories took place in suburban, rural and small town North Carolina, mostly in and around Lexington, Winston-Salem, Greensboro and Durham. Even though building techniques vary in different parts of the country, the people and their stories are universal.

This is also a book about people. I currently live in an area of the country that uses the number of degrees you have as a measure of who you are. What I have learned through the years is that the amount of education you have simply helps you get to where you want to go. Who you are is a measure of your character. In this book you will meet some extraordinary people who never made it past the tenth grade, but their intelligence, wisdom and strength of character are unsurpassed.

As far as the stories in this book are concerned, they are all true. I could not possibly make up some of this stuff. My wife claims I embellish the stories somewhat, but I am firmly convinced that the way I tell them is the way they happened. The names in the book will sometimes be fictitious. I would never want to embarrass anyone. Most of the times just a first name will do, and you will just have to wonder if that was the correct name or not. Other times you may wonder what a particular story has to do with housing. If I tend to stray off the subject at times, it may be more for the purpose of entertaining you than instructing you. I am convinced that when you spend your whole life in the building and real estate business, so does your family, and so do you during most of your non-working hours. In other words, most things in life are connected in some way or another.

The most important thing in my life is family. You will meet most of them somewhere in the book. I had a very happy childhood. Mom and Dad were great parents. Mom died at age 49 and never met my two youngest children. Her Mom also had died at age 49, and I only have one memory of her since I was just two years old at the time of her death. Mom's father was perhaps the most brilliant man I ever met and was known for his writing ability. I wish more of his attributes had rubbed off on me. Dad's side of the family was known more for their ability to work hard and apply their considerable intellect. I have one wonderful sister who is a whopping thirteen months older than I, and we remain close to this day.

I met my wife nearly half a century ago while we were both undergraduates at Duke University in Durham, North Carolina. We married after graduation and a couple of years later started a family that grew to consist of three girls and a boy. They must have had a happy childhood also because they are all happily married and have blessed us with 10 grandchildren.

Having had a 45-year career in building and real estate I am convinced that owning a home is truly an exceptional part of being an American. People work hard to provide for their families and in doing so provide stability to communities. At its boom, over 60% of Americans participated in the dream of home ownership. It seems, however, that the younger generations coming along now post-9/11 are not fully schooled on the importance of owning their own homes. They do not realize that one-third of our entire economy is driven by the housing industry. Accomplishing that "American Dream" of owning a home also fuels America's dream for a prosperous future, building opportunity for the next generation to participate and flourish.

≋ 1 ≋

FROM THE GROUND UP

Santa Claus never missed a Christmas at our house when I was a boy. The most anticipated special gift each year, however, was the gift from Mom and Dad. For my sister it always had something to do with dolls or clothes. For me, it was usually some kind of building set. I remember one year Dad was not around much for several weeks before Christmas. It turns out that he was over at "the shop" every night working on a hand-made set of "Lincoln Logs". About twenty years later I actually gained a true appreciation for the effort and the high degree of workmanship that he put into those logs. The presentation of these mom and dad gifts on Christmas morning was always something special. This year he had built a model of "the shop" as we referred to it, complete with a sign on top.

That Christmas morning Dad's Lincoln Log version of the shop had a full-length front porch, log walls and a sloped roof even though the real shop was a rectangular brick building with a flat roof and no porch. Since I was only six years old, I was not so much concerned with the exact details as I was with the sign on top that matched the real one on the building. One of the most important things about Christmas in North Carolina is that you can never predict the weather. The year I got my sled it was 75 degrees and the year I got my bike it snowed six inches. The year I got my custom made Lincoln Logs was the biggest snowfall of all. My Mom told me years later that, since our house was on a steep hill that tended to get too icy for driving in snowy weather, Dad had had to walk nearly a mile to the office that Christmas Eve and carry the building set back home in the snow.

"The shop" was my Dad's lumber yard and construction company office. It was a rather plain looking brick building which housed offices and a display and sales area. The displays were there for customers to select their cabinet styles, hardware, paint colors, and other items for a house "under construction". Dad's office was in the building along with the files and financial records maintained by the business manager, Max, a cordial, talented and loyal friend and employee. In the back of the shop was a large millwork area reigned over by the shop foreman who built cabinets and prefabricated walls, stored lumber and fine grade woods and all of the equipment necessary to build a home designed uniquely for each customer.

The huge woodworking shop was my favorite place in the whole world both as a kid and as an adult. Attached to the back of the shop was a series of lumber storage warehouses and bins, which, to a small boy, seemed to go on forever. Around every corner was always something that I had never seen before. I loved to climb the rickety, narrow stairs to the molding bins. The endless variety of moldings in various types of woods were neatly organized and ready to be loaded on to a truck for delivery to the job site. There were funny shaped pieces of wood and metal as well. I knew I would someday learn their usefulness. The shop was always dusty and dirty, which was a comfort to a small boy. There was little chance I could mess things up. Despite all of the dangerous equipment, I felt safe in the shop.

When it was cold outside there was an old pot-bellied stove that we would fire up. There was never a shortage of wood scraps, and, if there were not any scraps, we would just make some from leftover lumber. The crew would sit around the stove during breaks and at lunch, warm their hands and tell stories. Some were even true! In the summer time it could be unbearably hot in there, but there was a four-foot diameter home-made fan that always seemed to take your mind off of the heat. Besides, making things with wood was too much fun to worry about the weather

My Grandfather, who was also in the concrete block business, had built the shop and the warehouses during his days as a builder and his block plant, with a storage yard, was adjacent to the shop. He had produced the first concrete blocks made in our county, forming them by hand by pouring the mixture of sand, cement, water, and a binder into wooden moulds. He used handmade mallets to pack the mixture tightly around the round plugs inserted into the mould. Once the mixture set up and the plugs were pulled out, they created holes in the block. After letting the blocks set over night, the sides of the wooden moulds were knocked off with the mallets and the "green" block, still sitting on the wood bottom of the mould, was carefully placed on a rack and rolled out into the sunlight for drying. Sometimes it rained or it was cold and the drying process lasted longer. It took a lot of moulds and a lot of time to make blocks by hand. To this day it still amazes me that anything ever got built.

My Grandfather was a powerfully built man with broad shoulders who stood about six feet tall—a big man for his generation. I am built just like him except that he got the long legs. He believed in hard work and in working long hours. He loaded and unloaded many truckloads of blocks in his day by hand. If you are wondering why they made the holes in the blocks, it was simply to make them lighter. It also made picking up a concrete block much easier because you had a way to grip it. I learned this the hard way. During my first summer that I was old enough to work on the job, I got to unload an entire truck full of blocks by hand. When my uncle took over the block plant the next summer after my grandfather had died, the block plant bought its first boom truck. Watching the boom operator unload a truckload of blocks was one on my fondest early memories.

Over the years, as I talked to guys who had worked with my grandfather, I learned that he was both highly respected and, in some cases, highly feared for his toughness. However, he seemed to have a special place in his heart for the grandchildren. Whenever we went to visit, he was always sitting in the same chair in the corner of his den next to a big console radio. He always wanted me to sit on his lap for a few minutes. I think his most tender moments were the ones when I was sitting on his lap. He died when I was in high school but his legacy of hard work and production lives on in me.

⚙

When I was in elementary school, there was a nightly ritual in our house. Sis would give Mom and Dad a good night hug and kiss and then it was my turn. Before the sweet stuff however, Dad expected me to name the parts of a house, starting from the ground up with the footings. I worked my way through the foundation, the floor joist, the sub floor, the wall studs, the ceiling joist and rafters. Naming the ridge of the roof always brought a big smile to my face and an opportunity to go to bed.

Child labor laws prevented me from working on the construction sites until I was eighteen years of age. It did not stop me from working. My Dad was a designer. He designed everything he ever built. This meant a lot of evenings at home on the drawing board. In those days there were no computer aided design technologies, only drafting boards, pencils, compasses and templates. When I turned thirteen he decided it was time for me to begin to help with the plans, so he let me learn how to cross-hatch. Cross-hatching was an art form, I thought, until I realized it was the part of plan drawing that he least liked to do. When you want to draw a wall section, you do it by drawing two parallel lines representing the wall. If it is an exterior brick wall, you draw a third parallel line to represent the brick. All of this is done to a scale of one-quarter inch equals one foot. In other words these three lines were less than an inch apart. The symbol that distinguished the brick part of the wall from the wood part of the wall was the cross-hatch—a series of 45-degree angled lines approximately one quarter inch apart all the way around the outside of the house plan. I cannot remember whether the thrill of drawing these lines left before or after the boredom set in.

I remained the family cross-hatcher for at least a year before I graduated to closets. This was a bold step on my Dad's part. He designed the closets using a light touch so that the pencil lines were easy to erase if the client made changes. With my new responsibility, I could now darken in the pencil lines for the closets. Gradually I took on more of the standard parts of the design process. Meanwhile, I learned to be good with an eraser. Actually there was a neat toy called an erasing shield which I thought was a lot of fun to use. The erasing shield was a paper thin piece of metal with all sorts of cutouts in it so you could erase exactly what you thought should disappear. By the time I was a senior in high school Dad would lay out the design and overall size of the proposed house, and I would do the rest. He would take all of the credit for the plan, of course. I realized how much I enjoyed plan work when I found myself designing my own house plans just for fun. Plan drawing was not a job restricted to summer but was a year round job, because in North Carolina, weather does not limit the building process in the winter except in rare years. Since my sister and I were tennis players as teenagers, the summers were filled with traveling to tennis tournaments all over North and South Carolina. I quickly figured out that the more tournaments I entered the less time I had to draw plans in the summer. I guess my type A personality had not yet set in.

⚊⚊⚊⚊

Another part-time job I had during this period was to hold the dumb end of the tape. My Dad did appraisals for all kinds of folks in our area. In those days you did not have to be a licensed appraiser, even though he certainly would have qualified since he was a General Contractor and real estate expert. Today appraisers not only have to be licensed and be members of appraisal associations, they are strictly dictated to by the federal government as to the entire process, and most importantly, what can be used as comparable properties. More on this later. Dad used to say that when folks called him for an appraisal, the first thing he would ask was "is it for a divorce, a sale, or an estate?" You don't ask those questions today. Anyway, he did a lot of appraisals and a big part of each one was measuring the house.

Measuring is so much easier when you have someone to hold the dumb end of the tape. That was me. The dumb end of the tape is the one that starts with zero, and the other end requires you to read the actual distance in numbers. The holder of the dumb end was also the one that always got to dig their way behind the largest and thorniest bushes. Dad's first comment to me each time was to "pull it tight". To prove a point he would always give the tape enough of a jerk to make me drop the dumb end. This got old after a while. Finally we showed up at a house to be measured one Saturday afternoon, and he said, to my surprise, "I'll hold the dumb end". The temptation was more than I could stand. I jerked the tape just enough to make him drop it. I got one of those looks that silently said "cute, but don't ever do that again".

Along came my eighteenth birthday and the time was right to begin working on the job. The first summer I was a "go-for". If you are not familiar with the term, feel blessed. I was the person they would call and say "go for this or go for that". Have you ever been on a snipe hunt? If not, ask an old-timer to tell you all about snipe hunting. It did not take long to find out that construction crews had similar rituals. The guys on the job wanted to test my personality early. Actually it would be more accurate to say that they wanted to test my stupidity or ability to be gullible. One of our foremen, Terry, sent me back to the shop to fetch, as he put it, a left handed T-astragal. The guys at the shop were willing participants in this rite of initiation and provided me with what they called a left-handed T-astragal. When I got back to the job site, Terry informed me that I had brought him a right-handed T-astragal and promptly sent me back to the shop. This time, Max, the office manager, must have taken pity on me and informed me that there was no such thing as a right-handed or left-handed T-astragal. By the way, a T-astragal is a "T" shaped piece of wood the height of a door. It is used when you hang a pair of doors together by attaching the "T" to the end of one of the doors, thus forming a place for the other door to come to rest when they were closed and ensuring that the doors were plumb and would close exactly as needed. On the way back to the job site I marked "left-handed" on the T-astragal and gave it to Terry. Twenty years later Terry with a serious smile was still asking me about that left-handed T-astragal. That experience allowed me to be less gullible when the guys asked me to bring them "lumber stretchers" or "sky hooks". I must admit that over the years I have asked many a rookie for the same materials and equipment.

≋ 2 ≋

DAD

Dad was an interesting combination of personalities. He was born in Davidson County and attended Davidson College. He was polished and poised, but he had a feisty side which most folks never saw. After all, he was a salesman at heart. He began his business career on the drawing table as a draftsman. Most people thought he was an architect. He never spent a lot of time discouraging that rumor, but he never claimed to be anything that he was not. He was not as large a man as my Grandfather, but he did play high school football on a championship team. I suspect he was underestimated by his opponents who quickly learned some valuable lessons. He came to my defense once in high school with such intense determination that from that point on, I always knew he had my back.

He took great pride in his ability to judge people—I do not mean to pass judgment, but to sum up a person's character and intentions. It worked most of the time. But there was one time…..Max, who spent his entire career as Dad's office manager, tells a story that happened when I was a kid. It seems that three working class gentlemen, dressed for work in their bib overalls and covered with coal dust, came into the office late one afternoon. Max's office was open to the display area and you had to pass through his space to get to Dad's office. Dad's door was always open, unless he was in a private meeting, because he liked to keep up with whatever was going on in the outer office. Besides designing and building custom homes and developing subdivisions, my Dad designed and built fifty-five churches during his career, and these gentlemen were there on behalf of their congregation.

Dad's desk was placed in the back corner of his office at a 45-degree angle. His files were in cabinets and on shelves which were on both walls behind his desk. The old wooden swivel rocker that he used as a desk chair was often facing away from the door as it was on this occasion. Dad had glanced over his shoulder to make a quick assessment of his soon to be visitors just before they told Max that they wanted to speak to Mr. Craver. Max showed them into the office. Dad greeted them and asked what they wanted, but he kept right on working with his files. They said that they apologized for coming to see him straight from work but they were the building committee from their church, and they wanted to build a new sanctuary. That still was not enough information to make Dad stop facing his files. He asked what size church building they needed. After hearing the dimensions and doing a little math in his head, he said to the group that the building they described would probably cost around $100,000. In those days that was a lot of money. They responded by saying that was the figure they had guessed and that they had already raised $87,000 of it. Max said the next thing he heard was the 180-degree squeak from Dad's chair as he turned to face them. Appearances can occasionally be deceiving! He built them a church.

⊸⊸⊸⊷⊷⊷

He started from scratch, but he would have said it was because he had an itch. Dad was the master of the one line pun. He did have an itch to succeed. Up until the third grade we lived in a two bedroom duplex. He built the duplex before he got married and a nice older couple rented the other side. He decided one day that Sis and I would be better off at the other end of the structure, so we took over both sides of the duplex. This was my first taste of actually seeing construction first-hand. I was fascinated with the entire process. Before I entered Junior High, he had added a big family room off the back. This was a room that became a gathering place for all of our friends.

As his success gathered steam, Dad had visions of carrying out one of his most vivid dreams: to own a Cadillac. For a generation that grew up in the Depression, just owning a car was a big goal, but a Cadillac was the ultimate goal. I will never forget Mom and Dad putting Sis and me into the back seat of the old Chevy and driving 100 miles to Raleigh so Dad could buy his first Cadillac from an old friend. I am sure a discount was involved! With some gas in the tank we headed for home. In those days this type of adventure was an all day trip on two-lane roads. As we pulled into town 100 miles west of Raleigh the gas gauge was on empty. There was an underground gasoline tank at the shop for company trucks, and Dad was determined to make it to that haven.

Before I continue, you need to understand that all folks have competitors and rivals. Dad was no exception and his rival had a much bigger company and had owned a Cadillac for quite a long time. We were cruising through downtown on fumes when the engine finally ran out of gas one block past the square at the center of town. Dad was taking this little setback pretty well until the first person to pull along side of the car was, you guessed it, his arch rival. "What's wrong Leonard? Did you spend all of your money on the car?" was the comment he made, and then drove off. I did not know that people could actually turn that shade of red.

⸻

Dad was a man of many platitudes. He would say things like "the customer is always right", even when they were wrong. Once I was in his employ, he would tell me that he did not mind my making mistakes, but just do not make the same mistake twice. He really meant that one, and sometimes it was difficult keeping up with which mistakes I could repeat and which ones I could not. He also had a few sayings around on the walls at the shop. One of my favorites was the one declaring that this was a non-profit business. The phrase went on to explain that it was not meant to be a non-profit business; it had just turned out that way. Unfortunately, it was, and still is, the nature of the building and real estate business that occasionally turned that saying into a reality.

One of the most valuable platitudes he often used was one he learned the hard way. After accomplishing the Cadillac goal, he moved on to bigger and better dreams. After all he was a house designer, so he was convinced that he could design the perfect house. Well, at least the perfect house for his family. For four or five years, he spent endless evening hours at the drafting table drawing his dream house. This dream house not only required saving the proper amount of money, but it meant finding the perfect piece of land. Being in the development business, as well as the building and real estate business, afforded him the inside scoop on the availability of potential tracts of land before the rest of the world knew they were for sale. He found a large tract adjacent to the fifteenth fairway at the local golf course. It was by far more land than he needed but developers do not think that way. The first thing you do is pick out the site you want and carve the rest of it into lots.

This reminds me of two of his favorite declarations. One was that you always wanted to build for, or sell houses to, your friends because your enemies were not going to buy from you. What he was trying to teach me was that a lot of folks think they should avoid dealing with their closest friends. Dad's philosophy was just the opposite. He did, however, always maintain that you should not build your neighbor's house because they would always know where to find you when things broke. This one fell into the category of do what I say and not what I do. Actually I think this platitude was trumped by the desire to hand pick his neighbors. Later on in life I disobeyed that platitude as well, and was glad I did.

The road was graded and the house was started. It was a beautiful house with many hand-crafted parts. He called in some old favors in order to get some special types of wood and some special craftsmen to install them. Dad and I were sitting on the front steps late one afternoon about a week before we were supposed to move in. I was fifteen at the time, but I will never forget the moment. He looked a little down just when I thought he should be extremely excited about finishing his decade-long dream. I asked what was wrong. He said if he had it to do over again, he would change everything. He realized that your wants and dreams change over time and that your thought process evolves. There is always an ever changing list of new products, methods and ideas.

Out of this experience came a realization that where housing is concerned, the most important thing is not **what** type or size house you enjoy, but **how** you enjoy it that matters. I remember an old friend asking me a few months after I moved out of the city into the countryside, how long it took me to get used to country living. My reply was "About twenty minutes." I have spent a lot of time over the years trying to convince my clients that it is easier for them to adapt to a house than to find what they think is the perfect house. Learning to adapt to new homes and circumstances over the years has partly come from the lessons learned on that front porch when I was fifteen.

———

When I was young we always went out for Sunday lunch after church. In those days Sunday lunch was called Sunday dinner even though it occurred at the noon hour. After lunch we usually dropped by my Mom's parents' house for a visit. I am enjoying writing this book so much because my Mom's dad, E. E. Witherspoon whom we called Granddaddy, was the editor of the local newspaper. I guess writing is in the DNA. In fact he was the editor of the same newspaper for 55 years, a North Carolina record. He had plenty of offers to go to bigger newspapers, but he loved staying exactly where he was. My Mom was the first female sports editor in the state. Even though I think Granddaddy got her the job, I am sure that she deserved it.

Dad was naturally never quite as excited to visit Mom's parents as he was his own, so he bought the property next door to their house and built three apartment buildings. Now when we went to visit on Sundays, he would go check out his apartments after the obligatory greetings. Mom grew up in a modest bungalow that backed up to one of the many ante-bellum style homes that graced a tree-lined Main Street. Mom had told a lot of stories about growing up behind the Hinkle house and how her favorite thing was sliding down their stairway banister rail in their large two-story foyer. Sometime during the years of designing his dream house Dad bought the old Hinkle house just to have that railing to put in his new home. This pleased my Mom so very much.

Dad did not like the balusters or "pickets", as they are sometimes called, that supported the hand rail so he decided to make his own. We had a workshop upstairs in the old converted duplex. Dad designed the baluster he wanted to use and started to turn each one by hand on his turning lathe. This takes a lot of skill, patience and, above all, time. He had no idea how much time it was going to take. That is another thing he later said he would do differently. I also learned some new words for my future adult vocabulary during that period.

Dad was a sports fan but golf was not one of his favorites, even though he looked at a golf course every time he drove out of the driveway. He honestly believed that every golf course he ever saw could have been put to better use as a subdivision full of houses. I mention this because I will not be able to help myself later in the book. I will tell you some family golf stories. When you are in the building and real estate business and you finally find some time to sneak off and play golf, you tell your clients that you have to go out and walk some real estate. This is not lying, is it?

❦

In many ways Dad was a creature of habit. The first week of every June, we went to Cherry Grove Beach, just over the state line into South Carolina. It was just the four of us until Sis and I became teenagers; then we could each invite a friend. By the time we became seventeen that friend did not have to be of the same sex. Dad had a theory about courting. He said a week of close family quarters with a girlfriend would convince me to break up with her. He was right. He also said that the first girl I took to the beach twice would be the one I would marry. He was right there, too.

When I was eleven, I remember eating Sunday lunch at the hotel before heading home from the beach. Mom and Dad and Sis had roast beef and I had shrimp and French fries. The roast beef must have been bad because by the time we got home the three of them were violently ill. My sister, in particular, had a real close call and the family doctor told Dad that he needed to put her on an exercise program to build back her stamina. He suggested that he teach her how to play tennis. This became a life changing and life defining moment. Dad, being Dad, bought the land behind our renovated duplex and built a tennis court. Since I was just a year younger than my sister, I learned the game right along with her. In fact, the entire neighborhood learned to play tennis. By the time I graduated from high school, our high school team had a 33 match winning streak and a conference championship. Most of the players on the team had learned the game right in our back yard.

When we moved into Dad's dream house, he saw to it that we had a tennis court in that back yard too. I was always a little jealous of my sister's tennis career. We played each other all of the time. In fact, one Saturday morning we started playing and did not stop until we had played 17 sets. It makes me tired just thinking about it! I could beat Sis most of the time, but she ranked higher among the girls around the state than I did among the guys. I went on to play for Duke University but she won some state titles. Yes, I was a little jealous, but mostly I was proud of her. Dad had not been a tennis player when he started teaching the game to us, but he became a pretty fair player in his own right.

<hr />

It was his personality to look at a problem, figure out a solution, and charge straight ahead until it was solved. In the late sixties, a new plant was coming to town and Dad had secured a number of their executives as clients. Business was good. In fact it was so good that it was hard to tell some of the folks apart. I was spending a lot of hours on the drawing boards. Dad would meet with the new folks, make the deal, and hand me a light sketch of the plan. I would take that information and turn it into a set of blue prints ready to attach to a contract and set of specifications. A lot of this work was done at night because I was on the job sites during the day.

Our reputation had spread in a positive fashion among this company's execs and some of the deals were literally made over the phone. It was late on a Friday afternoon when a delightful gentleman bounced into the office, having just gotten into town from New Jersey. He asked to see Dad, and Max showed him in. He greeted Dad like a long lost brother and asked if the plans and specs were ready. Dad asked him to have a seat so he could check. He came out to Max's office and said to us "who is that?" Max and I did not recall ever having met the man before but we recognized the fact that he was ready to start building his house.

Dad went back into his office and told him that it would be Monday before everything was ready to sign. In the meantime he suggested that the two of them ride out to the lot and discuss the placement of the house. As they headed for the car I heard Dad ask the man if he remembered how to get to the lot, and he proudly blurted out the name of the subdivision and the lot number. It was a good thing he did because Dad did not have a clue where they were going. After an hour or so of wandering around the lot and the client answering several well-constructed questions, Dad had all of the information he needed to know. I worked all weekend on those plans and by Monday morning we were ready. I am still not completely sure whether it was a total lapse of memory on Dad's part or whether the client had just dreamed about the whole thing. He turned out to be one of our better customers. It is a good thing he never knew what really happened.

<hr/>

Dad had a special gift for looking at a piece of property and seeing the finished product in his mind. He often told me that very few customers had the ability to envision the finished product. With this ability buyers could have figured out the best place on the lot to put the house, which trees they wanted to save and which ones needed to go. Dad could visualize what height to set the house to maximize the amount of dirt available for grading the yard. I do not know if it is a genetic gift or just years of pounding the information against my thick skull, but I always seemed to have the same ability.

He and I went out one afternoon to locate a house on a lot. This was a ritual we did purely for the personal satisfaction of the client. We knew where we wanted to put the house, but we needed to make sure the client was happy with where he or she was going to be waking up for the next how-ever-many years. This particular day we were locating a house for an old high school pal of his. Our shop man had prepared several dozen wooden stakes we referred to as two by twos. They were actually an inch and one-half by an inch and one-half by four feet long. The same person who carried the dumb end of the tape also got to carry the two by twos at the same time. Dad told me to put one two by two where he thought the front corner should be. By the way, I also got to carry the ax for driving the stakes into the ground. Once we located that original stake, we calculated and located all of the other main corners. We had arrived at the lot an hour or so earlier than we were to meet the client so we could present the location of their new home to them upon their arrival. I was happy to be done a few minutes early when Dad told me to move all of the stakes ten feet toward the rear of the lot. That certainly seemed like a lot of useless work to me, but I did what I was told to do.

The client arrived and after the usual friendly greetings we guided him through the various corner locations. He and Dad stood at the front of the lot for a few minutes in deep thought–the kind of thought you can only achieve with your elbow bent so your hand is firmly placed on your chin. Finally the client turned to Dad and said, "Leonard it looks good but I think you should move it forward by ten feet." Dad said that we would do that, as the client turned and walked away. Dad winked at me and I went around and stuck the stakes back into the original holes. He told me later that he knew the client well enough to know that, wherever he put the house, he would want Dad to move it. All Dad had to do was to guess which way.

—◦◦◦—

Throughout my real estate career I have been to a number of personality training classes. The expert trainers usually divide folks into four different groups of personalities and proceed to refer to these groups as a "D" or an "I" personality and so on. I never knew what Dad named his various personality groups. I think he would have gotten a chuckle out of knowing that the exact same way he grouped people is how experts do it now. I wonder if he would also get a chuckle out of naming them with a single capital letter.

In his later years, his daily routine included his three great passions. He got up every morning and went to his home workshop until noon. His first cousin had been North Carolina's premier custom furniture maker, but Dad was pretty good in his own right. If he could not find a tool to do exactly what he wanted it to do, he would design a make-shift contraption to do the job. He hated to take the time to change drill bits so at one point in time he had seventeen drills lined up on a work-bench, each with a different drill bit in it. He had friends at the local furniture factories that would bring him discarded pieces of walnut, oak, mahogany and cherry. He stored them in what used to be our playroom in the basement. In his last years the entire lower level of his house was a maze of nice smelling exotic woods. He made a lot of fabulous pieces of furniture and miscellaneous things, but my favorite was the rocking horse. When I was small he had designed and built me a wooden rocking horse out of pine. It had a painted bridle and a bushy tail. In his later years he made rocking horses for his grandchildren out of mahogany. The grandchildren were too old to ride them by then but they were keepsake treasures. Before he died he cut out pieces for about thirty of the horses. Now, I have finished horses for my grandchildren and will pass on the remaining parts to the members of the next generation who are willing to do the work. I still burn his name on each one.

From noon until six in the evening he would be at his real estate office. From there he went to his dance studio and taught ballroom dancing. He had always been interested in ballroom dancing. I remember that Sis and I had to take lessons at an early age. It came in handy in college, but at the time I was not thrilled. It truly was a passion with him. He taught old folks, young folks, and middle-aged couples. He loved to go to the beach and shag. This really was a side of him I did not fully realize existed to the extent that it did. As a testimony to him, over 50 teenagers that he had taught at the local Cotillion came to his funeral.

≡ 3 ≡

LAYING THE FOUNDATION

My Dad always told me to be a builder for 20 years and then concentrate on real estate full time. I stayed in the building business for 28 years. He was right, of course. Just because you get out of building, you do not get building out of you. To me, relaxing is finding an excuse to lay a brick, putty some drywall, or build a cabinet. My kids are constantly calling me with questions about how to fix this or that. In some cases that evolves into my loading up the tools and going to their house for a day or two.

I really get tired when I think about it, but something made me volunteer to add a large addition onto the home of one of my daughters. This particular daughter married a young man who is a wonderful pastor, blessed with more good intentions than money, so they needed some extra help expanding their house. Besides, this son-in-law had missed the opportunity to work for me in the construction business during his college summers as my son and the other two sons-in-law had had the "good fortune" of doing. This addition presented itself with the opportunity for some on-the-job training. I made them this deal. I would draw the plans, figure the materials and do the work. Their part would be to pay for the materials, run the errands, provide me with lunch and soft drinks, and at least one of them had to match me hour for hour. We had a deal. At the time their boys were five and three and needed some more space. I designed a new family room and a walk in utility room as well as enlarging and re-arranging their master bath. This project was ambitious, but Mark and Amy were up to the task and supplied a lot of good labor.

The first rule of any construction project, I told Mark, was to learn about and to master cord management. This was a hard sell because it sounded ridiculous. By the end of the project Mark would be the first one to tell you that the first rule of any construction project is to learn about and to master cord management. Cords, by definition, also include compressor hoses, since automatic nail guns have become the order of the day. The first thing you do when you get to the job is unroll the electrical cords and compressor hoses and then you proceed to trip over them all day long. Murphy's Law says that wherever you need to be, the cord is always on the wrong side of you.

While I was in high school, Dad's crew was building a church with a three story base for the steeple spire. The third floor landing was about 10 feet by 10 feet and had a large arched opening on all four sides. Two of the crew members were installing oak flooring in this area and Slim, whom you will get to know well later in the book, was carrying the bundles of flooring up the winding staircase of the steeple tower. Slim always "toted", as he would put it, as much as he could possibly carry. This often meant that he could not see where he was going. Just as he crested the stairs, one of the crew hollered "watch out for the cor...." It was too late. Slim had just caught his foot on the electrical cord. As the two members of the crew leaned out of the arched opening, they watched Slim do a 360 in mid-air on the way to the ground. Have you ever thrown a cat out of a high window? The results were much the same. Slim landed on both feet and kept on walking.

When Amy and Mark first bought their house, my grandson Justin was just two years old. The house suited their small but growing family but it had a horrible squeak in the master bedroom floor. So, of course, I was summoned to fix it. I crawled under the house, which I will readily admit that I no longer like to do. Mark handed me tools and things through the crawl space door and Amy stayed in the bedroom to walk on the squeaky spot. I communicated with her through the heat duct in the floor. Justin spent his time in the bedroom with his

Mom observing the whole process. As it turned out, when the house was built, someone had failed to nail down the bottom plate under one of the bedroom walls. The result was that every time you stepped near that wall, the floor would move up and down under that wall, causing a lot of squeaks. From the bottom side I installed some long screws up through the flooring and into the bottom plate. That took care of the problem, but Amy said that for weeks, Justin would go into her bedroom and lean over to the heat duct and call for "Papa".

I donated almost every Saturday for about eight months to Amy and Mark's addition project and occasionally a weekday when I could get away. After we dug and poured the footings, my favorite part began. I love to lay brick. The foundation was about 12 feet by 25 feet and needed to be about 4 feet tall. Mark's job was to prepare the mortar mix and stack the bricks and blocks along both sides of the future foundation wall. Once the wall got above two feet high, it seemed like the bricks got further and further away. I convinced five year old Justin that he needed to help his Papa build the new room since he was going to be one of the prime beneficiaries of the project. Justin gladly agreed and took great pride in helping me by picking up the bricks one at a time so I would not have to lean over so far. Not only was it fun to work with Justin, but it really helped move the project along. After a couple of hours he would usually decide that he needed to go in and rest. About an hour into the fourth day of brick-laying, Justin looked up at me with a pair of very sincere eyes and said, "Papa, I don't know how you are going to get this room built with just one five-year-old helper."

———

Most residential houses are supported one of three ways. They either have a crawl space, a slab, or a basement. Not all stories about basements and crawl spaces are funny. While I was in college and doing my due diligence rotations in the summer with the different crews, I remember framing a floor system over a full basement. The politics of a crew went like this. The foreman worked out over the basement, making sure everything went according to the plans. The second in command, usually the carpenter with the most seniority, was the saw man. Being saw man was a big deal. If you were slow or made too many mistakes, the job would grind to a costly slow pace. Low man in the pecking order was the one who carried the various pieces of framing lumber from the saw man to the other carpenters on the crew who were actually nailing things together. I was working with the carpenters on this particular day, having already served time as the lumber distributor. I was assigned to the simple task of nailing four foot pieces of floor joist between two main support beams that ran down either side of the future hallway. After I marked the position and measured the length of three or four pieces at a time, I would yell the measurements to the saw man.

There was an inherent danger involved with the whole operation. We were all working over a basement. The ground was nine or ten feet below us. What made this so difficult was the fact that there was no floor on which to walk. The only way to get out to where I sat, straddling a beam, was to walk across the uncovered floor joist. This required paying attention. The guys had already told me that Pete, our lumber carrier, was the most accident-prone worker they knew. Most of the floor system was installed except for the four-foot section down the middle where I was working. I remember looking at Pete walking across the inch and a half wide floor joist with four newly sawn pieces in his arms. As I reached up to receive the first piece, Pete disappeared. He had walked right into the four foot wide opening and was lying flat on his back on the dirt floor of the basement, still holding the four pieces of lumber. He was out for a couple weeks.

It was not long after that incident that our insurance man came into the office and told us we had to let Pete go or they would cancel our worker's compensation insurance. Pete was costing them too much money. I am not sure that you can do that today. We had no choice then because you cannot do any work without insurance coverage. After he left us, Pete became a freelance handyman.

About six months later Pete was installing new insulation under an old house. A lot of houses that were built before the use of building codes had no standardized height rules for the crawl space. The house Pete was working under fit that description. The height of the crawl space was at its greatest where he entered and gradually diminished to just a few inches at the far end of the house. Pete worked his way under the house until he got stuck between the ground and the floor system. Unfortunately, he panicked, had a heart attack, and died. There have been a lot of changes in the building codes since then. Now there are minimum height requirements throughout the crawl space, minimum size requirements for crawl space door, and lots of drainage regulations. These changes are a result of such tragic incidents.

Slabs are a fairly simple and inexpensive way to support a house. In many large new neighborhoods, where developers tend to strip the land anyway, it is easier to grade many sites at once. After compacting the soil properly and setting the forms around the outside edges, you are ready to pour the floor. Before you pour the concrete, however, you must first install the plumbing and electrical piping. In a crawl space, these pipes can easily be installed later. The biggest drawback to pouring a slab is the problem you have if the pipes are in the wrong place. Digging them up is tough.

Another problem with slabs is that they are poured by concrete crews who are not nearly as precise as mason crews. I have seen a concrete crew foreman look at plans when a house is to be built on a slab and pour out handfuls of mortar mix to mark where the corners should be. That is getting it close but is not precise. The carpenter crew will build the outside walls to the edge of the slab and adjust the inside walls accordingly. So if you are trying to lay a do-it-yourself vinyl floor in a house built on a slab one weekend and cannot seem to find a wall that is square or perpendicular with another, now you know why.

When masons are laying the foundation for a crawl space, the accuracy burden falls to the crew who installed the batter boards. Batter boards are an accurate way of determining where to put the house. On a typical corner the crew would drive three 2 x 4 stakes into the ground in a position outside of the intended foundation wall. When this is done at all of the corners and offsets, the stakes are then all marked at the same level. The batter boards then are nailed to the stakes at that mark so they are all level with one another. Then strings are pulled across the batter boards indicating the exact location of the walls. When the mason crew arrives, they are going to lay the brick and block to the string. If the foundation is out of level or out of square, the mason crew will simply blame it on the batter board crew. You can imagine how complicated a set of batter boards can be when the house is large and has many angles and elevation changes. I have had mason crews lay the wall on the wrong side of the string. Suddenly, your family room just got bigger or smaller.

Basements could fill a book all by themselves. In the first half of the last century the term basement was generally used to describe what we would now call a cellar. A cellar was a hole in the ground just tall enough for you to stand up between the heating ducts. Its general purpose was to store things, especially things that liked a cool, damp environment, such as wine. There was not a premium on light nor was there an emphasis on a stairway that did not require a good grip or an occasional ducking of the head. In other words, these cellar-type basements were not candidates to be finished as a room for watching the Super Bowl. They were cool because they were not heated and damp because there was no real emphasis on waterproofing.

The quality of the modern basement is usually gauged on its ability to be finished into a usable, dry space. By the way, any time I use the term "modern", I am referring to the last 50 years. This requires sufficient height to finish an approximately eight-foot high ceiling that needs to fit comfortably under the plumbing pipes and the heat ducts. It also requires the area to be dry at all times so that you do not get your carpet ruined, or invite the dreaded "mold" word into your house every time it rains.

There are two types of usable basements. The first is the walkout type basement. This means that at least one portion of the basement floor is level with the outside grade of the yard. The real purpose here is to have a door through which you can walk out at ground level. Typically that door is located on the rear of the basement or on one end of the house. If the natural contour of the lot is not equal to the depth of the basement, then you have to rely on the bulldozer to do some extra grading. The customer simply wants to be able to walk out of the basement without going back up some steps to reach the yard. The real purpose of a walkout basement, however, is to have a natural gravity flow for the foundation to drain so that the basement will not flood.

To make a basement, first you have to dig a hole approximately three feet bigger in all directions than the exterior dimensions of the house. This extra space provides room in which the person or persons doing the waterproofing can operate. In our crew, that was Slim. Slim's first task would be to put a brick in his hand and rub the parging until it was smooth. When the mason crew finished laying the basement wall, they would plaster a layer of mortar mix on the outside of the wall. The height of this layer of mortar matched the proposed finished grade of the yard. This layer of mortar mix was called the parging, and its purpose was to provide a smooth surface for the waterproofing material. There were a number of different products on the market, but they were all basically liquid tar. Slim was a perfectionist when it came to waterproofing a basement. He always put two layers of tar on the walls and checked each layer carefully for bubbles between the coats. This took incredible strength because when I use the word liquid, I mean liquid in the same sense that molasses is liquid. Slim, who was an old-school Southern black man, used to brag that he was the only one on the crew who could get tar drops on him that were not visible to others.

The purpose of the tar was to create a barrier between the dirt on the outside, which got wet during a rain, and the block on the inside, which you wanted to stay dry. The water would reach the tar and slide down the outside of the wall, all the way to the bottom. The other equally important component to the waterproofing master plan was the drainage system that was designed to take the water away from the bottom of the wall. Slim would lay a four-inch plastic corrugated pipe around the entire bottom of the exterior basement wall, except for the part that was at ground level. This pipe has slits in the top side to allow the water to enter the pipe and find its way to the open end. On top of the pipe would be about two feet of washed stone acting as a filter to remove dirt from the water before it entered the pipe. The whole purpose of the system was to carry the water away. Slim would bury the pipe until it could surface somewhere in the yard, safely away from the house. This system when installed properly worked every time—almost.

In North Carolina about one-fourth of our average annual rainfall comes from the remnants of hurricanes or tropical depressions. They usually work their way inland from the coast or up from the Gulf of Mexico. I got a frantic call one morning from a couple saying that their furniture was floating across their basement floor. My life quickly flashed before my eyes because this man was a lawyer and building for lawyers always scared me a little anyway. After all, they did not have to hire anyone to sue you. It had rained all night to the tune of six or eight inches worth of water. After hanging up the phone, I called Max and told him to find Slim and send him to the lawyer's house immediately. When I got there the owner took me to the top of the basement stairs where I could see that they were not exaggerating. Toys, boxes, and pillows were floating by the bottom of the staircase. What made this scene worse was that this basement was finished in the same manner as the rest of the house.

When Slim arrived, the first thing I asked him was where the ends of the basement drain pipes were located. We did not keep a record of where every basement drainage pipe was located because we had Slim. He knew where each one was. It was still raining pretty hard but that did not matter. Out into the yard we went, shovels in hand. Slim went right to the location of the pipe but it was not there. Instead there was a nice mound with a big azalea planted on the top. I turned to the lady of the house and asked why she made the mound and planted the azalea. She replied that there was always a damp spot in the yard after a rain, so she thought it was the perfect place for the plant.

Part of our orientation lecture for new homeowners with a basement was to have them remember two essential things. First, never cover up the ends of the basement drain pipes, and second, never fill in dirt or mulch above the water proofing on the outside. I found over the years that new homeowners were usually so excited about moving in that they seldom paid much attention to the orientation lecture. Slim uncovered the ends of the pipe by digging up the azalea, and the water surged out like it was a fire hose. It ran at a full four-inch diameter stream of water for over an hour. It is hard to believe how much water pressure was involved. The water actually had gotten into the basement by forcing itself under the footings and seeping up between the concrete floor and the inside of the basement wall. This sounds impossible, but the pressure is that great. It was only a matter of time and rainfall before the water pressure would have literally lifted the house upward. The folks had lived there for several years when this happened, but I can guarantee that they have not covered up the pipes since.

⚒

Slim did make a mistake—once. He told us that he would stay late one Thursday to finish the waterproofing system on a house. He knew that we had the bulldozer scheduled for the next morning to backfill the job. Backfilling meant that the bulldozer would push fresh dirt into that three-foot wide space where Slim had worked so hard. The problem here was two-fold. Slim did not finish and the bulldozer arrived early. He started backfilling before Slim could arrive and finish the job. Slim had not laid the pipe nor had he put in the gravel. The gravel pile was behind the house and out of sight of the bulldozer operator, so he merrily continued working. When I arrived and spotted the gravel pile I knew we had a problem. Luckily this particular house was to have only the front yard filled in and the side yards were to be tapered down rapidly. Nonetheless, Slim dug out all of the newly filled dirt by hand. It took his entire weekend, but he was always careful to be sure that the gravel was spread before a bulldozer came again.

It is almost inevitable that when you fill dirt into a space three feet wide and ten feet deep, you will have some compaction take place. You always hope that this compaction, or settling, happens while you are finishing up the building process. Unfortunately, it can take a lot longer on some occasions. Sometimes the homeowner will ignore this settling. Every time it rains, water pools against the foundation, putting pressure on the drainage system. In other cases they will overfill the settled areas, packing dirt against a part of the exterior wall that has not been waterproofed. Brick is surprisingly porous and water will seep through the wall where there is no waterproofing, and create damp spots on the inside. These damps spots, unfortunately, usually do not show up until the holes inside the concrete block are full of water. The good news is that this is an easy fix. Simply lower the dirt on the outside. The most common abuse of the system is the over-ambitious family gardener. After a Saturday trip to the garden center, the homeowner will pile lots of mulch in flower beds next to the house. After all, mulch holds water and makes plants grow. Mulch also holds water and makes basements wet. Once again, this is an easy fix and can be accomplished by either lowering the mulch or raising the waterproofing line.

❦

The second type of usable basement is the one without a direct walkout at basement floor level. This type of basement requires a sump pump to carry the water up to ground level so it can then drain off naturally. Here is how that works. Since there is no natural downhill flow for the drain pipe that goes around the outside of the basement wall, the pipe has to go somewhere. It goes into a collection point that is usually located somewhere inside the basement area. The collection area or sump pump well, can usually hold about twenty gallons of water. Suspended about half way down in this well is a sump pump. The sump pump motor is run by electricity and is turned on and off by a floating switch. When enough water fills the well, the switch floats up to the on position, and it turns on the pump motor. The pump then removes the water from the well and pumps it up and out into the yard.

The system works well, most of the time. The real flaw here is that when the system has to work the hardest, for example, during a huge thunder storm, the odds of the power going out are at its highest. I do not have to tell you the consequences of a lot of water entering this well, located inside of the basement, at the same time there is no power to run the pump that takes it out. You get the picture. During my building career I never built a basement with a sump pump.

This same technology also applies to sewage systems that are located below where the sewage would naturally flow into the public sewer. The sewage is collected and pumped up to a point where gravity can take it away. I remember when the first high rise hotels were being built in Myrtle Beach, South Carolina. One of the most famous hotels was right downtown and sitting on what locals would call a high piece of ground. What this actually meant was that you walked into the hotel from the street at the second floor level, and went down one flight to the beach level. All of the sewage from the fifteen or so floors of the hotel fell to the bottom floor and was pumped up one level so it could enter the city sewer system at the street level.

Have you spotted the flaw in the design yet? The grand opening week was going well until the night of the big thunderstorm that knocked out power to all of downtown Myrtle Beach. The guests at the hotel were not aware of the design flaw so they continued to flush and shower. The entire beach level of the hotel filled with sewage. The hotel re-opened weeks later.

⎯⎯⋘⋙⎯⎯

Before I tell you one of my favorite stories I need to educate you on how a septic system works. A properly engineered septic system has a high rate of success and rarely causes problems. The county health department has dictatorial power over the location of the septic tank, as well as the location of the drain field. This also means they have a lot of say over where the house is actually placed on the lot as well.

For the benefit of you city folk, here is how a septic system works. Sewage, which always flows downhill, travels through the solid drain pipes in the house until all of the pipes become one. After exiting the house the pipe flows downhill into a septic tank. These tanks come in various sizes, but they can best be described as large concrete boxes capable of holding several hundred gallons of sewage. The pipe from the house enters one end of the tank at a point near the top of the tank. On the opposite end, near the top, is another pipe which heads out into the drainage field. I will have more about that in a minute. The purpose of the septic tank is to separate the solids from the liquids, or number one from number two, as you were taught as a child. The solids, of course, sink to the bottom of the tank forcing the liquids to the top and out the drainpipe at the far end of the tank. The solids are constantly being eaten by bacteria, hopefully at the same rate as they enter the tank.

When the bacteria fail to keep up with their job description, it is necessary to have someone come and pump out the solids into a truck and haul them away. It is a noble profession but not one for which I would stand in line to fill out an application. It is recommended that you should have your tank pumped every year but few people do. Most folks will do it every three to five years if all is working well. I have known people who never pumped their tanks. Sometimes it is necessary to dump some packages of yeast down the drain to increase the amount of bacteria working in the tank.

The most important part of the septic system is the drain field. The drain field is a large area of land where the liquid is distributed in a zig-zag pattern. The lines are usually no closer than twenty feet from each other and are buried in ditches several feet deep. They use the same pipe Slim used to waterproof the basement. This time you face the slits down so the liquid can gradually drain out of the pipe as it passes, always downhill, through the pipe. The washed stone is also on the bottom of the pipe as well, to filter the liquid before it is absorbed into the ground. The size of the ditch, the length of the ditch, and the amount of stone to be used is determined solely by the ability of the soil, on that particular piece of ground, to absorb water.

Determining this soil permeability is the duty of the county health department. Once the builder picks a spot for the house and applies for a septic permit, the county health inspector will come out to the property and take a lot of soil samples to see if the land perks. The inspector will determine where the best place to put the drain field would be, and he also will determine where you would have room to put a backup system if the first one fails. You can imagine the uproar that was caused when the requirement for a second drain field became the law. It meant that property in rural areas now had to be twice as big as originally planned. This sometimes meant redrawing plats of existing subdivisions. It also affected the profit ratios for future subdivisions.

Thirty years ago the perk test consisted of digging six-inch diameter holes about thirty inches deep in various places around the property. After digging the holes, you then filled each hole about two-thirds full of water. Then you placed a nail in the side of the hole to mark the original high point of the water. Twenty-four hours later the health department inspector would come out and check to see how far down the water had gone. The rate of decrease determined how ready the soil was to accept a septic system. This system had a lot of flaws. First of all, there was no proof as to how much water was in the hole to begin with. Secondly, it was too easy to dip some of the water out over night. I had an old farmer tell me one time that he could even make rocky soil perk. Once he got the hole dug, he simply set off a small stick of dynamite in the hole, creating cracks in the rock, guaranteeing an escape route for the water. It was practices like that which caused the health departments to train their people to do a soil analysis on site.

Now I will tell you the story. We built a house for another one of my Dad's high school buddies on a sloping wooded lot. This was a long ranch style home with a half basement. The basement was a natural fit on the lot so waterproofing it was not a problem. The problem was that the property was not in the city, and therefore it did not have access to city sewer. This simply meant that we needed a septic system in lieu of public sewer. The basement was never intended to be finished because there was not a practical way to put in a bathroom on the lower level. The health department had determined that, due to the permeability of the soil, the septic tank had to be placed on the high side of the lot meaning only the main floor could have gravity access to the septic tank.

Once the foundation was in, the client could walk around in his future basement. It was large, and had a number of windows and a walkout door. He thought it would make a nice place for a recreation room, guest bedroom, and yes, a bath. Dad explained to him that the only way to put a bath in this basement setting would be to use a sewer lift pump, which works much like the sump pump. The sewage would be gathered into an enclosed collection tank buried in the basement floor. This tank would contain a pump that would turn on as the tank filled up, thus lifting the sewage up to the main level where it could flow out of the house by gravity. Dad warned him that the system could be a problem if the power was out. All was understood.

Dad's friend and his wife had been in the house for about two years when he suddenly burst open the front door to the shop so hard that I thought the glass in the top half of the door was surely broken. "Where's Leonard" he shouted. I told him that he was not in so he turned his anger toward Max and me. "I've got sh… floating in my basement bathtub" he said as he continued to shout. He repeated several times that Dad had told him that the sewer pump system would work just fine. I figured that he felt that being a big time executive entitled him to shout orders to everyone who would listen. In this case that was limited to Max and me. Before slamming the front door on the way out just as hard as when he came in, he issued his final edict saying "Here is what you are going to do. Within one hour you will have the plumber at my house. By noon my sewer pump will be fixed, and the plumber will have explained to me why it will never happen again."

The silence was deafening except for my dialing the phone to call the plumber. I do not remember exactly how I said it, but the plumber was in our office in twenty minutes. That must have been a new land speed record for plumbers. With explanation in hand, the plumber headed toward the client's house. At some point during the morning Dad arrived at the office and Max and I filled him in on the events of the day. We all decided that it would be best if the plumber handled it from here. About two o'clock in the afternoon the plumber came into the office carrying a nice sized cardboard box. As he placed the box on the sales counter I asked him if he had fixed the problem. To our great relief he said that he had. Then I asked him if he had called the client and explained, as the client put it, why it would never happen again. His answer was a simple one. "Nope," he said, "That's your job."

Max asked the plumber what had caused the problem. He reached into the cardboard box and lifted up the burned out lift pump motor. It was completely encased with condoms that had been flushed down the toilet. The plumber looked at me and said for me to call the client and explain. I looked at Dad and said, "He's your friend. You call him." Dad looked a little paler than usual as he proclaimed that he thought he would call the wife, because his friend had had a vasectomy.

≋ 4 ≋

THE BEST OF THE BEST

Before I go any further, I must tell you about some of my favorite people. These are folks I worked with over the years. My wife and I have always believed that getting a good education was the first key to success. In fact, my son, sons-in-law, daughters and daughter-in-law have more degrees than Fahrenheit, as my Dad would say. If the truth were known most of the folks in this part of the book had very little formal education. However, a lack of education in their case had more to do with a lack of opportunity than a lack of intelligence.

⸻⫸⫷⸻

Peabody was a very short man—hence the nickname– but he was the best finish carpenter I ever saw. He was so short that he always carried a little stool with him everywhere he went so that he could nail across the top of doorframes. Peabody could not read or write, but he could measure. I remember him telling me to cut a piece of baseboard six foot three inches and thirteen little black marks. When he finally let me case my first door, I could not wait to get it finished. I was so proud despite the fact that it took me three times longer than making a profit would allow. He did not look at it for long before saying, "take it down and do it again." Besides being crushed, I was curious as to what I had done wrong. Peabody told me that he did not mind a crack between the two pieces of wood being big enough for a flea to crawl through, but he just did not want the flea to be able to crawl through piggyback.

We had a number of employees like Peabody in the old days. These folks were craftsmen in their respective trades. Clients would call for years after we built their houses and ask for Peabody to come over and do some work. We would often tell them that Peabody was busy, but we would be happy to send someone else. They would always say that they would wait until he was available.

One of the largest houses we ever built was for an old friend of Dad's who was in the lumber business. Dad designed the house and furnished the crew on a modified cost plus basis. The client furnished most of the materials. Dad assigned a foreman to the job knowing that there was no real time limit as to how long they would be on the job site. The house was completed in about a year and a half but the client asked Dad if the foreman could stay on and do miscellaneous jobs as they came up. Knowing the foreman was nearing retirement age, Dad agreed. I remember the foreman coming into the shop one day and proudly announcing that it was the third year in a row that he had staked up their tomato plants. Our guys were very versatile.

We had a painter named Charles that had the same reputation as Peabody. Charles was an artist in his own right. He always had an artist's kit with him. He would paint heating grills or light switches to match the grain of the wood in which they were placed. They looked more like the wood than the wood itself when Charles was finished with them. Charles always had two sayings that stuck with me. First he said that the most important part of painting was the preparation. He was referring to patching, puttying, sanding and caulking. Unfortunately they are the least fun things about painting. They, therefore, often get less than their proper amount of attention. The second thing Charles believed was that it was the painter's job to make the carpenter look good. And he could.

Charles would meticulously clean his brushes every day or soak them in something so they would be ready to go the next day. These brushes were his tools of the trade and without them being at their best, he could not be at his best. He always carried tubes of raw paint color with him in case he needed to change the shade of some paint or mix some special putty. There was always a little jar of white sheetrock putty dust with him also. He would mix this dust with putty to make the putty a little drier, if necessary, so it would not stick to his fingers or smear on the surface around the hole he was trying to fill. I have tried to remember all of Charles's helpful hints over the years and have tried to pass them on to my kids. They sure do make the little tasks associated with owning a home much easier to do—and do well.

As time passed it became harder and harder to financially justify keeping such meticulous craftsmen on your payroll. We were able to get a great many jobs over the years because these folks worked for us, but gradually the art of home building was slowly giving way to the production of home building. The buying public still wanted the craftsmanship, but they wanted it at production prices. Peabody and Charles worked with us until they retired. Even though I missed them personally and professionally when they retired, it was the entire housing industry that would miss them, and craftsmen like them, the most.

⸻

Our shop man was named Artis. He was the best and probably the most valuable employee we had. If I could have traded jobs with anyone on our staff, it would have been Artis. As I said earlier, the shop was my favorite place. Artis, unlike most perfection-minded tradesmen, was just as concerned about production and speed as he was about producing the best product. These were traits seldom seen in the same person. The most used piece of power equipment in the shop was an industrial grade radial arm saw. The ball bearings in this saw were so good that it ran for several minutes after you cut it off. Even though Artis gave you a full and complete day's work, he knew when to quit. We had a large clock on the wall in the office that had a sweep second hand. Artis's day ended at 4:30 pm. By the time the second hand was thirty seconds past four thirty you could hear the sliding door to the shop being pulled shut. Artis's car would be out of sight, but you could still hear the blade on the radial arm saw slowing down on its way to a good night's sleep.

My Grandfather had built the shop. It was the most important cog in our building business for three generations. We built our own cabinets, fancy entrance doorframes, mantles, and wall panels. When Artis took his products to the job site for installation the rest of the crew would often look for other things to do. Artis expected the job site to function as precisely as his shop. There was definitely a rhythm to the shop and there was a rhythm to the job site. It just was not the same rhythm. What upset Artis the most was when something he built did not fit once it arrived on the job site. You needed to hide if you had prepared the site wrong, but you did not want to be between the job site and the shop if Artis had measured it wrong. He would race back to the shop and feverishly work until he fixed the mistake. I never figured out if he was more upset because he had made a rare mistake, or if he was just mad, as John Wayne would say, because he was burning daylight.

⚊⚊⚊

Max was the glue. He worked his entire business career for my Dad as office manager. Max will always be in that special category with Slim. Dad hired Max after he served in the Army during the Korean War in the intelligence branch. Max had been at the top of his class in college. When I was a kid, I thought Max knew everything. I remember one evening my Mom was cooking dinner and all of a sudden there was a grease fire on the stove. Did she call the fire department? No, she called Max who calmly told her how to put it out. Sis and I were really impressed. I have always been convinced that no business of any size could possibly be successful if it did not have someone like Max keeping everything straight, not just the billing and finance paperwork, but the people, the supplies, the overall operations and the coordination of personalities.

Max is a practical philosopher who loved the simple life. He loved living in the rural setting where he grew up. I could not describe Max as a country boy, because that would not adequately describe who he was. Max loved the countryside, loved his fruit trees, loved mowing his several acres of grass, and loved to hunt. Some of my fondest memories are of Max teaching me to hunt. I did not know it could be that cold so early in the morning. If I were a rabbit I would not have gotten up that early either.

Slim usually went hunting with us. In the fall, when dove season started, Max knew all of the fields where his neighbors and friends had planted special food just to entertain doves. Of course we were not the only ones privy to this information. As the doves flew in over the field, it resembled something like the battle of Gettysburg or Clint Eastwood running the gauntlet. Dad would have given me three or four boxes of shells for the hunting trip, and I made sure I used up and fired every one of them. It sure was fun. Slim would be a little way down the hedgerow from me. He usually brought six or eight shells with him. When the day was over, he took six or eight doves home for dinner. I was lucky to have hit one.

The only time I saw Max get really mad was on a hunting trip when Slim brought along an uninvited friend. When hunting, Max, like any good hunter, preferred knowing the skills and habits of his hunting partners. I was fairly near Max when Slim's friend mistook Max for a deer. It was a good thing the man was using a shotgun and not a rifle. By the time we dug a few pellets out of Max, the friend had thought of some things he needed to do elsewhere.

Max was a good judge of people. I always valued his opinion. Max had two sons who were both bright and capable students. "B's" never crept onto their report cards, whether it was in high school or college. When his oldest son was around ten, I remember Max coming into the office and telling us about the little league baseball game he had watched the night before. Max told me to write down a certain name. He said he had spotted the best little athlete he had ever seen. This kid must have been really good to impress Max so much. Being a sports fan, myself, I kept up with this particular kid's career. Max was right. He became an All-American at Clemson on their national championship football team and then advanced to become a star for the Buffalo Bills. Max had him pegged much earlier.

Max was one of the most conservative people I have ever known when it came to handling money. Dad was not as conservative and occasionally I would see Max roll his eyes when Dad decided to buy something like the first color TV or the first central air-conditioning system in our town. Max's financial philosophy could best be summed up with a comment he made when I asked him how his oldest son was doing in his first job. The young man was a new CPA working in Charlotte and Max had just gotten back from a weekend visit. Max told me that his son was making enough money to buy the things he needed and not enough money to buy the things he did not need. Max was more than an employee or a friend–he was part of the family.

⟶◦⟵

Probably my favorite fellow worker and friend was Slim. His name has come up a lot already. Slim was a proto-type southern black man with a southern dialect and a few "yes sirs" thrown in. I have never known a time in my life when I did not know Slim. Slim was not completely sure of his age, so he adopted my Dad's birthday. Slim had three sons. One was a couple of years older than me, one was my age and one was several years younger. Every Saturday Slim and the boys would come by the house. Slim would mow the grass and do whatever else needed to be done and the boys and I would play. My eighth birthday fell on a Saturday and my parents asked me what I wanted to do special that day. Since my favorite thing in whole the world was building roads in the sand box, I told them that I wanted to ride out to see where they were building the new bypass highway around our town. Dad thought that was a good idea so we all piled into the pickup truck. I told them that I wanted Slim's boys to go with me. After some pretty lame excuses, my Mom tried to explain to me that that just was not done. I did not understand it then, and I never did understand it later in life, either. It was one of life's truly profound moments for an eight-year old to understand.

While I was in college, Slim's youngest son was a star basketball player at the local all black high school. This was just a couple of years before school integration took place in our state. I was home from school for the weekend when Dad got the call that the young man had collapsed and died during a game in his local high school gym. Dad turned to me and said we need to go over to Slim's house and see if we could help him in any way. Even though I was in college, and these boys had been friends for my entire life, I had never been to their house. I was a little reluctant to do so even then. Slim was bigger than life to me. He was the strongest man I had ever known and he always took special care of me. I will never forget seeing Slim that night, as Dad held him, giving out a primal cry straight from the heart. I did not know that such heart-felt pain existed. Since that moment, I have never questioned the unexpected sources of life's greatest lessons.

Just about my favorite event of the year was the office Christmas party. Dad started taking me to it at an early age. The shop man would clear off the worktables and cover them with plywood and fresh paper. Around this large table would be benches made from 2 x 12's lying across stacked up concrete blocks. He always strung a few extra lights so we could all see what we were eating. What we were eating was always barbeque. Our town was known as the barbeque capital of the state, so nothing else would do.

Dad was a soft touch at Christmas and gave away a lot of money and gifts at the office party. Slim, whose specialty was not English grammar, was always called upon to deliver the blessing. Slim was a man of few words, except when he prayed. And when he prayed, somehow the King's English flowed off of his tongue. In my early years of attending the Christmas party, Slim usually sat at the end of a bench on one side of the table, a little to himself. I always sat with him. As times changed, so did Slim's seat at the table.

Construction crews are probably a little more macho than most work settings. Just because you liked someone did not mean you did not pick on him if he had a weakness or a sensitive area. In fact, I always felt that the more the rest of the crew liked you, the more they felt free to pick on you. If they did not like you, they just ignored you. Everybody liked Slim.

Slim had four primary duties with our company. He waterproofed our basements. He cut trees. Slim was the best person I ever met when it came to using a chain saw. Emergency room doctors can tell you how dangerous chain saws can be when weekend warriors get hold of them. Slim was the only person I ever met that I would let drop a tree right next to me. Trees always went where he wanted them to go. Slim's third function was to deliver materials. This duty placed Slim on just about every job site every day. The fourth function was to be a truck driver, especially when the bulldozer man was working.

Slim, who was not afraid of anyone, was afraid of snakes. I honestly do not think a bear would have bothered him at all, but a snake terrified him. When you cut trees, clear lots, and hang around bulldozers in the South, you are going to run into a lot of snakes. The first snake story I remember the crew telling happened when I was still in school. Dad was building a new neighborhood called Rosemary Park and our bulldozer man, Duck, was hard at work clearing the land along a creek that ran through the property. Just after lunch Duck's bulldozer unearthed a large copperhead snake which he killed immediately. A large copperhead can be about three and one-half feet long and as big around as a muscular forearm. This one fit the bill. The dead snake happened to be lying on its side with its mouth wide open.

When Slim came back after dumping a load of stumps, the crew could not wait to show him the snake. Slim did not want to have anything to do with the snake, dead or alive. Then someone came up with the idea of betting Slim that he would not stick his finger into the open mouth of the dead snake. They were right. He would not do it. As the day progressed the bet got bigger and bigger. By the end of the work day, even Slim was interested in the size of the pot he could take home if he just had the nerve to stick his finger in the dead snake's mouth. Slim trusted Duck, sort of, and Duck reassured Slim that the snake was indeed dead. Slim, who had spent his adult life avoiding snakes, was really not familiar with the fact that the muscles in dead snakes sometimes twitch and reflex hours after they are dead. Just as Slim slid his finger into the mouth of the snake, it twitched. The Chevrolet dealership is about eleven blocks north of Rosemary Park. That is where the crew finally caught up with Slim. Slim was on foot and they were chasing him in their cars.

During one of my college summers I was working with the crew in Greensboro. We were building a brick ranch with a full basement. The driveway was on the left side of the house and was level with the first floor. The right side of the house was over the open end of the basement area. That made the ridge of the roof quite high off the ground at that point. We had finished putting the roof sheathing on the rafters and had nailed down the felt underlayment that morning. Slim arrived about ten o'clock in the morning with a truckload of roofing shingles and proceeded to unload them. He would carry four bundles of shingles at a time up the ladder and across the sloping roof. He would spread them out in a way that made our job easier. I was pretty strong but quite content just to pick up one bundle. I wanted no part of carrying four bundles up a ladder.

Even though the roof on the right side of the house was a long way off of the ground, it did not look so high because a large tree stood just off of the end of the roof's ridge. It looked like one could reach out, grab the tree branch and climb down if it ever became necessary. Our foreman, Billy, had been working at that end of the ridge when he looked up and saw a decent sized green garden snake hanging by its tail. It was just about where you would reach out to grab the tree.

About the same time Billy saw the snake, Slim reached the top of the ladder with four more bundles of shingles. Billy turned to the crew and hollered that it was lunchtime. The whole crew quickly scrambled down from the roof, and Slim said he would be down in a minute. When Billy got to the bottom of the ladder he pulled it away from the house and put it on the ground. Having seen what Billy had done, Slim said, "Ah Mr. Billy, I'll get down." Slim placed the last bundle of shingles on the roof and headed for the tree. With his hand stretched out and his eyes wide open, he came within inches of grabbing that snake. I do not remember which was louder, Slim's scream or the sound of him running full speed across the top of the roof. My mouth dropped wide open as Slim ran as fast as he could off the left hand end of that roof. It was a thing of beauty. Slim never missed a stride as he hit the ground running. It only took two blocks to catch him this time. I still do not know who was more scared, Slim or Billy.

Slim was out working on one of the job sites one morning when he ran across a snake. Slim was all alone meaning no one else was around to kill the snake. In a moment of immense courage, Slim killed the snake. At lunchtime Slim came by the shop to tell Max and me that he had killed a snake all by himself. History had never recorded a previous snake killed by Slim. Max and I quickly decided that this unique event deserved a road trip. Max spent virtually all of his time in the office and, more times than not, knew every thing about a job site except where it was. He actually knew where it was supposed to be, but rarely ever went to the site itself.

This one was going to be an exception. Before we arrived at the site we asked Slim just how he managed to kill the snake, and he described how he threw a rock at the snake and killed it. What he failed to mention was that he threw a rock, and another rock, and another rock, and another rock. The rock pile was two feet high. The snake was only sixteen inches long, but he was definitely dead.

Slim was my friend so I never picked on him. Temptation can be a powerful sin, however, and I succumbed one day. Shortly after Cathy and I bought our first house I was doing some Saturday morning yard work. Slim had agreed to help me and had brought one of the company dump trucks over to haul away some rubbish. At the end of our front walk was a low, ugly block wall running parallel with the edge of the road. It was only one block high for the most part, but there was a two-inch thick solid cap block on top to cover the holes in the eight-inch blocks.

Slim was working in another part of the yard. I told him that I was going to bust the solid cap block off of the top of the other block with a pick and sledge hammer. Then he could help me load them on the truck. The truck was parked right next to the wall so all we would have to do was pick up the loose blocks and throw them into the back of the truck. After I loosened the first cap I reach down and picked it up. To my startling surprise, both holes in the eight-inch block were filled with large black snakes. I loosened the next cap and discovered the same thing. This is when the Devil grabbed me for sure. I put the caps back and called Slim. I told him that I could not get the cap loose and asked him to give it a try.

It is really difficult to describe what happened next. When Slim picked up the first cap, total panic set in. His natural reflex was to run. The only problem was that he ran straight into the side of the truck that was so conveniently parked next to the wall. He hit the truck with tremendous force. Undeterred, he back off and ran into it again. After the fourth encounter with the side of the truck I was able to calm him down. I killed the snakes and loaded the block on to the truck myself. Until the day Slim died, he did not know I did that on purpose, and I am glad he never found out. I still feel bad about it, but seeing him run into the side of that truck time after time was still one of the funniest things I have ever seen.

Slim had a little showman in him. I drove up to a job site in Clemmons one day about noon and nobody was anywhere in sight. A few doors down I could see the back end of what looked like a pretty big crowd. It was summer time and all of the kids were out of school. The entire neighborhood had gathered to watch Slim. One of our previous clients had come over to the new job site to ask Slim if he would take down a large limb that was hanging over their house. Slim agreed to help them during his lunch hour, which was really only thirty minutes long. This day it stretched into two hours. Slim had tied a chain saw around his waist and had climbed up the tallest tree in the entire neighborhood. Ringling Brothers had nothing on Slim. As soon as he untied that chain saw and yanked real hard on the starter rope, the roar of the running chain saw brought out all of the neighbors. Collectively they sighed, gasped, and cheered as he went about his work. When he came down from the tree his celebrity status rivaled that of Babe Ruth after hitting one of his famous home runs. Slim just said, "Shucks, it was nothing."

Slim did not have many faults but he did take a week off of work five different times to go to Georgia to bury his mother. I assume he just thought we were not counting. On another occasion Slim's work capacity had started to slack off for a period of a few weeks. We asked him if he was OK, but all we got was a "Yep." Then, one afternoon Max asked Slim to replace a burned out light bulb in a fixture that hung over the side entrance to the display area of the shop. Slim opened the eight-foot step ladder and climbed up to do the job. About a half an hour later Max noticed that Slim was still up on the ladder. Max went out the other door and walked around the building to see what was going on. He found Slim sound asleep on top of the ladder. Why he did not fall off and hurt himself is still a mystery. As it turned out Slim confessed that he had gotten behind in some bills and had taken a second job, so he was not getting any sleep. Max and Dad somehow worked out that problem since we had even taller ladders.

≡ 5 ≡

STUDS

Most guys on a carpenter crew might think this chapter is about them. Actually it is about a piece of lumber and all the things you can do with it. A stud is a 2 x 4 cut to a length equal to the height of any particular wall. I did not know they were so valuable until one Sunday afternoon when Cathy and the kids and I were riding home from church. Our kids were little then and in a hurry to get home and do the things little kids do. They were not too happy when I pulled into one of our job sites. I had spotted a station wagon backed up to the front door of one of our houses under construction.

This particular house was one of my new designs and it had taken a great deal of effort to persuade Dad to build it. The projected sale price was $52,500 and no one in our town had ever built a spec house for that much money. In fact the local paper had run an editorial about how daring a venture this was. My Grandfather, the editor, had died by this point in time, but when I think about it, he would have written the same editorial. A spec house, if you are not familiar with the term, is a house that you build on the hope that someone will buy it. In other words, we were speculating that someone would come along and purchase the house by the time we finished it. The other type of building we undertook was referred to as custom building. This meant that you not only had a customer from the beginning but that you customized the house just for them.

I had the family stay in the car because I was not sure what I was going to find when I got inside the house. It was not unusual to see a car parked at one of our spec houses on a weekend. In fact we were always delighted to see folks looking around. But this car was backed up to the front door, so I went in through the back. When I got to the foyer area I found a stranger loading 2 x 4's into the back of his station wagon. "What are you doing," I asked? He told me that he was building a playhouse at home and he knew the builder would not miss the lumber because they had plenty. Then he asked me if I would help him load the car. After hearing who I was and listening to some not so friendly advice concerning how quickly he needed to unload the 2 x 4's, he jumped into his car. He sped off so quickly that all of the 2 x 4's slid out of the back of his station wagon.

⸻⁂⸻

My wife and I bought our first house about three months after we got married. Dad called one evening after work and asked us to meet him out at the country club, which was actually a municipal golf course. It served the same function as a country club in our small town. Through a bizarre set of circumstances, the smallest house on the golf course had suddenly come on the market. Dad had heard a rumor that day that the owner was going to sell, so he went by to see him.

After hearing the price, he asked for, and was given, a four-hour option on the property. Then he called me. Cathy and I met him at the house not knowing exactly why we were there. After touring the house which faced the sixteenth green and sat on one and one-quarter acres of land, he asked me what I thought it would sell for. As you have figured out by now, I was used to this type of house quiz. Even though the house was old, having been built in the 1920's and not updated, it was made of brick, was a 1500 square foot, three bedroom house and had a gorgeous setting. I was sure from the beginning that we could not afford it, because I had spent my entire $350 fortune on our honeymoon, and it was worth every penny. I guessed the house's value at between

$25,000 and $30,000. When Dad said that the owner was asking only $15,000, all I could say was "Wow."

In those days there was only one kind of home loan. You had to put twenty percent down and you then possessed a twenty-year mortgage at six per cent interest. Real estate agents did not have to remember many loan multipliers back then. By now my mind was wandering all over the place. I could just see us living there. Dad asked us what we thought, and of course, we said we loved it. He then told us about the four-hour option, at which point I reminded him that we did not have any money. That was the polite way of saying that he did not pay me enough to buy the house. It seems he had already made another call before we arrived. This call was to his good friend at one of the local savings and loans. Since the house was so under priced, and I am sure, as I think back on it, that Dad guaranteed the loan, the savings and loan had agreed to loan us the entire amount. "Where do I sign," was the next thing out of my mouth.

We were living in those apartments Dad owned next to where my mother grew up. We were paying the same rent as everyone else. It would be a few more months before we could move in because the house did need some renovation work. It was during this period that we learned that, of all things, my Grandfather Craver had originally built the house in 1928 for a bootlegger named Toots. Not long after we moved in, the doorbell rang one evening and to my amazement, a drunk was standing there. He wanted to see Toots. Toots had not lived there in over 25 years. However, while we were renovating the house, we had discovered that most of the closets had false back walls. Instead of being two feet deep, they were actually four feet deep. This extra space was where Toots hid the fruits of his trade. There was a false ceiling to the stairway leading to the basement. The little one-car detached garage had a false back wall which led to a four-foot wide space. No, they were all empty by the time we bought the house. The day we tore down the garage brought an interesting response from some golfers. We had taken the roof off and had pulled the nails out of the corners of the walls. When we pulled the last nails out we let the walls drop. I was not playing golf in those days so I really had not noticed the golfer on the seventeenth tee located directly behind the garage. He happened to be at the height of his backswing when the walls hit the ground with a tremendous thud. After watching his drive disappear into the woods down the left side of the fairway, he turned and shouted to us, "I hope you get the damn thing fixed." As my kids grew up, they learned a lot of choice language from the golfers.

The studs in our first house were actually full 2 x 4's, measuring two inches by four inches. By the 1960's we were using 2 x 4's that measured an inch and five-eighths by three and five-eighths inches. I remember the lumber salesman coming into the office one day to announce to us that starting with our next shipment of studs, they would measure one and one-half inches by three and one-half inches. When I asked him why, he said it was simple. Every thirteen studs they made, they got an extra one at no cost to them. Actually I thought that was brilliant. Besides, laying off walls in inch and one-half increments was a whole lot easier than using inch and five-eighths increments.

Size does matter. The 2 x 10's supporting the floors in our old house were actually a little larger than 2 inches by 10 inches. They were rough sawn. When a tree goes to the sawmill, the first thing the miller does is trim off the bark. Then the tree is cut into the desired length. After that, it is run through the rip saw over and over at two-inch widths. Depending on the size of the tree, you get several different widths of lumber from 2 x 4's along the outside edge to 2 x 12's in the middle. The top and bottom edges are trimmed to square up the lumber. Then it is passed through a planer to make it smooth. The floor joists on our 1920's era house had skipped this last step, which left the outside very rough and full of splinters. It also left them super strong. The sub floor, or first layer of flooring, was made of full one inch thick boards of varying widths, nailed diagonally to the floor joist for extra strength. The same was true for the sheathing on the exterior walls. I mention all of this because the old saying about houses not being built like they used to be is often entirely true. In many ways, old houses were built stronger and better.

⚒

After our three daughters were born over a four year period, we decided to add on to the house. I had cleverly designed a playroom on the second floor of the addition, not knowing that by the time it was finished, it would be my son's room. The original part of the house had what I described earlier in the book as a partial cellar. It could not be made into a recreation room for the kids, but it made an adequate workshop and hobby room for my model railroading habit. I planned a grand, wide-open full basement under the new wing. To achieve this we had to excavate about four feet lower than the adjoining cellar and crawl space. This was tricky because in order to put the stairway next to the original part of the house, we needed to make the new basement right against the old one.

The bulldozer had done a good job and now it was time for me to put up the batter boards. When the backhoe driver arrived to dig the footings, I carefully walked him through each step of where the ditches needed to be dug. He started on the wall that was furthest from the old part of the house and slowly worked his way around the basement. I dropped into the ditch behind him with my flat point shovel and began the backbreaking job of cleaning out the ditches. Where was Slim when I needed him? This was a low budget operation, so I was doing it by myself. Did I mention that masons are not the only ones that occasionally go to the wrong side of the batter board string? Backhoe drivers are just as guilty. I was concentrating on cleaning out the ditch when the backhoe made the turn next to the original house. Instead of digging where I showed him, he dug on the side of the string next to the house, thus literally digging under the existing footing for the old part of the house.

The original house's compact 1500 square feet had about 1200 of those feet on the first floor. It was all brick and had a 12/12 pitched (very steep) roof that encompassed the second floor. Above that was a small attic. When you stood in the new basement looking at the end of the old house, it was an impressive three and one-half stories tall being supported by a footing that now was not being supported. When I spotted what could be a looming disaster, I quickly had the backhoe dig a parallel ditch where it was supposed to be. This left me with a ditch that was twice as wide as normal. I stopped working on the ditch along the back of the house and decided to go ahead and clean out the extra wide ditch. I was halfway across the area, or in other words, directly under the tallest part of the end wall of the house, when my wife walked out to the far side of the excavated basement and offered me a tall glass of Coke. It was summer and that was a welcome site. I walked over to her and reached up and took the glass. Before I could turn around I heard and felt a strange noise and vibration. Half of the brick on the entire 3-story end of the house fell all at once into a pile, exactly covering the spot where I had been standing. The cloud of mortar dust encased us like a dense fog before heading to the neighbor's yard. We stood motionless for a while. The pile of bricks was at least six feet high. It would have taken them an hour to even find me under there. Timing can be a wonderful thing.

After gaining my composure I realized I had another problem. Not only was the entire end of the house exposed, but nothing was holding it up. The foundation wall on that end was completely gone. The nearest pier under the main girder of the house was eight feet back into the crawl space. On that end of the house, right in the middle, directly over that girder that was now cantilevered out over nothing, was a ceramic tile bath which we had redone when we first moved in. I was already picturing it as completely full of cracks. It was almost dark, so we had no choice but to wait until morning to prop things up. We gathered up the kids and spent the night out. The next morning, I gained a real appreciation for the strength of the house my Grandfather had built. Nothing had settled or cracked. It was amazing to see. Had that happened to one of today's houses, it would have fallen into the basement on top of the brick pile.

The only way to accomplish that desired wide-open basement that I could some day finish into a recreation room for the entire family, was to install a giant steel "H" beam that spanned the entire area. This piece of steel was thirty-five feet long and sixteen inches tall. When the truck from the steel company arrived in front of my house late one afternoon, the driver decided the easiest and quickest way for him to go home early was to simply encourage the steel beam to slide off the end of his truck. It landed right next to the road. I am quite sure that somewhere in the state where they do such things, there was a recording on a seismograph when the beam hit the ground.

There were some folks in the next county that had a welding shop. They made wrought iron railings and steel flitch plates that you spliced between two pieces of lumber when you wanted to span a reasonable distance. The span of this basement area was not a reasonable distance. They also had a crane. Now that I think about it, I think they built the crane themselves. It had always worked well on our job sites. When I explained to them what I needed the crane to do, they said it would be a piece of cake.

The masons had finished the basement walls and we were ready to set the steel. The wall away from the original part of the house was a solid wall and level across the top. I had marked the spot where the steel beam needed to rest. On the end next to the house, we had built the wall to just above the level of the dirt in the adjoining crawl space. Above that point we built a masonry pier up to the floor level in the original part of the house. The masonry pier now had a dual purpose, to support the girder as well as to support the other end of the steel beam. It had seemed like a good idea when I designed it; the top of that pier was starting to look like an awfully small landing area for that big steel beam.

When the crane arrived the only place for it to set up was on the road in front of the house. The crane operator immediately began to add the extra extensions he had brought for the boom of the crane. Cranes are more stable when they can keep the boom at a high angle. The closer the beam can stay to the base of the crane, the easier it is for the crane operator. We presented the crane operator with two problems. Three, actually, if you consider how much the beam weighed. The first problem had to do with the distance from the base of the crane to where the steel beam needed to come to rest. The second was the huge tree in our front yard that prevented the boom from rising too high. The whole operation sort of resembled the launching of a hot air balloon. We had two heavy duty ropes tied to each end of the steel. We had a man on the other end of each rope to gently guide the beam to where we wanted it to go. I was on the wall and another man was next to the top of the pier. Our jobs were to see that the beam landed exactly where it needed to be. Once the steel beam got airborne, controlling it was similar to docking an aircraft carrier or trying to stop an ocean liner on a dime. It had a mind of its own. The base of the crane, which was actually an old truck with the boom mounted on the truck's bed, had four stabilizer feet that had been deployed. The purpose of these stabilizers was to keep the truck from turning over if the boom became extended beyond the tipping point. Those of us guiding the beam had to be extra careful to keep the beam from swaying back and forth in the direction of the original house. I do not care how well my Grandfather had built that house; this beam could have knocked it over.

The boom on the crane was fully extended and the beam was about 12 inches above its target. We were having a difficult time getting the beam to stop moving so it could be gently lowered into place. I glanced up at the crane operator and he was really sweating and did not look all that good. Then his eyes got real big and he hollered, "Line it up. Here it comes." The beam had suddenly over-powered the crane, and the stabilizers on the far side began lifting off the ground. Down came the beam. By the grace of God, the beam happened to be floating over the exact spot it was supposed to land when that final twelve inches were covered in a split second. The only thing that kept the crane from turning over was the weight of the beam coming to rest on top of our basement walls. The crane operator had a nice tan when he arrived but was really pale when he left.

———

In our region of the country, in the middle of the 20th century, most building companies were relatively small and localized. Wages were paid by the hour. In the 80's and 90's most hourly wage jobs in construction in our area had been eliminated in favor of subcontracting. This meant that you agreed to pay a crew a fixed amount to do a certain phase of the job, such as framing, exterior trim, or interior finish. In theory this method produced more speed and cost controls. Quality suffered, however.

Studs are used to build walls. Before I had joined the company officially after college, Dad had begun the process of panelizing walls. This was not something he invented but it was a process that no one else in our area was using. Since our crews were on hourly wages, Dad wanted to be able to keep them working when the weather was bad. He added a wing on to the shop which allowed us to store materials at one end, have a huge layout table in the middle, and have an assembled wall storage area in the front. I mention all of this because about ten years after joining the company I decided that I would rather have Dad as a Dad, than as a boss. There is no loyalty like family loyalty, but it can get in the way of living. Besides I knew that I would pay myself more than he would. The biggest change in my new company's operation was that we did not have the shop, meaning we did not have a place to panelize walls. We had to build walls the old fashion way: by hand on the subfloor.

Dad's life had changed. Mom had died much too young of a brain tumor, and Dad was realizing how much he had depended on me to do all of the things that he did not want to do anymore. He took his own advice after a couple of years and went into the real estate business full time. I got the shop back. For those couple of years without the shop, we built wall sections directly on the subfloor and stood them up in place. After you nailed a wall section to the floor, the next thing you did was to level it and brace it so it could not fall down.

⚒

We were building a large house out in the country one extremely hot summer. Believe what you want about global warming in the 21st century, but I think it peaked that summer. For the only time in my life, we had five straight days over 100 degrees. The worst part about it was that the days were Monday through Friday. We would take breaks every thirty minutes or so and quit at whatever point in the afternoon that we ran out of water. This particular house was over 100 feet long and had a wing out the back for a screened porch and two-car garage.

Our nails came in 50-pound boxes and we would tear the top off of the boxes so we could grab the nails quickly. We also put the boxes on the foundation wall of the garage because we were not going to frame the garage walls until after we had the main house under roof. Also, that part of the garage foundation was in the shade. If it had not been in the shade the nails would have been too hot to pick up.

At that particular point in time, we were using three-quarter inch styrofoam for the exterior sheathing. This was not nearly as strong as the diagonal one-inch boards my Grandfather had used on my house, but the general public was all excited about its energy saving potential. When we left the job site in the late afternoon, we simply put a piece of styrofoam over the nail boxes to keep them dry. A piece of styrofoam weighed a pound or two at the most.

Friday was the hottest of this stretch of days, reaching a high of 105 degrees. We stayed on the job long enough to finish the last of the walls for the main floor. As we covered the nails and left the job site, I noticed one of the darkest clouds I had ever seen approaching from the west. Not five minutes after completing the 20 minute drive home, the phone rang. The man who lived next door to the job site was on the line to tell me that they had experienced a really bad storm. He suggested that I come out to the site. I could not believe what I saw when I arrived. All of our studs that had so recently been walls were scattered all over the several acres of front yard. The owner's tool shed that had been behind the house was in a tree across the road. Our job sign, which was planted in the ground via two 2 x 4 stakes, was twisted so that it faced the house and not the road. After surveying all of this damage I walked around to the garage, and to my amazement, there was the piece of styrofoam still covering the nail boxes. We never knew for sure if the wind had been a tornado, but you definitely do not want to fool with Mother Nature.

⚊⚊⚊

One of the most interesting employees I ever had was a guy named Ray. Ray had an extremely good heart and soul, but had experienced poverty in his childhood. Ray was from West Virginia. In fact, over the 18 years I was in construction after I left Dad's company, I would guess that more than half of our employees came from West Virginia. We used to kid them by saying that our area was one tank of gas from West Virginia. When they ran out of gas, they looked for a job and settled down. Most were in search of a better life than the coal mines and desolate valleys of the West Virginia mountains had to offer.

Ray had five kids, no money, and few skills. We taught him a lot over the years. In the first few years after Ray joined us he had a regular problem with attendance. When you are running a four-man crew as we often did in those days, one man's absence was noticeable. We were in the process of trimming the exterior of the same house that the tornado had leveled. As I explained earlier, the make up of each crew was typical. It consisted of a saw man, two carpenters and a "go-for." Ray was the go-for. When you are nailing 16-foot long flexible boards over your head, you need the go-for to also be the middleman once he has brought you the material. The middleman's job was to help hold up the long boards and keep them from sagging in the middle while the other two carpenters nailed the boards in place.

One day, when we needed ol' Ray the most, he did not show up. After an hour or so of frustration and choice language, I had an idea. I grabbed a 2 x 4, cut it the right length, and wedged it between the scaffolding we were on and the board we had wanted Ray to hold up. It worked just fine. A few minutes later I wrote "RAY" on the side of the 2 x 4. From that day forward, all of our crews carried a 2 x 4 named Ray. I still have one in my attic. Ray was not sure what to think of this necessary work aid, but over the years I actually think he became proud of it.

After a series of chats with Ray, I found out that the reason he periodically missed work was because he was constantly moving. Ray would rent a house for a couple of months, live in it free for a couple of months, and then be forced to move out and find another place. This was not a sinister plot on his part, but just the only way of life he knew. To help him with his dependability, I looked around and found a little lake cabin that needed some work but was livable. It even came with a boat and a dock. I bought the house and sold it to Ray on contract. That meant that I was his bank since he did not have one. I required him to get a bank account and make the monthly payments to me and I, in turn, paid the bank. Ray immediately took great pride in the house. Most of his evenings and weekends were spent fixing up the place.

One of the least pleasant jobs in construction was installing insulation, whether it was in the walls, underneath the floors, or in the attic.

It was sort of like putting tar on the basement walls. No matter how careful you were, it was going to get all over you. I would guess that at least 90% of the people I have ever met broke out with the hives every time they rubbed against fiberglass insulation. Ray, on the other hand, loved it, and it did not bother him at all. It did not take me long to figure out that installing insulation was a job I would gladly subcontract to Ray. When a construction job was ready for insulation, Ray's entire family would show up after quitting time and work like bees at a honey farm. He got a few other builders to hire him as well. Ray became the first person I ever knew to pay off his house in less than five years. He was so proud to have been able to accomplish this—perhaps one of the first people I ever saw realize the American Dream in such a dramatic way.

⟨⟩

Second on my list of favorite days, behind working in the shop, were the days we rented a Bobcat. A Bobcat is a mini bulldozer that can turn on a dime and get into places big machines cannot. They were great for moving small amounts of dirt or filling in awkward places. Since I was paying the rent, I insisted on being the driver. I always told the crew that it was a liability issue. The truth could actually be found way back in my early days in the sand box. I went with the crew one morning to the equipment rental company to rent a Bobcat. When they hitched it to the back of our old Chevy Suburban, I asked the rental dealer where the safety chains were. He asked how far we were going and I told him about fifteen miles. I got those famous last words, "No problem." Safety chains must have been an afterthought in those days!!

It was about four o'clock in the afternoon when I reluctantly climbed off of the Bobcat and packed it up for its journey back to the equipment company. Ray and the guys left in the Suburban and I told them I would be along in a little while. The way Ray told the story was that he was driving down Peace Haven Road, a busy two-lane tree-lined street in Winston-Salem, when he was passed by a Bobcat on a trailer. He commented to the boys that the Bobcat sure looked like the one they had been using all day. It was.

I still do not know how the Bobcat, proudly riding atop the trailer, managed to cross through the busy lane of on-coming traffic without hitting anyone. After missing all of the on-coming cars, its luck turned. The trailer hopped over the curb and headed through a previously well-maintained yard. This particular yard was a corner lot and luckily the Bobcat's path was headed diagonally across the front yard toward the side street, thus missing the house altogether. Between the Bobcat and the side street were two trees. The distance between these trees happened to match the width of the trailer but not the trailer and its tires. The Bobcat was chained to the trailer so well that wherever the extremely heavy Bobcat wanted to go, the trailer went also. Unfortunately the tires did not make it past the trees. They were sheared off and left lying in the yard. Since the tongue of the trailer was no longer attached to the Suburban, the Bobcat set its sights on a fire hydrant next to the side street. It hit the hydrant dead center, rolling it out into the middle of the road. This entire event created quite a scene, and a whole lot of explaining on my part when the authorities arrived. The only thing missing was the column of water shooting up into the sky like you see in the movies. This hydrant happened to have a safety release valve under it. They must have known Ray would be coming by one day.

Ray was big friends with our large and friendly golden retriever named Butter. Ray came by the house often and always made a point of playing with Butter. Butter looked forward to his visits. Much to my kids' dismay, Butter got out of his pen one afternoon and we had no idea where he had gone. A couple of hours later Ray came by driving one of our dump trucks. I suspect he was planning on a short chat with Butter. It upset him to find out that Butter was missing, and he immediately set out to look for him. About an hour later, Ray and Butter, both on the front seat, drove up in the truck. Ray had found him about three miles away sitting on the front stoop of a bank. I am still not sure which one was driving when they arrived at our house.

≋ 6 ≋

THE VIEW FROM THE TOP

I always admired the mason crews. It took a lot of nerve to cap out a chimney top, especially on a two-story house with a basement and a steep pitched roof. I had just pulled up to one of the larger homes we ever built, with the full intention of climbing to the top. The masons were working on finishing the final part of the chimney cap, and I knew this would be the last time there would be a climbable route to the top. Dad was standing there talking with the client, so I delayed my climb and joined the conversation. Up drove the client's wife and she was not happy.

After some private exchanges, I could see that her husband wanted to get away from whatever was on her mind. He looked at Dad and me and said he was going to the top. I followed. So did she. I was paying a lot of attention to how I was going to get up there. The masons' scaffolds were set up in the front of the house so the climb to where the roof started was not as difficult as it would have been from the backside of the house. There, you would have had to start from the basement level. Once I reached the roof the climb became more difficult because one had to lean forward and scale a make-shift ladder at a 45 degree angle. Once I reached the ridge of the roof, I found myself at the base of the chimney cap. The actual top of the chimney rose about six feet above the ridge. I was 56 feet in the air and could see half of the surrounding county.

I had been very diligent in making my climb, because with one wrong move, someone would put me six feet under the surrounding county. When I reached the top, I looked back to see that the client was just a few feet behind me. Much to my surprise, a few feet behind him was his wife. She had no idea where she was because she had been fussing at him the entire way up, and paying no attention to anything else. Suddenly her expression changed and her eyes got really big. The client paused, looked around, and said, "It sure is a long way down." I have never seen anyone climb down such a treacherous distance in so little time as that wife did. I stayed for a while to enjoy the view.

◆

Roofs are a fascinating part of the house. Most folks do not fall off of them as gracefully as Slim and land on their feet. They are steep and dangerous yet totally essential to the final product. They protect the building materials and the occupants from the weather. Unfortunately, there is nothing to protect the roof from the weather. Weather probably plays the most critical role in building a house. It does not snow a great deal in North Carolina but when it does, it messes up everything. If you are a kid in school, there is no possible way to get there. But, if you are a carpenter being paid by the hour, you show up on time. We had been putting the shingles on a roof for a couple of days, and the crew needed to finish that job so they would have a dry place to work in the cold, wet winter weather.

When I got to the job site the crew had built a beautiful bonfire, and they were all standing around it, rubbing their hands together and telling stories. Several inches of snow were on the ground. When they saw me pulling up, they decided it was time to pretend they were working. After surveying the situation, I told them to pack it up and head home. They insisted that they could clean the snow off of the roof and work the entire day. I said no. I was young and these guys were all veteran carpenters. Deep down inside them, they occasionally took great pleasure in displaying their long earned wisdom over the young college kid.

One of the guys, Harold, said he would show me how easy it was to clean off the snow. Up the ladder he went before I could stop him. He took a broom and a flat point shovel with him, and immediately began to push the snow off the roof. He hollered to me, "See, I told you I could clean it off.........." He first landed on the ground and then in the hospital. The crew took the rest of the day off.

I have seen more changes in construction over my career than did my Dad and my Grandfather combined. This is true, simply because technology advances change exponentially. The transition from hand built or stick built roofs to trussed roofs was a major change. From the beginning, Dad had carefully taught me the principles of hand building a roof truss. I will always be convinced that the way we built them was far superior to those trusses built today in factories out of 2 x 4's. Factory–built trusses were designed by licensed engineers who never left the classroom. They went by the book. On the job, we always over-designed for the individual situation.

The building code changed during the 1980's requiring us to use engineered roof trusses. Just before that change went into effect, we experienced one of our most challenging situations for truss design. I had designed a house just like the client wanted. The center section of the house was wide open from front to back. It was one-story on the outside but two stories on the inside. The house had a steep roof pitch to allow for the existence of bedrooms on the second floor on both sides of the open area. We used steel to build a bridge from one set of bedrooms to the other set of bedrooms across the open living space. It was a neat design. The roof system, however, had to be self-supporting and made of wood. The roof design could not allow any outward pressure on the front or back walls.

This was probably a roof system I would not have designed had I not been able to consult with Dad about how to build the trusses. He had been out of the construction business for a number of years at that point, but he was thrilled to get to offer advice. The moment of truth with any roof truss system occurs when you remove the artificial props used during construction of the truss. We always pulled a tight string next to the bottom of the truss so that we could measure how much it sagged when you removed the props. They all either sagged just a little or remained tight against the string. We held our breath and removed the props. Any sagging at this moment meant that there was outward pressure on the exterior walls. When the props came out, the truss actually rose one-quarter of an inch. I was impressed.

The ultimate test for that particular roof system came a few years later when a series of tornados and straight-line winds blew through the area. A large tree fell on the roof, right in the middle of the truss system. The walls on the inside of the house did not even show any cracks. The force of the falling tree was so great that one of its limbs poked a hole through the roof and penetrated all of the way into the master shower just five minutes after the owner had finished using it.

———

Clemmons is a suburban community outside of Winston-Salem. We did a lot of our building in this area. A subdivision named Waterford was our main focus. It contained between two and three hundred upscale two story brick homes, most of which had basements. We built over 10% of the homes there. About a year after I retired from building and moved to the Triangle area of North Carolina, I got a phone call from one of my former carpenters. First, he wanted to be sure I knew that he was running his own crew now. He was another one of those good ol' boys from West Virginia and I was (and am) proud of him and his success. Mainly, he wanted to know if I had heard about the tornado that had plowed through Waterford during the late afternoon on the day before. I had not. He insisted that I come see for myself. I could almost feel his chest swelling up when he told me that every house we had built was still standing and had suffered little damage.

I grabbed my camera and headed for Clemmons. The path of the funnel had dissected the neighborhood almost down the middle. Every home had experienced some trauma, even if it was just moving the newspaper from the front yard to the back yard. Insurance reports later said that at least 80 homes had suffered major damage, and nearly 40 had to be bulldozed to the ground. The most startling sight to me was seeing how many of the homes were completely missing their roofs. It was as if the roof had never been there. The first house we had built in this particular section of the neighborhood was ground zero for the funnel. Every house surrounding it had to be bulldozed. It had suffered only missing shingles and blown out windows. It was another one of those houses we had built for a lawyer, so I guess we inserted some extra nails.

The truth was that we hand built the roof system so that it was an integral part of the entire structure. You could not separate the roof from the house. The other builders in the neighborhood all used pre-engineered truss systems for their roofs. It was a faster and cheaper way to get the house dried in. When the crane arrived on the job site, it lifted the trusses, one by one, up to the top of the second floor. The carpenters would then nail the trusses to the top of the walls along the outside edge. The trusses are then tied together internally and topped with roof sheathing. Essentially, this created a large wooden hat on top of each house. When the big wind came, the hats blew off.

It was a big wind, too. After flipping off the entire roof section on one house, the tornado sucked all of the drywall off of the walls on the now exposed second floor. On another house, the funnel snapped off the brick chimney top, lifted it up and turned it over, sending it downward through the roof and both floors. It came to rest, buried six feet below the basement floor. The family was hiding in the basement about ten feet from where the guided missile that they used to call their chimney top penetrated the concrete floor.

There was only one house in the neighborhood that was not made of brick. I remember the builder putting up a sign out front saying that they were going to build it from start to finish in ninety days. It was the only house that did not need to be bulldozed after the storm, because it was nowhere to be found. I was tempted to stick up a sign on that lot saying from finished to nothing in ninety seconds.

<hr />

Working on roofs can be dangerous work. You needed to trust the person working beside you. While working on one of our roof projects one day, we had a good view of the folks putting the roof on a house in the next block. We could also hear them when the argument started.

They were working on top of your typical Waterford two-story with a basement. Unfortunately, these two guys were working on the side where the basement was exposed. Not ever having been a sailor, I was asking my crew what a couple of the phrases I heard actually meant. All of a sudden, one of the guys ripped up a 2 x 4 and swung it at the other guy. Off of the roof he flew, three stories down. We had a great view of the EMS squad arriving to haul away the unlucky recipient of the 2 x 4. We also had a great view of the police arriving to take away the other guy.

We built a number of homes with two-story foyers. We had just gotten one house under roof and the crew was bracing the roof from the inside. I was up in the attic designing the various bracing patterns when one of the crew had a question in another part of the attic. The closest way to get there was to walk across the top of the two-story foyer. I hesitated before venturing out over what looked like the Grand Canyon, even though it was only a 20-foot drop. The first rule about heights is not to look down. The first rule about walking on inch and one-half wide framing lumber is to always look down. This combination is what made me hesitate. What I should have been concerned about was the fact that these ceiling joists were not as strong as they would eventually be once the bracing was completed. Half way across, without warning, the joist beneath me snapped in two. I suddenly was going straight down, as my old physics teacher had taught me, at a rate increasing by 32 feet per second squared. It is amazing what you think about at such times.

As the adjacent ceiling joist flashed by in front of me, so did my entire life. Something made me reach out and grab that ceiling joist. I caught it with both hands, but my troubles did not end there. The joist that had broken in two was recoiling and heading right for me. The places I had to go were limited to none, so I braced myself for a blow. My main goal at this point was to not let it knock my hands loose. I held on but the sharp, splintered end of the joist hit me in the face just missing my eye. With that sequence over, and the crew standing there stunned, all I could do was to yell at them to get me down. The clock was ticking on my grip, like it does on your final Jeopardy answer when the answer is on the tip of your tongue. One of the crew ran out to the truck and grabbed a 24-foot extension ladder. He quickly set it up next to me so I could climb down. I took the rest of the day off.

———

I had other adventures with extension ladders. We had some unspoken rules on the crew. Never go up an extension ladder that you did not set up and test, and never work on a scaffold that you did not personally help build. It was not that you did not trust your fellow worker; it was that no one was going to be as careful about setting up these things as you were.

Sometimes you got in a hurry. We were in the finishing stages of an elaborate South Carolina low-country style house. The exterior was covered with rough sawn cedar siding. All of the siding and trim, therefore, was painted with a solid color penetrating stain. There were some places that needed touching up along the trim just under the roofline on the front of the house. Everyone was busy doing tasks that I had already assigned to them, so I decided to do the touchups myself. The extension ladder was already in place so I opened a fresh one-gallon can of stain, grabbed a brush, and headed up the ladder. When an extension ladder is fully extended, the weakest point is where the two parts are joined together. The two clamps on the upper section must be firmly hooked over the rungs of the lower section. These were not. I passed this section not paying any attention to it because I was concentrating on the open, and quite full, can of stain in my right hand. Maybe it was a macho type thing, but I liked to carry a full can of paint or stain in an unconventional manner. Instead of just holding the wire handle the manufacturer provided, like normal people, I would fold the handle down on the side. My thumb would hook over it with my fingers on the bottom of the can. This way, I could carry the stain at a higher point in relation to my body, thus allowing me to keep a better eye on the bucket as I climbed. I did not want to spill any of the stain on the trip to the top.

The further I advanced up the upper section, the more pressure was being placed on those hooks that I had ignored. Suddenly, the top section of the ladder, and I, went straight down. Twenty feet can be an eternity. I had a firm grip on the can of stain and I carried it all of the way to the ground. The problem was that I just had the can; the stain remained exactly where I had left it, twenty feet up in the air. The stain also remained perfectly motionless, in the shape of a one-gallon can, for what seemed like an eternity. Then it exploded. The stain that got all over me was going to have to wait a while to be removed. Removing the extra stain from the nearly finished house was now top priority. We had a paint-spraying machine that we filled with paint thinner. Then we literally pressure washed the front of the house with paint thinner. It worked. I took the rest of the day off that day, too.

≋ 7 ≋

WALLOON

When you design and build houses for a living, you cannot look at another house without using a critical eye. There are some really ugly houses out there. They are like ugly dogs; somebody must love them. Another trait you pick up over the years is a "level" eye. It was always my job to spot things that were out of level when I pulled up to a job site. Being plumb and level were necessary traits in building a good house. After checking after your crews for years, it becomes so ingrained in your mind that you notice every picture hanging on anyone's wall. There are only two ways to go through life with this disease: you become a compulsive picture straightener or you just chuckle. I chuckle.

When you build and sell houses for a living you also become a resource for your clients, forever. This is not all bad. You want to become a resource, especially if you are primarily in the real estate side of the business. On the building side, your clients tend to expect you to fix their houses......forever. I once had the fourth owner of a 17 year old house, with a 15 year old roof, call me and expect me to replace it. I was polite.

If you want to take a vacation, you need to really get away from everything, and everyone. North Carolina is a great vacation state. From where we live, it is three or four hours to the ocean. That is where most folks around here go in the summer. The only trouble with this theory is that it is hot in the summer, and you tend to get hotter at the beach. The mountains are two to three hours in the other direction and the temperature is a lot more comfortable. The only problem with the mountains is that they are only two or three hours away. If anything comes up, your clients will find you. That makes it too easy to go back and fix whatever the problem happens to be. We have spent our fair share of time in the mountains and at the beach, but every year we really got away by going to Walloon.

———

I am going to tell you about Walloon but you have to promise not to tell anyone else. Walloon is Walloon Lake, Michigan and it is a long way from North Carolina. My Dad went to Walloon with us once, and he said that you go to the end of the earth, park your car and swing in on a vine! It is special to my wife because her father's parents met there as children "summering" away from the heat of the Midwest before air-conditioning. Most of the members of her family have been spending part of their summers there ever since. It is special to all of us because of the sheer beauty and tranquility of the place. Until this year we had no Internet at the cottage where we stay. To get cell service, you had to lean out over the front steps and hold your teeth just right. Even the FedEx truck could not find us for 4 days one summer when we were expecting a package. Walloon is a place where children spend days outside, in the water, away from television, video games, I-pods, I-pads, and on and on and just play. It's a place that celebrates bonfires and marshmallow roasts, brilliant sunsets, water-skiing and sailing, enjoying nature—a little piece of the past before they return to the hectic 21st century life that they must live!

The lake was dug by a glacier millions of years ago, and I think the influence of all of that ice still affects the water temperature. We took some friends up one year and, after hitting the water for the first time, the wife yelled, "Does your heart stop!" My kids still laugh at me each time I methodically go down the steps of the dock. Each step requires more courage. Once I finally get in the water, it feels great and is really a quite refreshing 70 or 71 degrees (in August, mind you, when it's been heated all summer by the sun). Then, the problem is getting me out of the water. I never want to get out of the water—or leave Walloon, for that matter.

A few people over the years have known about Walloon. Tom Watson learned to play golf at the Walloon Lake Country Club and Earnest Hemmingway's family once had a house on the lake. Michigan, for those of you not from Michigan, is divided into upper and lower parts separated by the Straits of Mackinaw. Spanning the straits is one of the world's greatest and most beautiful bridges, the Mackinac Bridge. Walloon is about fifty miles southwest of the bridge and just seven miles from Lake Michigan itself.

Lower Michigan is flat, busy, and full of car manufacturing companies. Once you pass through the lower half of the lower half of Michigan it becomes a different place. Towns are few and far between and the rolling hills begin. As you approach the upper part of the lower section of Michigan, the hills become mini mountains with ski slopes and extremely lush golf courses. And of course, there are lots of lakes. The resort towns of Traverse City, Charlevoix, and Petoskey are harbors for fabulous boats and for shops full of things you really do not need, but tend to buy just because you are on vacation. We think Walloon is the prettiest lake, although I am not looking to debate the folks who frequent all of the other beautiful lakes in northern Michigan.

Walloon is lined mostly with seven-figure and up summer homes. A few are used year round, but it is mostly a summer place. I gave up snow skiing years ago but the ski business in northern Michigan is thriving. The standard joke is that there are two seasons, winter and July. Cathy's grandfather built a cottage on the lake in the early 1900's. He did so by pulling an icehouse, with a team of horses, across the frozen lake in the dead of winter. A lot of the old houses were built that way. That house lost its one hundred year battle with termites a few years back. Since then we have been renting what is now the oldest house on the lake. It was built in 1890 by dragging a boathouse across the frozen lake. The original boathouse still forms the living room portion of the cottage. Numerous additions have been added over the years. Even with all of the new luxurious homes on the lake, to me the Walloon experience is directly connected to old, quaint cottages.

The caretaker of the cottage told me that last year the old "over the ice" method of construction is sometimes still in use. A large two-story house was being moved from one part of the lake to another. One truck was pulling the house and another truck was pushing. Luckily they were fairly close to shore when the ice decided it was not thick enough to support such a load. The house and both trucks fell in. They got the trucks out, but the house had to be cut up into pieces. They used chain saws to cut it into small enough pieces to get most of it out of the lake. The caretaker says he has an under water camera capable of going down one hundred feet where you can see some of the interesting things have been left on the bottom of the lake over the years. Closer to the top, you do not need a camera because the water is crystal clear. You can see the bottom at a depth of twenty feet.

⋘⋙

Fifty miles to the northeast, on Mackinac Island, there is a sign saying that the EPA has declared it to be the cleanest air in the world. Mackinac Island is located in the Straits of Mackinaw with a perfect view of the bridge. On the island, which is eight miles in circumference, is a village as quaint as any New England fishing village you will ever see. The big difference is that no cars are allowed on Mackinac Island. At night the tranquility is breathtaking!

The village is lined with fudge shops, restaurants, novelty stores, and hotels. The houses in the village and up on the bluffs are primarily Victorian in style. Those of us who visit the island are called "Fudgies" because I defy you to go to the island and not purchase some of its famous fudge. Once folks arrive on the island, transportation is by horse drawn wagon for supplies, and horse drawn carriage if you are wealthy. If you are like most of us, you settle for renting a bicycle.

The people and the supplies for the island must all get there by ferry. When your supplies have to arrive in this manner, building a house can be a slow and painful process. This is further complicated by a short building season. The ferries do not run in the winter because the straits are frozen solid. A row of Christmas trees marks the way across the ice to the island for the snow-mobilers who venture back and forth. The island has rock cliffs, spectacular vistas, an arched rock to be climbed for the best view on the island, an old fort to tour, and lots of history. The Grand Hotel is a magnificent structure and features the world's longest wooden colonnade porch. It is truly one of my favorite places on earth.

⤙⤚

Dealing with such extreme temperatures is not something we do in North Carolina. I had a client once from Wisconsin tell me that they were riding in a new home subdivision over the weekend and made the decision never to buy a new house in North Carolina. I asked. "Why?" They told me that they had seen a crew pouring the footings for a new house and the footings were only twelve inches deep. Back in Wisconsin, they said, the footings were four feet deep. I had to explain to them that a 12-inch deep by 24-inch wide concrete footing was more than adequate to support a two story brick house. In the central part of North Carolina, the freeze line is only five to eight inches below the surface. That means that the ground does not freeze solid below the 12-inch point. When the ground freezes, it lifts the dirt upward. Therefore you must make sure the bottom of the footing is on stable ground in the winter. In Wisconsin, that means a four-foot deep footing.

My daughter Ginny was living in Minneapolis while her husband Steve was doing his ophthalmology residency. She called me one morning while she was on her way to work just to tell me that the guy on the radio had just said, "It is clear and twenty-six below zero. What a beautiful day." Ginny's response to me was, "Dad, don't these people know they can live somewhere else?"

I learned a lot about extreme weather when I visited them in Minneapolis. We arrived on the hottest day recorded in years in July. No one has air-conditioning adequate for those temperatures except the airport, and it was broken that day due to an overload. All of our windows in North Carolina have been double glazed since the 70's so I was not surprised to learn that in Minneapolis the windows were triple glazed. What amazed me the most was that their apartment had two sets of triple-glazed windows in every opening. The garage even had electric blankets for the cars so they would not get too cold in the dead of winter. All of these things made me think about Ginny's comment about living somewhere else.

One of my trips to Walloon was similar to some of the trips I have made to my kids' houses. My father-in-law had decided to build a house on the land he owned adjacent to the cottage his father had built. He wanted the whole family to be able to be at Walloon at the same time, so he decided he needed more space. I understood his sentiments because now we have to rent three cottages to accommodate all twenty of our family members.

We had interested him in a unique style of octagonal shaped house called a "Topsider". The design had originated in North Carolina. The parts of the house were manufactured in North Carolina, also. Those parts were then shipped to the job site in a kit, much like those swing sets you buy. You know the ones that say "can be assembled by a child in thirty minutes or a parent in six hours." Before the kit arrived at the job site, the concrete pedestal foundation had to be poured. My father-in-law, John, had hired a crew to clear the site and pour the pedestal. The pedestal was also eight-sided and contained a utility room, an entry way and a spiral stairway that took you up to the main floor. The bolts to support the cantilevered beams that held the main structure had to be placed precisely where the plan said they should be, or the project would be doomed from the start. The crew John had hired had done an excellent job. Everything was ready when I arrived at Walloon.

When the original cottage arrived via the frozen lake, the crew and the horses pulled it on to shore and placed it in a beautiful valley between two hills. One of the hills belonged to some nice folks from Illinois and the other hill belonged to John. It was at least a 60-foot rise from the lower cottage to the site on top of the hill. The view of the lake was almost indescribable. I never saw anyone walk into the Topsider after it was finished that did not stop in their tracks and become overwhelmed with the view. The Topsider was designed to have a minimal footprint on the land. It thrust upward from its pedestal foundation and projected outward into the surrounding treetops. Just enough limbs were pruned to fully expose the view of the lake.

The kit arrived about three days before I did. We arrived on a Saturday evening so I had one whole day of vacation before the crew arrived. First, we installed the cantilever beams by bolting them to the pedestal and attaching the pre-cut braces. Everything fit exactly as it was supposed to. Next to be installed were the prebuilt floor sections complete with insulation already in place. The entire house came neatly packed on a huge tractor-trailer rig. The biggest challenge for the delivery guys, other than just finding the place, was maneuvering the hilly and often one lane road with that big rig. I was sorry that I had not been there to see them turn it around.

Each of the bathrooms was a completely finished unit. I had seen one-piece fiberglass tub/showers many times, but this was the first one-piece fiberglass bathroom I had ever seen. The floor, walls, and ceiling were a single fiberglass pod with the vanity and commode attached and ready to go. Not literally ready to go, because you still had to hook it up to water and sewer. We laid down some boards and slid the bathrooms out to the floor system and into place.

The interior and exterior walls came finished on both sides. The outside was stained cedar and the inside was stained wood or wall-paper. It looked ready to live in after this phase was complete, except for the fact that it had no roof. The rooms all had vaulted ceilings with angled wall sections to separate the bedrooms from the living spaces. The kitchen cabinets came prefinished with the sink and appliances already installed. This was truly better than any swing set kit I had ever worked with.

The triangular shaped roof panels already had the cedar shake shingles attached. All we had to do was to install the ridge caps between the roof panels. In the two weeks I was there we had completed the structure. All that remained when I left was to connect the utilities.

A day or two before I left the bulldozer man showed up to grade what there was of a yard. This was no place for a bulldozer man to be cocky. This guy was. He was working on the lakeside of the house when he suddenly backed up too fast. I cannot describe the size of this man's eyes as the bulldozer careened backwards down the sixty feet toward the lake. The only thing that saved him, and the lake, was a path, carved into the hillside, as it ran along the shoreline. It was just wide enough to give his bulldozer traction since he had already shifted the gears into forward as he was sliding backwards down the hill. He came back up much slower than he went down.

That two-week experience taught me a lot about building that I did not know. It also taught me that in the future, Walloon was going to be that special place reserved only for vacations.

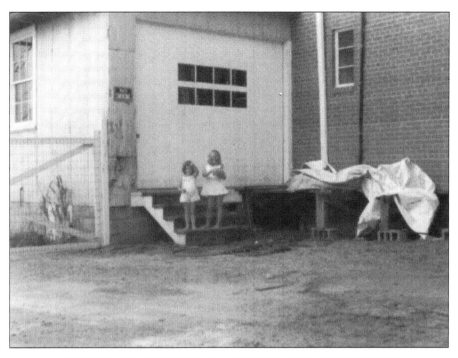

CARRIE AND GINNY AT LOADING DOCK AT THE SHOP

DAD, MAX AND I EVENTUALLY WORKED FROM THE
NEW REAL ESTATE OFFICE.

DAD'S EARLY YEARS WERE SPENT IN A COTTAGE
ACROSS FROM THE SHOP UNTIL MY GRANDDAD
DREW THIS HOUSE ON A MATCHBOX COVER.

DAD GOT HIS FIRST BIG BREAK WHEN HIS BEST
FRIEND HIRED HIM TO BUILD THIS PLANT.

IN THE 1950'S DAD STARTED HIS FIRST MAJOR DEVELOPMENT WITH
HIS BUILDING PARTNER, CLYDE, AND HIS FRIEND WOODROW.

YEARS LATER THE HOUSES GOT BIGGER AND BIGGER.

THE INDOOR COURTS – WHERE I WAS CHAMP FOR A DAY

THE RACQUET CLUB WAS THE FIRST OF ITS
KIND IN THE STATE. DAD LIKED BEING FIRST.

DAD

TOOTS WOULD HAVE BEEN PROUD OF HIS HOUSE
AFTER I ADDED A NEW DOOR FRAME AND A BAY WINDOW.

IT WAS A GREAT FEELING NOT TO BE BURIED
UNDER THAT PILE OF BRICKS.

JEFF EAGERLY AWAITS THE ARRIVAL OF THE CRAVEN HOUSE.
WE WERE JUST HOPING IT WOULD FIT BETWEEN THOSE TWO POLES.

A YOUNGER ME INTRODUCES OUR U.S. SENATOR
AT THE DEDICATION OF OUR HISTORIC SHOPPING VILLAGE.

CATHY'S GRANDFATHER BUILT THE COTTAGE AT WALLOON
IN 1922 BY DRAGGING AN OLD ICE HOUSE ACROSS THE FROZEN LAKE.

**I LEARNED A LOT BUILDING THE TOPSIDER ONE
SUMMER, MAINLY THAT VACATIONS ARE FOR RESTING.**

**GENERATIONS OF OUR FAMILY ENJOYED TIME
SPENT TOGETHER AT THE OLD AND NEW COTTAGE AT WALLOON.**

WALLOON

⇛ 8 ⇚

KEEPING UP WITH THE JONESES

The founder and CEO of Exit Realty International, Steve Morris, the firm from which I purchased my current real estate franchise, always says that you should give out at least three thousand business cards a year. He says it is the best and cheapest way to get your name out to the general public. He also admits that most real estate agents do not hand out anywhere near that many for a variety of reasons. Even though it is the cheapest form of advertising, most agents are reluctant to spend the extra money. Some are just shy, and some just do not want to bother.

One summer I was working with the crew on a job site at the end of a cul-de-sac. We were building a large transitional house for a couple, both of whom were doctors. I noticed a car pull into the cul-de-sac and park. A woman got out and started looking around. The house we were building was the only one in the cul-de-sac. The rest of the land was undeveloped. She looked a little perplexed, so I put down what I was doing and walked out and introduced myself. She said that she was thinking about building a house in a year or two and was scouting out vacant land. I told her what I knew about the lots in that area and a little about the process in general. She thanked me, and as she started to leave, I gave her my business card and told her to call me if she ever had any further questions.

Two years later, I got a phone call from a lady who started the conversation by saying, "You probably don't remember me, but you gave me your business card in a cul-de-sac in front of a house you were building for two doctors." Actually, I did remember her, but not her name. Unfortunately, names are never etched into my brain. If you tell me where you are from, I will remember it forever, but your name is a lost cause. Anyway, what's-her-name told me that she and her husband were ready to build. They wanted to talk with me about the process since I had been so helpful. She also said that if I had not given her my business card, she would have had no idea who to call. Thus began the largest and best project I ever built.

The design process was fun. The clients, whom we will call Mr. and Mrs. Jones, were prominent in the business community. He was one of the top executives of the region's largest employer. He was also an excellent golfer and represented his company in the Pro-Am golf tournaments which his company sponsored across the country. His first request of me was to design the three-car garage with a tall enough ceiling so that he could practice his golf swing indoors on rainy days. This requirement literally involved having him stop his swing, club in hand, at the top of his swing motion, so I could climb up a ladder and measure the minimum distance we needed. Mrs. Jones planned the rest of the house.

⚜

Once the permits were obtained, we were ready to break ground. It was time for the bulldozer to arrive. This is the moment on the jobsite when chance really begins. I was fortunate during my building career to have worked with two of the best bulldozer men in the business. Duck did our work in the first half of my building career, as he had done for much of Dad's career. I only remember Duck making two mistakes. The odd thing was that they both occurred on the same street, but on two different pieces of property. Bulldozer men pride themselves on always knowing what they are pushing over, where it is going, and what is behind them when they are backing up.

Usually when I came on to the job site, Duck would stop his machine so we could hear each other talk. He was running a little behind one particular day. Obviously, he had promised to be somewhere else before the day was over. He continued to drive, and we shouted at each other over the noise of his powerful engine. He was backing up at full throttle, talking to me, and not paying attention as he hit a large tree dead center. I had never seen anything stop a bulldozer cold in its tracks before. I had also never seen that expression on Duck's face as he desperately made sure his eyeballs were both where they needed to be.

About a year later we were building a house on a lot where we probably should not have been building a house. Dad had a philosophy that any lot could eventually become a good lot once you figured out how to fix it. This particular piece of ground was extremely low with two creeks running through the property. Flood insurance was not an issue then, but I do not think this lot would have required flood insurance even today, because once the two creeks merged, they continued downhill for quite a distance. The lot, therefore, was not really in a collection area for water. There was a nice little section of the property right in the middle that was ideal for a house. We just had to be able to get to it. We brought in a backhoe to dig out the two creeks and install 36-inch diameter concrete pipe. Then we dug a ditch around the three upper sides of the lot. We filled the ditch with washed stone and a smaller concrete pipe, thus lowering the water table for the entire piece of property. With all of this planning we were able to create a stable lot for the house we wanted to build, but not before one of the funniest sights I had ever seen occurred.

Duck was working on the property along with the backhoe driver. He was clearing the areas along the creek banks so the backhoe could set up next to the creek and dig. There was an area between the two creeks, just before they merged, that did not look too stable. Duck and I discussed not going into this area, but he decided it would be all right. Duck had no sooner straddled the first creek on his way to this part of the lot, when he hit what could only be described as quick sand. He desperately tried to work his way free, but it was of no use. Once he realized it was hopeless, he told me to get someone to help him get out.

There was only one firm in the area with a piece of equipment large enough to help us. That machine belonged to Duck's former employer.

I do not know the full story about why Duck no longer worked for these folks, but I quickly got the impression that, if there was anyone else in the whole world that could rescue Duck, that person would be his first choice. I think pride was involved as well as bragging rights. Anyway, time was of the essence since the dozer was slowly disappearing.

This event happened before the cell phone, so I jumped in the car and headed for the rival's bulldozer shop. Luckily, when I arrived the owner was there. After telling my story, which was followed by a lot of laughter, they loaded up their largest machine and followed me to the site. Upon arriving at the site, at first glance, I could not find Duck. Then I spotted him, standing ankle deep in mud, with only the vent stack of his bulldozer above ground. The look on his face was pitiful. Duck was not a tall man so I am glad we did not get there any later. After a lot of grunts and groans, and strained engine noises, and a few chuckles, they got the bulldozer out. Duck spent the rest of the day washing it off.

—⟨⟩—

My second bulldozer operator was Bill. He was closer to my age and we became good friends. He was the one I hired to clear the lot for the Jones's house project. Other than the great Northwest, trees in North Carolina are as tall as anywhere in the country. Interestingly enough, Mrs. Jones chose a cul-de-sac lot in Winston-Salem. It was several acres in size and had big, beautiful trees. Most of them had to come down since the footprint of the house and its extensive driveway system took up most of the lot. We left a row of trees along the right side of the property, not too far from another large house.

The trees were close to one hundred feet tall, which means they took up a lot of space when they fell. It was always easier to push over a tree that had not been topped because, once you got the tree to start falling, the weight of the top brought it down even faster. Sometimes a tree will have one particular root system that is stronger than any of the others. Sometimes a root is embedded in some underground rock system. When you encounter a tree like that, it will often twist as you start to push it over. The real problem with pushing over trees is that you do not know which trees will create trouble for you.

You always have to work from the perimeter of the lot toward the interior of the lot when there are houses on the neighboring property. Bill started pushing against a very tall tree that was in the path of the future driveway. Just as it started to gain some momentum, the tree started to twist ninety degrees to the right, sending it toward the neighbor's lot. It did not make it to the neighbor's lot because it landed right in the fork of another tree. The tree we were pushing down was stuck at almost a 45-degree angle. That meant it had fallen too far to stand back up. Besides, we could not have pushed it back up without getting on the neighbor's exquisitely landscaped property.

Even though the tree in which it was caught belonged to the Joneses, they did not want it cut. Bill and I scratched our heads for quite a while and could not come up with a solution. The only thing that I could figure out was to hire a crane—one big enough and probably expensive enough to lift the fallen tree out of the forks of the tree that had so cleverly captured it. I knew the steel beams I had designed to span the two-story family room, were going to take a modest sized crane to set them in place. I decided to leave the tree alone for a while. I did not want to spend the extra money for the super-sized crane any sooner than I had to. The one drawback to giving a contract price on a house project was, when something like this happened, there was no one to send the bill to.

———

A couple of months later, the basement was in place and we had just finished the main floor system. It was a Friday and by the end of work that day we had raised about half of the first floor walls. It was May, and May was always the busiest month of the year when you had four kids and three of them were girls. There was always an endless supply of ballet recitals, piano recitals, singing recitals, and plays to attend. This Friday night was no exception, except that I also had to go to Guilford College in Greensboro to move my oldest daughter home for the summer. Cathy and I split the duty. I took Jeff with me to get Carrie at college; Ginny was still in Durham at Duke; Cathy had a music rehearsal and then went to pick up Amy from a play she was appearing in at the Salem College auditorium.

During the many trips up and down the stairs from the dorm room to the car in the parking lot, I noticed a storm system building to the west. It really was not like any I had ever seen. The rolling and angry clouds were tall and overwhelming. Our pace quickened. Once we had loaded everything, the two-car convoy headed west toward Winston-Salem. I turned on the car radio to see if there was any news about the storm. To my surprise, a tornado hit the radio station's studio shortly after I started listening to the broadcast.

I immediately stopped the van and flagged down Carrie and Jeff in the other car. I told them we needed to turn south and go through High Point on the way home. Halfway across High Point, the storm hit. The sun had set so we could no longer see the storm clouds barreling down on us. As we pulled up to an intersection, I was in the outside lane, and Carrie was in her car to my left. All of a sudden the stoplight that had been hanging innocently in the middle of the intersection was being blown by such a fierce wind, that it was now hanging parallel to the ground instead of vertical. The street signs blew over and a gust of wind lifted up the right side of my fully loaded van. For a moment, I was about to land on top of my kids and my car, in the lane beside me. Then, with a thud, the van fell back to its normal position.

About a block down the road we pulled into a church parking lot. I gathered the kids and we ran through the rain and the debris to find sanctuary in the church. I will never forget opening the door to the darkened church and seeing only hundreds of candles being held by others who were also seeking shelter. When I got home, I learned that Cathy and Amy had had a similar experience as a tornado passed right over the auditorium, which luckily was located in a well-defined valley. That same storm also then made its way all the way to Durham 90 miles away where Ginny was.

She luckily escaped any damage.

The next morning, I loaded my chain saws and axes in my Jeep and headed to Winston-Salem to check on my job sites. Numerous times, as I got closer to the city, I had to stop and clear away trees that had fallen across the road. I spent all day clearing debris at several sites before I got to the Jones's house. When I pulled up to the site, I absolutely could not believe what I saw. The storm had picked up the tree that had been wedged in the forks of the adjacent tree. That was the good news. The bad news was the storm had carefully laid the tree directly through the front door of the Jones's house. Fortunately, we only had to rebuild one wall and replace a few floor joists. Mother Nature had solved the problem Bill and I could not solve in just seconds. I was extremely amazed and pleased.

⚶

Masons are truly a different breed. In residential construction they have historically worked and been paid by the brick and not by the hour. That simply means that the more bricks they laid, the more money they made. Our masons were the best. Most mason crews were so messy that, when the job was finished, the builder had to hire a crew to wash the brickwork with acid so that it would look neat and clean. We rarely, if ever, had to clean the brick when our crew finished. I use the term "our crew", but these guys were independent. They occasionally worked for other builders, especially if they were paying more and the work was easier. Our jobs, which usually included a lot of specialty work, often involved special negotiations with the masons. Masons do not like fireplaces and chimneys because it is slow work. The Jones's house had six fireplaces in three different chimneys. Two of the chimneys were extremely tall and would require a lot of time-consuming scaffold work. On the plus side, there was an awful lot of just plain brickwork on which they could make a lot of money.

As was so often the case, there was some continuity between my crews and my Dad's crews. The father-in-law of one of my masons had been Dad's head mason for years. A number of my carpenters' fathers had worked for Dad at one time or another. Most of my crews had some family connection. Even one of my West Virginia guys was the nephew of one of Dad's former clients. His uncle appeared at the shop one day and asked me to give his nephew a job. I did not know the young man but I liked the uncle, so I gave him a try. He turned out to be one of the best hires I ever made and now runs his own construction company.

The masons were at the Jones's house for a long time. They finished all of the outside brickwork. They built and topped out the three chimneys. Five of the fireplaces were typical fireplaces. Some were prepared for a marble surround. Some had a brick surround, and the face of one was bricked to the ceiling. The fireplace in the two-story family room, however, was to be faced with stone. The masons had built the chimney and the firebox. The face of the two-story chimney was covered with metal wall ties which the masons had inserted to secure the stone to the chimney itself.

I had figured into the price of the house an allotment for the stone, and waited for Mrs. Jones to make a selection. I was hoping that the rest of the house, and especially the family room, would be far enough along to start the stonework before the masons left the job site. It wasn't. Most stone for fireplace facades usually falls into one of two groups. One is what we called stacked stone. You lay stacked stone by placing the stone pieces on their sides and inserting the mortar along the back edge of the stone pieces where it cannot be seen from the front. This produces a contemporary effect and definitely would not have been compatible with this traditionally designed house. The other look you achieve with stone is created by fitting the various shapes of the stone pieces together like a puzzle, flat side out. Stone comes in all shapes and colors and I assumed that Mrs. Jones would choose a stone that fit this type of façade. However, she did not.

She chose a round river rock. This is when I learned there was a third type of stone façade. This was indeed a beautiful stone and promised to look great all the way up the 19-foot high façade. It seems that the problem with round river rock is that it is round. It is easy to secure a jagged edged stone in a wall with mortar. A round stone, however, only tends to roll out of the wall before the mortar has had a chance to set up. I had made several trips to the stone company in Greensboro to personally hand pick each stone for Mrs. Jones. Once the several tons of stone had been unloaded outside the nearest door to the family room, I brought the masons back to the job to show them what they had to work with. They were good stonemasons and had faced a lot of fireplaces for me in the past with stone. They took one look at the stone and said emphatically "No." A lot of begging followed, but the answer was still no.

They explained the difference to me between laying conventional stone and laying round river rock. It seems that with conventional stone, even though the work goes slowly, they can still get in a full day's work. The word "slowly" is a term meaning they were going to charge me a lot more money. With round river rock, they explained that you could only stack it two rows high at a time. Also, the mortar had to be a special blend with a high component of Portland cement, which is the lime-based powder that makes everything stick together. Oh yes, the round stone had to be laid with your hands and not with typical masonry tools. After laying the stone, you had to wait approximately five or six hours before you could tool the joints. Tooling the joint meant coming back to the job site once the mortar had cured long enough to become firm, but not fully set. Then, you scraped off the excess mortar and made sure the visible joints were smooth. I was beginning to understand why the masons said "No".

My next step was to call every mason I knew, as well as talk to some of my competitors about the possibility of hiring their crews. Those who did not laugh at me just simply said "No". That led to one more shot at my regular masons, but to no avail.

Most mason crews had at least one helper or assistant for each mason. Often a two-man mason crew had three masons' helpers. My two-man mason crew had Luke. Luke could do the work of three people. He was a large, strong man of few words. A more accurate description would be a man of no words. Luke never looked like he was working hard, but he never wasted a motion. He sat down every now and then because he would get ahead in his work. I remember when the masons bought a forklift. After that, Luke got to sit down even more because he was very efficient with the forklift. It was a thing of beauty to watch Luke toss three or four brick at a time up to the masons, standing 10 feet above him on a scaffold. Each toss was just perfect and the brick would stop in mid air, hanging there just long enough for the mason to grab each one, and stack it on the scaffold. The forklift, unfortunately, made this talent obsolete. Luke would just lift a pallet of brick up to the scaffold and place it in the right spot. The masons would not even have to turn around. This was more productive but not nearly as entertaining to watch. Building the tall chimneys, however, brought out a renewal of Luke's tossing talents, because the tops of the chimneys were far beyond the reach of the forklift.

My main job description could be summed up in a simple phrase— solve the problem. My personality description usually meant that solving the problem was accomplished by doing it myself. I figured that it would take twenty-two sessions of laying stone to complete the façade and the hearth. I visited the job site every day anyway so why not stay most of each morning. I could come back late in the afternoon and tool the joints. I had a conversation with my masons about the technique for laying round river rock. They were helpful and I also got the feeling that they were very happy not to be doing the job. The hint came in the form of a slight hidden chuckle now and then. Their last piece of advice was to talk to Luke about preparing and handling the mortar. This promised to be a short conversation. Luke told me what ratio of sand, water and Portland cement to use. More importantly, he explained that the mixture needed to be the consistency of soft clay or bread dough. As he turned to leave the room, he looked back and said "You had better get some gloves."

I was way too macho to wear gloves. Besides the cool, soft, lime enriched mortar felt good to my hands. The first thing I did was to pick out the member of my crew, Johnny, that looked the most like Luke, and fill him full of instructions. I taught him how to mix the mortar, which he did one batch at a time in a wheelbarrow. He was told how many stones to have next to the fireplace each morning. As the job progressed he would also have to build scaffolds, which I thoroughly examined, and stock them with stone. To do that task, I delegated to him the responsibility of picking an assistant. This made him feel important. Each morning, I would arrive about an hour after Johnny, so that work could start immediately.

The first day was a little bit of an experiment. The fireplace was designed to have a raised hearth so that the Joneses could sit on it if they so desired. This also meant that the first two or three rows of stone would be hidden behind the raised hearth which would be built as the final step in the process. The first day was spent learning how the stones, with different sizes and shapes, reacted to the stiffness of the mortar. I quickly learned how easily they rolled out of the wall. The cure for that was a drier, stiffer mortar and always placing the fattest side of the stone toward the bottom. I was quite pleased with the first day's work and convinced that I had learned all I needed to know about the stone laying process. My goodness was I wrong.

When I woke up the next morning there was no skin on the ends of any of my fingers. Besides the pain, I could not pick up anything or hold a pencil. In the back of my mind I kept hearing Luke's final words, "You had better get some gloves." If only he had told me why I needed the gloves, I might have paid more attention. The reality was that high concentrations of lime and skin do not mix. Yes, I was embarrassed the next day when I was late to the job site. Even worse was the fact that all ten fingers were taped on the ends. Johnny had to throw out that batch of mortar because day two of the project was definitely on hold. On the way home that evening I stopped at the grocery store and purchased the biggest, ugliest pair of bright yellow dishwashing gloves you have ever seen. The long sleeves of the gloves practically went up to my elbows. They were thick and bulky but I was convinced they would protect my hands from the flesh-eating mortar. I wished Luke had been a little more verbal.

After a few days of healing, the project re-started. It was a lot of fun creating such a thing of beauty. The higher we got, the more demanding a job it was physically. Mrs. Jones would come by each morning to check on the progress. I could tell by the way she stood there admiring the stonework that the efforts were worthwhile. Every now and then we would run across a stone that was a little flatter on one side. We would set that stone aside to be used on the surface of the hearth. As we neared the top, the scaffold would shake and sway a little more with each section we added. One fear I had was dropping a stone, or having one roll off the scaffold. I wasn't sure how far into the earth it would penetrate. Each day when I finished, I would survey the façade from every angle in the room to see if there were any stones that did not look like they should be there. If there were, I would climb back up and take them out.

Once we reached the top, we tore down the scaffolds and got our first look at the façade. Our entire crew was proud of what we, and not the masons, had done. We still needed several more work sessions to finish the hearth. It took more stones to complete the hearth than I thought it would. That is why you always order a little extra material when doing a job like this. I did not want to have many stones left over though, because I did not want anyone else to be tempted to use this stone again.

Late one afternoon, I laid the last stone! Mrs. Jones was present for the installation of that final stone. This time, when I finished, satisfied but really tired, I did not check it out from all of the angles. I took off the big yellow gloves, which had begun to show signs of wear and tear, and tossed them into our big trashcan. I nodded to Mrs. Jones and walked out the door with a feeling of great relief.

<hr />

The Joneses were special people. They were efficient and business-like in their dealings with everyone, but at the same time, they were very generous. My son was a golfer and so was Mr. Jones. Mr. Jones asked my son, Jeff, to caddy for him in one of the annual golf tournaments that his company sponsored. As a high school golfer, Jeff was thrilled to get the opportunity. He ended up caddying for Mr. Jones throughout his high school years and got to meet many of the big names in golf, as well as many famous celebrities and sports figures. These times gave him memories for a lifetime. I always got to tag along inside the ropes of the tournament and meet the same folks.

A year or so after the house was completed, I was meeting with Mrs. Jones about the one-year punch list items. Somewhere in the conversation I was bemoaning the cost of sending four kids to college. Since the Joneses had no children, she said they had sadly missed that experience. I mentioned that the foreman on her job had a bright high school senior who wanted to go to college, but they did not think they could afford anything more than the local community college. A few days later she asked me to bring my foreman by the house. The three of us sat in the family room, in front of the massive stone façade of the fireplace, and she told him that she and Mr. Jones were going to pay for his daughter's college costs for all four years. Wow, you don't meet folks like this every day!

We had done our best to give the Joneses the type of customer service they deserved. When you hired us as your builder, you not only got a custom designed house, but each facet of the house was custom designed. We designed and hand built the kitchen cabinets. The Joneses each had closets the size of a normal bedroom. Each closet was specially catered for their own personal needs. A prominent design feature on the front of the house was the front door frame. This is one place size does really matter. On a house this large, the doorframe had to stand out and be a focal point. I knew what I wanted it to look like, as far as the various moldings were concerned, but just how big it should be had to be site tested.

In the shop I drew an outline of the top of the doorframe on a piece of four-foot by eight-foot by one-quarter inch plywood. The top of the frame was the key element because the legs, or side pieces, would be directly proportional to the top. After sketching the shape on the plywood, I used the band saw to cut out the image. It would not fit in the back of my Jeep so one of our big trucks had to haul it the twenty-five miles from the shop to the site. After tacking it up above the door, Mrs. Jones and I put on our imagination hats and stood in the front yard. We stood in every part of the front yard before deciding which parts of the top of the frame pattern needed to be changed. Back to the shop for version number two. Version number six was perfect. The next couple of days were spent in the shop crafting the doorframe. We made it in three parts and took it to the job site. Immediately upon assembling the frame we coated it with white primer so the various moldings would show their depth properly. It looked great and Mrs. Jones was pleased with the results and the finished elegance that this entrance created.

<hr>

I have been invited to a number of house warming parties that took place after one of our creations was completed. I have even been invited to a house blessing and dedication. Mrs. Jones told me at the final settlement meeting, which took place around their breakfast room table, that they wanted to have the entire crew and subcontractors over to celebrate the house being finished. I had no idea what she had in mind. A couple of months after the house was completed, the Joneses asked me for a list of every one who had worked on the house. This list was to include all of the subcontractors and their employees who actually worked at the house site.

The invitations went out and all of the workers' families were included as well. We all gathered on a beautiful spring Saturday evening on their extensive network of brick patios, which many of us had helped lay by hand. They had brought in several barrel-topped outdoor grills, on which cooks were grilling barbequed chicken and filet mignon. They had all of the trimmings and an open bar, even though, many, if not most, of my employees did partake of adult beverages, they did not show it in excess that night. It is hard to describe how proud I was that a client of ours was so pleased with what our entire crew had done. I just relished the moment.

Then it became time for the Joneses to say their "thank you" to everyone. After complimenting the electrician, the plumber, the bull-dozer folks, and each of my carpenters, Mrs. Jones said she had a special presentation. She unveiled an 18-inch by 24-inch framed glass shadow box in which had been placed my yellow gloves. It seems that immediately after I had nodded to her and walked out the door after laying the last stone on the hearth, she reached into the trash can and retrieved the worn out yellow gloves. They were no longer yellow because she had had them "bronzed" in pewter. There was of course an appropriate inscription. Those gloves and a 2 x 4 named "Ray" are the type of things you keep forever,

It was the most unique gift I had ever received. I was very proud of what we had accomplished and how truly grateful and appreciative our clients were. As I reflected back on that event in the coming months and years, I was also a little sad knowing that that particular moment had to be the pinnacle of my building career. Times were starting to change, and finding clients that truly appreciated good craftsmanship was becoming more difficult. Even more difficult in the future, would be finding clients who appreciated the effort you put forth in building their house. Something inside me told me that no one else would ever be able to keep up with the Joneses.

≋ 9 ≋

THE BRIGHT SIDE

If you are lucky with your life, you work at a job that you love. That does not mean you love it all of the time. Every job has its ups and downs, good days and bad days. Looking back, there were a number of things that I consistently liked about the building business. I liked getting started and I liked getting finished, especially getting paid. None of us is willing to work for free, at least not intentionally.

The first time I went to Disney World, one thought stood out in my mind as we rode the monorail into the Magic Kingdom. Where did they start? Where did they drive the first stake? I always enjoyed driving the first stake on a piece of property. The finished product was already engraved in my mind before the first tree was cut. Before you could drive the first stake, you had to establish where the lot corners were. The standing joke at the office was that the first thing you wanted to do was to make sure you built the house on the right lot. In a large cabinet at the office was a collection of recorded plats of all of the major subdivisions where we frequently built. A description of the proposed lot was extracted from these maps to identify the property on the contract documents. The plat always accompanied me to the site to locate the corner stakes.

We had opened a new street in a subdivision call Glenwood. There were about ten lots in a row on the west side of the street that were just perfect for houses with basements. In the middle of this stretch of lots was a 20-foot wide cleared easement for a sewer outfall line. An easement of this type actually occupied ten feet of each of the two adjoining lots. The homeowners still owned the property but they were restricted in the way they could use the land in the easement. Essentially they had the right to mow it, pay taxes on it and walk on it. They could not build anything on the land. The sewer line usually ran underneath the street, but at some point it needed to find a way to reach the main sewer outfall line that served as a collection system for all of the sewer lines in the area. In this case the main outfall line, the big line that took all of the "stuff" to the sewer plant somewhere down stream, ran behind the lots in question.

My clients had chosen the lot to the right of the cleared easement area. Since all of the lots were heavily wooded, it was easy to spot which lot they wanted. The contract was signed and the permits were bought. I headed out to the lot with the plat under my arm. This time someone else was carrying the ax and the two-by-twos.

The first thing I always did when I arrived was walk up and down the street until I found an established corner iron. There were two types of homeowners in every neighborhood. One type could care less about where their corners were, and threw away the iron stakes as soon as their lawn mower hit them. The other type meticulously maintained their corner irons, often protecting them with a small shrub. These folks usually had every iron in place.

I had to walk a long way up the block, past the new lots, to the third existing house. The new lots had iron corners, but it was easier to find them in a nicely mown lawn than in the briar patch that existed before the lots were cleared. I carefully measured off each lot as I came down the street, placing a two by two at each corner until I arrived at the sewer easement. Something was wrong. Either the sewer easement was in the wrong place, meaning we had sold them the wrong lot, or the plat was wrong. I measured again. And again. Now I was beginning to doubt the plat which was recorded in the Register of Deeds office. Having the plat recorded made the plat as close to being the map gospel as you could get.

I sent the crew to another job site and headed to the city engineer's office, plat in hand. After a long explanation from me, and trip to the lot, the city engineer scratched his head and said, "Well, I'll be damned." His departmental draftsman had put the sewer easement in the wrong place on the plat. Even though it was going to take a few days to correct the plat and get a new one recorded, he gave me permission to change the lot number on the building permit and start the project. But that was only half of the solution. I had to meet with the client next, and explain not only what happened, but that they were contractually obligated to buy the wrong lot. Luckily, the client did not care what lot number it was. They just wanted the lot next to the sewer line. Luckily too, we still owned all of the lots on that side of the street and could easily switch the numbers on the contract.

⎯⎯⎰⎱⎯⎯

I prided myself on being a good reader of maps as well being a good detective when it came to finding lot corners. We had signed a contract to build a house on the only vacant lot remaining on a street in a popular middle class subdivision. Vacant lots are easy to spot when there is a house on all of the other lots. The tricky part was always being accurate when finding the corners. The neighbors usually knew where their corners were. At least they thought they did. When they had been mistakenly using part of the lot next door for a few years, they were reluctant to give it back.

I always carried my amateur surveyor's gear in the truck when making that first visit to the lot. The City Manager happened to live next door, and I knew him quite well. I really wanted to be right on this particular occasion. After considerable checking and re-checking, I placed the front right corner stake where I was confident it should be. "Houston, we have a problem." My stake was a couple of feet into what the City Manager had obviously thought to be his yard. He had planted a beautiful row of shrubs to mark the edge of his yard and my stake was on the wrong side of the shrubs. My crew looked at the stake and said "That can't be right." I glanced toward the City Manager's house and saw his wife looking out the window. She did not have a happy look on her face.

I told the crew that we were going to proceed with what we were doing, and that I had a feeling we would know if we were right within ten minutes. They did not understand why I said that, but within ten minutes, a surveying crew from the city arrived. They set up some real surveyor's toys and went to work, never saying a word to us. After about an hour, they left and another crew from the city arrived and dug up and replanted the entire row of shrubs. Again, no one said a word to us. Being right can be lonely sometimes.

⟢⟣

Old Beau was a dog. They say you can learn to love even an ugly face. That applied to Old Beau. Beau belonged to a gentleman named Billy who was responsible for creating two of my favorite golf courses, Bermuda Run Country Club and Old Beau Golf Club. Bermuda Run is near Clemmons, NC, and for years was the home of the Bing Crosby Charity Golf Tournament. I have many fond memories of watching Bob Hope stroll up the 18th fairway toward the hilltop clubhouse. When Billy decided to build a golf course just off of the Blue Ridge Parkway in the North Carolina Mountains, he named it after his best friend, Old Beau. It is a spectacular course with hundreds of feet in elevation changes and breathtaking views of the region's mountains and valleys. The best view on the course is the one Old Beau has for eternity. Billy buried him just behind the 15th green in a spot where you can see the entire Piedmont region of North Carolina.

There was a vacant lot next to Billy's house in Bermuda Run. This was one of the choice lots in the entire gated community, situated on a bluff over looking the Yadkin River flood plain. Several beautiful golf holes and lakes meandered along the river's banks. A widow had contracted our company to design and build her a new home. I told one of our crews to meet me at the property about two o'clock one afternoon with 2 x 2's and string so we could locate the house.

As usual, I was running a little late. When I arrived at the site the crew was gathered at the back right corner of the bluff next to Billy's house. Billy had installed a large plate glass window on that corner of his house and it stretched almost to the floor. The purpose of the window was to take advantage of the spectacular view. I knew that I had left the crew with nothing to do for at least a half an hour, so I had no idea what they were up to. When I asked, they pointed to the plate glass window and the large, short-legged bull dog behind it. "We're trying to get that bulldog to jump through the plate glass window," one of them said. I did not know whether to laugh, cry, or get angry.

I said to them, "Do you know who that is?" They all shook their heads in the negative. I asked them if they had seen the billboard on I-40 in downtown Winston-Salem that featured a picture of a dog. The picture of Beau was as big as the billboard, and the only words on the billboard were "Old Beau." They all had seen it. I told them that the dog they were trying to get to jump through the window was the most famous dog in North Carolina. "That's Old Beau," I said. They were stunned and quickly apologized. For the next six months Old Beau came over and played with the crew during his daily walks. They all became great friends.

⟻⟨⟩⟼

Dad told me a story about what happened to him while working in Richmond, Virginia during World War II. The government had him designing and building warehouses at a huge storage facility just south of the city. These warehouses were several hundred feet wide and at least five hundred feet long. He told me this story while teaching me to use a piece of surveying equipment that he had used during the war. The most common use for this particular instrument was to determine a 90-degree angle over a long distance. When you are set up over point A, and locate point B through the magnified lenses, your next job is to locate point C. Point C needed to be a 90-degree turn from point B. The goal here is to be absolutely accurate when you turn the scope 90 degrees. It is pretty easy to be accurate when you are dealing with numbers used for a single-family residence, but an Army warehouse was a different matter. It seems that Dad got one of the buildings a little off when he laid it out. After the walls were built and the two hundred foot long trusses arrived, the cranes started installing them. At first they fit just fine. The further they went down the length of the building, the more overhang appeared. By the time they got to the far end, the roof trusses were 30 feet wider than the walls.

I was never 100 per cent sure this story was true until our family was taking a vacation one summer through the great state of Virginia. I thought it might be fun to see if we could get into the Army's supply depot. The guard at the gate who was both official and pleasant said we were not allowed to enter. I told him the story about the warehouse with the extra wide overhang at one end. After having a big laugh he said, "That's a well-known landmark in here, but I still cannot let you in."

⁂

While I was in college, Dad built a lot of houses in Greensboro. Split-level style houses were popular in those days. He had a contract to build a split-level for a couple who were transferred to the area. Their lot was one of only two vacant lots left on that particular street. The other vacant lot happened to be next door, but it had a creek running from front to back, right through the middle of the lot. It was owned by the man who lived on the other side of the vacant lot. The foreman of the Greensboro crew located the corners and established the set back point. The set back point is the minimum distance that either the subdivision covenants, or the city zoning laws required you to be away from the street. This was not a big lot so the crew was told to set the house exactly on the setback point.

The foreman marked off the house and proceeded to pour the footings. He did not realize when he poured the footings for the lower level at exactly the set back point, that the upper floor of a split level would usually hang over the lower floor by a foot or more. This one did, and that made the house too close to the street. The neighbor who owned the worthless lot next door spotted the mistake the day they staked off the house.

On the day the house was finished, Dad and the happy couple showed up at the lawyer's office to take care of the final settlement, the neighbor appeared with an injunction to prevent them from moving in. He claimed, and correctly so, that the house was too close to the street. Dad, understanding that this guy must have some motive besides never being invited to a backyard barbeque, asked what it would take to remove the injunction. He demanded that Dad buy the worthless lot next door at the going rate for the good lots.

After considerable conversation, the formerly happy couple said that they only could afford to buy the half of the lot next to their house. Dad agreed to buy the other half, knowing that he would be stuck with it forever. About eight years later, Dad got a call from the happy couple saying that they had set aside a little money each month since they moved in, and now they wanted to buy the other half of the lot from Dad. Needless to say, he sold it to them. There is just no way to describe how gratifying it is to work with folks with such great character.

The biggest financial blunder I ever made while working for Dad occurred while building a house for another one of those lawyers. This particular lawyer and his wife were great folks from the start. Some people appreciate what you do. Others stay up late at night trying to figure out how to get something from you for nothing. I designed these folks a classy two-story brick home on a new street we had developed. In those days, not everyone built a garage. After all, this was the South and it just did not get that cold in the winter. As the rest of the country began to figure out that it did not get that cold in North Carolina, they began to move here in droves. Then everybody wanted a garage because "that's the way they did it back home." This particular lawyer and his wife decided that they would have the house designed for a future garage to be built when they were better able to afford it.

Part of my job description during this period was to keep the job file up to date by recording all of the expenses, such as labor, materials and subcontractors. When we got to the end of the job, I had to prepare for the closing by assembling all of the extra charges from the change orders and allotments. Somewhere along the way my lawyer client must have won a big case, because they had us add the garage wing with a bonus room above. This amounted to an approximate 20 per cent increase in the overall cost of the project. Since this was more than your average change order, I kept the statistics in a separate job folder. When I put together the closing statement, I forgot to include the entire garage addition.

After arriving at the closing, I went over the closing statement with them. They signed the loan papers and we gave them the deed to record. Everyone was happy, including me, because I still did not realize that I had forgotten the garage. As we got up from the table, we shook hands and exchanged pleasantries. The client looked at me and said, "You forgot to charge us for the garage." Just before my stomach completely sank to the floor, he reached into his coat pocket and handed me a check for the full amount of the garage. That moment is still one of the most profound examples of honesty and good character I have ever experienced. He later became a judge, and you can be assured that we are all a little better off since he was appointed to the bench.

⚬⚬⚬

We all have things we do, think, and feel, that we just keep inside ourselves and do not share with others. I have mentioned how much I enjoyed staking off a house. Another time that I always liked was being present on the job site when the first load of lumber arrived. The foundation was always in place and ready for a house to be placed upon it. The truck from the lumberyard would be packed beyond capacity with the lumber for the flooring system. Dumping that first load was like dropping the green flag at the Indy 500. We used to laugh as a crew, saying that if the driver had been more talented, all of the lumber would have landed in the right place. Then, we would not have to do as much work.

Another ritual I did for years was to ride by the job on the night the clients moved in, just so I could see the lights on. It was more than the lights being on; it was seeing the results of all of that effort coming to life. The house we had taken so long to build had finally become a home. I do not remember when I stopped riding by on that first night, but whenever it was, it began the countdown toward getting out of the building business.

When I teach continuing education classes to real estate agents about the fundamentals of construction, I always tell them that my Grandfather drew plans on the back of a match box, and agreed to the terms with a handshake. Dad always drew detailed plans and had a one page typed contract. By the time I got out of the building business, I tell them that we would not start a project without detailed plans, a seven page set of specifications, a sixteen page contract, a lawyer and a faith healer. I do not think that we changed that much over time, but the world certainly did.

Another favorite time was getting that final payment. When you build large custom homes, this special time was often a personal moment. The final meeting for some of my largest and best clients was often at their breakfast room table. We usually had built the house on their lot, so there was no deed to be passed and recorded. We would simply go over the final numbers. They would write me a check, and we would share some sweet rolls.

With only a handful of exceptions, when we were building a custom house, we built the house for the wife. She made virtually all of the decisions about design. She picked out all of the appliances, bath fixtures, paint colors and wallpaper. When the wife came to us with an idea for a big change or redesign, we would explain to her what was involved and what it would cost. We usually got a comment like "I will get back to you tomorrow." When she left the job site the crew would always laugh about what they envisioned to be an upcoming fun evening for the husband. By the next day, the wife always had permission for that change order. However, she never wrote the check.

Sometimes the only involvement by the husband was to pay the monthly bill. I think the feeling of writing the check made them at least think they were involved. A large house I designed and built for a good friend fell into this category. About six months into the project I called him one afternoon to see if he wanted to be a fourth for tennis. When he heard my voice on the phone, the first thing he said was "How much do I owe you." About six months later he wrote the final payment as we sat around their breakfast room table.

⚊⚊

I built for a lot of friends, and for a lot of people who became good friends. You always tried to separate the business part from the friendship part. Even when you got the job because you were a friend, from that point on you wanted keep business as business. We always preferred to work on a detailed contract and a guaranteed price. The price always changed during the course of construction because everybody changed something. In my career and my Dad's career, we never finished a job without change orders. The closest we ever came was one couple who only added a screen door to their rear entrance.

One thing I spent a lot of time counseling people about was change orders. Each change order did not seem very significant at the time, but the running total could end up becoming overwhelming to the client. We had a cartoon on the office wall at the shop. It showed a draftsman placing his signature on the final version of the plans as the customer walks in the door. In the customer's arms was a stack of plan books that towered over his head. The caption said, "Are you far enough along to make changes?"

One of my good friends was my veterinarian. George took care of our dog, Butter. George had found a house plan that he and his wife liked in one of the many house plan magazines available at your local newsstand. He ordered the plans and brought them to me once they arrived. I redrew them with the customized changes they had wanted. I also redrew them because my crews were used to reading plans the way I prepared them.

After figuring a contract price for the job, George informed me that he wanted to do some of the work himself. I really hated to do that and often tried to discourage this practice with my clients. George was so enthusiastic, and was honest as the day was long, so I worked out a system. We settled on a wage rate comparable to what I paid some of the crew members. We also agreed to credit him that amount for every hour he worked. I gave him a time book and each day I left him some assigned tasks. These jobs were in the realm of clean up tasks and repetitive nailing assignments, such as nailing subfloor. George did good work and put in a number of hard hours. A few weeks into this process, I got a call one evening from George. He said, "Tony, I'll make you a deal. You build my house and I'll fix your dog." He and I were both relieved.

⁓

As much as I enjoyed working with the crews on the job sites, especially on beautiful days, I enjoyed the thousands of hours I spent on the drawing board. Designing a house on paper was as much of a thrill as was watching the house grow on the job site. From dumping that first load of lumber, to turning on that first light on the night they moved in, both building and designing were equally thrilling to me. After years of cross-hatching and filling in the details, I could not wait for my first real opportunity to take the lead on a design project. Dad called me into his office one day and told me it was time to manage a project from beginning to end. I was certainly excited and pleased that he was ready to show that much confidence in me. As I look back on the situation now, I think he just did not want to deal with these folks. It was sort of like the old commercial, "Let Mikey do it." So I got the job.

Dad did not dislike these folks at all. He just knew they were going to take a lot of time. As for the client, I think they were pleased to have their own personal project manager. This couple still ranks as one of my favorite couples that I dealt with over the years. They were detail-oriented and full of ideas. I am sure the cartoon on the office wall concerning design changes was written about them. He was a salesman and a glorious one at that. He had the gift of gab, as we used to say. I soon learned that they were going to be exhausting to work with. I understood why Dad did not want to take on this type of project. It was a perfect learning experience for me, however. They tested my design skills, my creative imagination, my patience, and my perseverance. I loved every minute of it. They were honorable and creative and together we created a spectacular house.

I designed a lot of different styles of houses over the years, but my favorite was always the Williamsburg style. Williamsburg is such a wonderful place to visit and to admire the architecture on display there. Some friends of mine wanted me to design them a true Williamsburg style home in a neighborhood that already had some pretty impressive houses. Luckily they could afford to do it right, so I had a fairly free reign in creating the design details. They had two things that were a must. One was that all of the paint colors had to be authentic Williamsburg colors. Grey is not grey in Williamsburg-ease, because the word grey has to be proceeded by the name of a famous house in Williamsburg. A gallon of grey paint with a Williamsburg prefix costs a whole lot more than the exact same color of grey without a fancy name. Having the real thing often makes a lot of people feel better, but the truth is, most paint stores have the formulas to match the fancy named colors.

The other request concerned their chimney. They wanted it to be the focal point of the house. There were two main interior chimneys that protruded through the roof in the symmetrical center section. The chimney in question was a side chimney that has the famous Williamsburg offset just above the firebox, so the upper part of the chimney was separated from the siding on the surface of the house. This was a safety issue originally, I suppose. My friends gave me the name of the house in Williamsburg that had just the chimney they wanted to duplicate. Since this was before the days of the Internet or the digital camera, there was only one thing left to do: "Road Trip."

Cathy and I loved going to Williamsburg, so this road trip was not as much of a hardship as it was an excuse. After arriving in Williamsburg and having a meal at Christiana Campbell's Tavern, we went looking for the house. The chimney in question happened to be on the side of an occupied house. Access to the chimney could only be obtained through a lovely, thick garden, surrounded by a fence. With Polaroid in hand, I managed to sneak into the garden and take some pictures. It took a while however, to sketch the chimney and count the number of bricks used to make each offset. I was glad to be finished so we could get out of there before anyone caught us. It had been fun sticking my head through the gallows at the old jail, but I had no interest in doing it at the new jail.

The house turned out to be a striking design and this side chimney, unlike the original one in Williamsburg, was totally visible from the street on the corner lot where the house was placed. I had scheduled to meet my friend and client at the house on the morning of the closing to go over the final bill. The bill included a long list of many extras they had added during the year-long building process. After going over the list, my friend started complaining about the additional cost of each item, and how he did not have the money to pay for all of them. He wanted me to give him a break since "I" had taken all of his money. He was quite good at making me feel sorry for him, so being the good guy that I was, I gave him a few breaks. The whole thing did not feel just right, but all I wanted was for him to leave, so I could finish the final touchups.

He really did not want me to walk him out to his car, but I did anyway. I wanted be sure he left and did not shed any more poverty tears. There it was, parked in the driveway, a brand new Mercedes sports convertible, which he had just bought that morning. No wonder he did not have any money left. I felt like I had just contributed to the purchase price.

Fate has a way of evening things up sometimes. About an hour later I spotted a gentleman out in the street taking pictures of the house from several different angles. With my curiosity on the rise, I trotted out to the street and asked what he was doing. He quickly told me that this was his favorite house in the entire county. I proudly told him that I had designed the house and pointed out how the chimney was a perfect replica of an original one in Williamsburg. Then I asked him what he did for a living. He told me he was the county property tax assessor. I then thought it was my civic duty to point out to him every custom detail in the house. I may not have gotten paid in full, but I think the county did.

In the early 1980's I became convinced that the building market in our small town was not going to be sufficient to supply our future needs, so I ventured to the big city in the next county. Breaking into a new market can be tough. This also meant a longer commute. After a few years of supporting the oil company's ever-rising stock by buying all of that gasoline, we sold our house and moved to the country. It was a part of the country much closer to our new market in the big city.

Our company was the new kid on the block, as far as building in the big city was concerned. Dad had suggested that I meet with an old friend of his named Lewis, who also just happened to be the biggest developer in the region. He had given many a new builder their first start. We were not new but we needed a new start in that market. Lewis provided the land and the financing, and we built the houses. Our first few projects were successful, and Lewis really liked some of our designs. His real estate firm marketed our products, and we were content to grow. Lewis quickly moved us into some larger subdivisions where we would have more exposure to the public.

This move also meant more exposure to the other, more established builders in the area. There was only one way to get your foot in the door, so to speak. You needed opportunity, good designs, and a competitive price. Lewis offered us the opportunity. Our designs spoke for themselves. Our pricing was less than our competition because we were small town guys. The wages we paid were gauged toward a less competitive market, and our profit margins were less ambitious. This did not sit well with the more established builders. Our biggest competition became a builder named Bill. He was a big, tall fellow with slightly graying temples that made him quite distinguished looking, even though I do not think he was any more than a couple of years older than me. He built an outstanding product that I personally thought was a little over-priced. At least it seemed over-priced, when compared to the market I came from.

I had been eager to meet Bill and become his friend, because I admired his work. Our first meeting did not go exactly as I had envisioned. I was building a spec house on a cul-de-sac in the neighborhood that was struck by a tornado years later. Our house was just under roof and really starting to look good. Bill had just started a spec house two lots away. Our houses had a lot of similarities in style and square footage, but not in price.

I was standing in the middle of the cul-de-sac one afternoon staring intently at our spec house. I do not even remember what decision I was trying to make. I had not seen Bill drive up and get out of his Jeep. All of a sudden a large arm stretched across my shoulders and gripped my upper right arm. Before I could react, the tall gentleman had me firmly in his grip and said, "I am Bill. I am sure glad to meet you." I quickly responded that the same applied to me as well. I expected him to let go, but he didn't. Actually the grip became more firm. "You build a great product" he said. "The other builders and I are proud to be building in the same neighborhood with you. There is only one problem. Your prices are too low." He asked what I was asking for the house in the cul-de-sac and I told him. "You need to immediately raise that price by at least ten thousand dollars."

I said thanks for the advice and he let go of me and walked away. I went over to my car phone and called Lewis. I did not tell him about the incident. I told him to raise the price of the house ten thousand dollars. Two days later the house sold for the new price. I did not know whether to thank Bill, send him a commission, or just consider it a lesson learned. We were friendly competitors after that, I think.

A few years later, a major national company was sending in a new CEO to its local plant and one of Lewis's agents was working with him. After a number of days of research, the new CEO had decided he wanted to build rather than buy an existing house. He narrowed his choice of lots down to two. I owned one lot and Bill owned the other. Bill and I had each already figured out what type of house we had planned to build on our respective lots. The client wanted to meet with each of us to see with whom he felt more comfortable.

My Dad had grey temples in college and always looked more mature (older) than he was. I, on the other hand, had a boyish look and looked at least ten years younger than I actually was. This is a curse when you are young and trying to be mature. Later in life, it can be a blessing. I spent an entire afternoon with this particular prospect, showing him some of the houses we had built and discussing our plans for the lot he liked. He sat in the front seat with me. He was splendidly attired in a pin stripped suit with tie and vest. His well-dressed wife sat in the back seat. I was dressed casually. When we finally got back to the real estate office where I had picked them up, we sat in my Jeep for a while longer discussing the project. I had a feeling that something was causing him to hesitate. Finally he said, "I need to ask you one question. I am impressed with your work, but how old are you?" I told him I was 38. Immediately his wife began laughing hysterically in the back seat. When she finally gained control of herself, she looked at me and said, "Look beside you and see what you are going to look like in two years." He turned red. We said our "Goodbyes". Bill built the house.

≡ 10 ≡

THE DARK SIDE

In the interest of fair play we must tell the bad with the good. Some of these stories you may find funnier than I did at the time they happened. Injuries are part of life. When you work around sharp things that turn very fast, they become a bigger part of life. Some injuries just cause pain for a little while, and some cause pain for a lifetime. I remember eagerly awaiting the arrival of a home gym set that I purchased at the National Homebuilders Show. You would think that I would have bought some helpful tool or building system, but no, I thought this four station home gym with lots of weights and pulleys was just what I needed. It was not like I did not get enough exercise on the job.

The delivery truck pulled up behind the real estate office one morning with my long-awaited delivery. The driver raised the rear tailgate and exposed about ten different boxes. It looked like a swing set on steroids. I offered to help unload the truck but the driver explained that it was his job to unload his freight. He started with the largest boxes, which we later discovered contained the center framework sections. They were surprisingly light. The smaller the boxes got, the lighter they became. This fact made the driver speed up his work and pay very little attention to what was in the boxes. After all, there were only four relatively small boxes left on the truck. He reached in and grabbed the next box, expecting it to be light. The only thing that moved was something in his lower back. As it turned out, the weights were in the four small boxes. About a year later, we were asked to fill out some paperwork for a workman's compensation claim. The truck driver had been declared permanently disabled.

⚜

My wife Cathy and I graduated from Duke in the first week of June in 1966. She went home to the North Shore of Chicago, and I went to work on one of Dad's crews. Four weeks later I drove to Chicago, and we were married. After a wonderful week long honeymoon in the North Carolina Mountains, it was time to go back to work. We were living in the guest suite in Dad's basement for a few weeks. One of his apartments was scheduled to become available in late August, so we were temporarily camping out.

The first week after I returned from my honeymoon, Dad and I were playing in the city tennis tournament as a doubles team. By week's end we had reached the semi-finals and were scheduled to play my doctor and his partner who were defending champs. I was really excited about the match. Some days I got really frustrated having Dad as a partner. I never knew which tennis player would show up, the focused one or the distracted one. Sometimes after a match he would look at me and say "I just did not have it today." About 25 years later I finally understood what he meant.

On the day of the big match I was working with a crew trimming out the interior of a house; we were installing paneling. This was the real kind of paneling that was three-quarters of an inch thick and had some beautiful grain in the wood. Peabody was nailing up the paneling as only he could, and his assistant, Shorty, was helping me saw the pieces of paneling. The blade on the table saw was set at one and one-half inches above the bed so that the person actually doing the sawing could see it clearly. I was pushing the paneling through the blade and Shorty was "tailing" the wood. That meant he was supposed to make sure the wood came through the blade at a steady pace and did not drop down as it finished. Just as my hand was pushing the final few inches of wood through the blade, someone hollered at Shorty and he turned away, letting the end of the board drop down. The piece of wood acted like a seesaw on my end and knocked my hand off of the piece of paneling and into the saw blade.

My hand hit the spinning blade palm up and popped right out. It didn't even hurt. Then I noticed that my middle finger on my left hand had been cut off. Only about a one-quarter inch strip of skin on the bottom side of the finger kept it from falling to the floor. I did not panic, and I remained surprisingly calm. Shorty was bouncing up and down and muttering, "Oh my, oh my!" All I could think of was my tennis match and making sure I could still play. After all, I was right-handed and this finger was on my left hand. Calmly, I asked Shorty to take my handkerchief out of my back pocket and soak it in the ice water from the water barrel. After carefully lining up the two pieces of my finger and wrapping them with the handkerchief, I asked the foreman to drive me to my doctor's office. I didn't ask Shorty because he was still muttering "Oh my, oh my."

I went in the back door of Dr. Bill's office and luckily caught him in the hall. I said, "Bill, you need to sew up my finger so we can play our match this evening." He took one look at it and called the hospital to talk with the only surgeon in town. He told me to get to the hospital as quickly as I could. It still did not hurt. I sat in the emergency room for about a half an hour while the surgeon finished sewing up someone else. In the meantime, Dad showed up to see how I was. I took the handkerchief off of my finger and bent it down to show him the cut. He actually staggered briefly. It still did not hurt. They brought a little girl into the emergency room that had gotten her big toe caught in her bicycle spokes. That looked like it hurt, so I told them to take her on up. I would wait because my finger still did not hurt.

When it was finally my turn, they rolled me into the operating room where I became quite talkative. They laid me on my back flanked by two of the biggest nurses I had ever seen. After laying my left hand on a separate surgical table, the nurse on that side unwrapped my damaged finger and bent it down. She then proceeded to squirt some soap into the wound from a plastic bottle. That started to sting just a little. Then she picked up what looked like a toothbrush and started scrubbing the wound. That hurt so much that I clinched my right fist and instinctively started to take a swing at her. I am not a violent guy, but that hurt. That is when I found out why the nurse to my right was so big. She reacted in a split second and sat on my right arm.

The surgeon and I had a nice conversation for a few minutes, and then he told me to be quiet so he could concentrate. Weeks later, he told me at one of my follow up visits that mine was the first finger he had successfully re-attached. I think that made me feel good. The saw blade had hit dead center on the knuckle joint and eliminated both the ball and socket. My middle finger on my left hand is forever straight. Even though the surgeon re-attached the nerves and tendons in the finger so that I have feelings and movement in the end joint, whenever I dance a waltz with my wife, I insult the entire dance floor.

One of my two biggest regrets about the entire incident was that we had to forfeit the tennis tournament. The other was that the doctor's instructions were that I could not break a sweat for three weeks for fear of infection. I said to the doctor, "You have to be kidding. It is July and I just got back from my honeymoon." I reluctantly agreed, but I will confess to cheating a little. And by the way—it did hurt a lot for several days!!

⚊⚊⚊

Sometimes injuries look much worse than they really are. My eldest daughter was dating her husband-to-be during their college days. He needed a summer job and I needed to find out if he would pass the "Dad Test." Rick was a hard worker and got along well with all of the guys. We were building walls in the shop one afternoon and Rick was using the nail gun. Nail guns are very reliable when you hold them perpendicular to the surface into which you are nailing. Two of the rules of using a nail gun are first, try to avoid putting the nail in at an angle and second, always avoid holding the wood below the point of entry. Right after Rick violated both of these principles, I heard a loud "Uh oh". At least I think that is what he said. The phrase may have just started with "Oh." Rick had put a sixteen-penny nail right through the center of his hand. Off to the hospital we went. Rick told the doctor that he had a hangnail. The doctor was not amused. I do not know if I was more worried about Rick's hand or how I was going to tell my daughter that Rick had gotten hurt on my watch. Sometimes things turn out well. Amazingly, the nail came out after having done no damage. Today those skilled hands deliver babies and perform surgery.

⸻⸺⸻

There are certain rules that are absolute. One of them is that you do not hold a board in one hand and a circular saw in the other, while trying to cut the board you are holding. Always place the board on the sawbuck or bench. Ray grabbed a four foot long piece of 2 x 10 one day and started to cut an angled piece off of it. I was only standing ten feet from him when I saw him pick up the board. I offered to hold the board for him but he refused help. Before I could finish warning him not to cut the board he was holding, the saw blade got pinched in the wood. That caused the saw to rapidly reject the board in one direction, and send the spinning blade in the other direction, right over Ray's open hand. At first I thought he had cut his hand off completely, but then I realized the blade had not gone all the way through his hand. Unlike my finger, this really hurt.

We were 20 minutes from the nearest hospital. We did not have time to wait for them to come to us, so we went to them. After wrapping Ray's hand tightly, I had one of the crew sit in the back seat and put pressure on the wound. With lights flashing and horn blowing, I did my best Dale Earnhardt impression and got us to the hospital in what must have been record time. It was one of the nastiest wounds I had ever seen. Ray must have been living right that day, because every part of himself that he cut that day could be sewn back together. After a few weeks of being out of work he was as good as new. During that period, however, we did make a lot of use of that 2 x 4 we had named "Ray."

⸻⸺⸻

When I go to the doctor now, they ask me to describe my pain level on a scale from one to ten. I asked them "whose threshold of pain are we using?" Folks who have worked on construction crews for any length of time have a different set of standards for pain than most people. We were completing the framing on one of the five largest houses we ever built when the guys called me to the attic for advice. They were trying to nail the final board outside of the hole they had framed for the gable ventilator. We were on the basement end of a two-story house that had a tall roof. I figured that we were over 50 feet in the air. The crew said they could not figure out how to finish nailing the final board. The real truth was that no one was volunteering to hang out over the 50 plus feet of open air to drive in the last couple of nails.

Partly because I did not want to waste any more time on this problem, and partly because occasionally the boss had to prove he had not gone soft, I said that I would do it. I placed my left foot on the bottom of the ventilator opening. I reached up with my left hand and grabbed the end rafter. Then I placed my right foot firmly on that open air. I clutched the rafter in my left hand tightly because it was the only thing protecting me from the ground below. One of the other members of the crew reached out and placed four nails in the proper place so I could tap them enough to get them started. Once that was done, all I had to do was drive them in with the hammer I was holding in my right hand.

Just about the time I had the first one completely nailed in, I felt a tremendous pain in the center of my left hand. Your natural instinct is to let go with your left hand. I quickly realized that letting go was not an option. The last thing I wanted to do, other than let go and fall to the ground, was to have to climb back out there at a later time. With my teeth gritted, I just kept nailing until I was finished. The guys had no idea I was even in pain until I climbed back into the attic. When I had grabbed that rafter, I picked a spot where a wasp was starting to build a nest. The wasp did not appreciate my presence, and I certainly did not appreciate the wasp's stinger. That really hurt.

⟞⟝

I have only had a handful of times when the pain scale reached a ten. Two of them involved kidney stones. I cannot explain that kind of pain to you, but those of you who have had them understand. My second kidney stone attack hurt so bad that the EMS was called because my son-in-law, whom we were visiting, could not even get me out of the bed. On the way to the hospital in one of those bouncy EMS trucks with the red lights on top, the EMS Tech told me that she was going to insert an IV. When she told me it was going to hurt, I just grinned and said, "No it's not."

There were a number of times when I reached a nine on the pain scale. Pain just does not happen by itself. Usually, either you, or some one around you, messed up. I had some errands to run one morning so I instructed the crew to build a set of scaffolds across the entire end of a house. I wanted the scaffolds to be ready for us to work from when I got back after lunch. By the time I returned, the scaffolds were built. Remember the rule about never going on a scaffold you did not help build? Well, I forgot it, or at least I was in too big of a hurry to remember it.

Just as soon as I got to the top set of scaffold boards, the one board I stepped on decided it wanted to be somewhere else. I did not simply fall to the ground. I took the same route that a pinball takes in a pinball machine. I bounced on each layer of board all the way to the ground. If I missed landing on a board on the way down, then it proceeded to land on me. By the time I got to the ground, and everything stopped falling, I thought I was dead. When I discovered that I was not dead, I then became convinced that I had broken everything. The guys picked me up and sat me down for a brief rest. Then, like an idiot, I drove myself back to town to see my friend, the orthopedist. It took him a while to convince me that I had not broken anything. I took the rest of that day off, too.

<hr />

Not all of the on the job accidents happen to the crew. We always warned our clients about the dangers of messing around the job site after hours. When the client owns the property on which you are building, warning them does not do much good. Late one afternoon, after he had gotten off of work, one of our clients went to his property to see how much we had accomplished that day. He walked into his family room to see how much drywall we had hung that day. Leaning up against the wall of the room was a stack of 4 x 12 foot drywall boards. His curiosity wanted to see if a rough-in box for a TV was behind that stack of drywall boards.

Another in that long line of absolute rules is never shift the weight of a stack of drywall. It really was not that difficult, the client thought, to pull each individual piece of drywall toward him. Once the stack of drywall was standing straight up, and not leaning toward the wall, the entire mass of material shifted its weight toward my client. The homeowner became like a large stone on a medieval catapult, and he was sent hurling backwards across the room. He stopped his flight when both of his elbows penetrated the newly hung drywall on the other side of the room. He was stuck there until a neighbor heard the screams.

⤚⠶⠶⤙

Enough about physical pain: sometimes people can just be a pain. I had learned that lesson as a young boy when customers came to the shop to make selections for their new house. Often there were lively conversations and some fairly telling arguments. Over the years I gained lots of evidence that building a house can be stressful on marriages! I remember one couple breaking up over the type of hardware they should use on the kitchen cabinets. Another couple got into an argument over who was going to move the furniture into their new house. The lady informed her husband, while they were sitting in our office to make the final payment and take possession, that she had decided to purchase an expensive dog, and had, therefore, canceled the moving company. She expected him to move everything himself. That marriage ended shortly thereafter in a divorce. Building a house was and still is serious business.

For years we had a phrase in our specifications describing the make and model of the heating and air-conditioning equipment that we planned to use in the house we were building. The specs said that we would use "Lennox or equal." The whole idea behind using this phrase was that we were not as concerned about the manufacturer of the unit, as much as were concerned about who the technicians were that installed and maintained the units. The companies we let bid on our heating and air-conditioning (HVAC) work all used acceptable national brands.

Our HVAC contractor had just finished installing the unit on a job one morning. Later that day the client came by the office and told

Dad he was not happy with the brand of HVAC units that we had just installed in his house. He said that he would not accept them, and he wanted them changed. Dad reminded him that the specifications said we would use "Lennox or equal." The client looked at Dad coldly and said, "To me, Lennox has no equal."

I am sure that this would have pleased the folks at the Lennox plant, but it did not sit well with Dad. Rarely had I seen him that mad. Dad took a deep breath and told the client he would give him his money back if he would just go away. The client said he loved the house and did not want his money back. He just wanted a Lennox HVAC system. It cost us a lot of money to switch out the installed units and replace them with Lennox units. From that moment on, our specifications said that the make and model of the HVAC unit was "To be determined by the contractor."

Most of our clients were really wonderful to work with. I can only think of about a half dozen or so that I would never have built for again. I have no idea how many of them felt that way about us, but hopefully the numbers are similar. We used to joke among other builders that the best client was the one who came into town, signed the contract, gave you a down payment, and did not show up again until closing. Those were few and far between.

Probably the part of the building business that I disliked the most occurred after the job was done. It is referred to in the business as "touch ups" or "call backs." A lot of things happen naturally to a house, especially in its first year. In our climate, which can be described as hot and humid in the summer and cold and less humid in the winter, the materials go through a lot of changes. A house built in the winter tends to swell up in the summer season and vice versa.

I had a client once who was obsessed with the humid climate. He bought a de-humidifier at the local hardware store. They told him to run it about three days a week and to be sure to empty the water it collected on a regular basis. He went on a trip and left it running. His cup runneth over, so to speak. When he got back there was water all over his basement. His next move was to get a better model and plumb it directly into the sewer system. He was so pleased with how the system worked that he left it on all of the time, despite the manufacturer's warning.

This house had over 5,000 square feet, and he extracted the moisture out of every single foot. Every piece of hardwood floor separated from the one beside it. Every miter joint looked like it had been cut with a chainsaw and not a miter saw. To solve this problem he mopped water on the hardwood floors in an effort to add moisture throughout the house. All this did was make the wood floors buckle. They all had to be replaced. This was an expensive lesson, but the fellow did not learn a thing. He sold the house and moved back to Arizona.

A house has to season. Literally, this means a house needs to experience all four seasons before the material starts to stabilize. The first year will create cracks that need to be caulked. The changing seasons will cause drywall nails to pop out. None of these things are the fault of the builder, but the builder always gets blamed for them. Builders used to hate to go back and fix things that were not their fault because they were not getting paid for it. The large tract builders have created a one-year touch up policy, and the smaller builders have uniformly had to accept the same concept. Car dealers learned years ago to factor in the cost of financing into the price of the car. Now the consumer has a choice between a big discount on the price of a car, or a low or non-existent interest rate. Builders now factor in the one-year touch up cost as well.

The worst thing about touch ups in the old days was that, after the owner had lived in the house for a year, it was difficult to distinguish between touch ups and abuse. Years ago I finished a small house for a single lady. I personally did a thorough walk through right before the closing to be sure everything was just right. About two weeks after she moved in, I received a fairly abusive phone call from her claiming that the window grilles were defective. I knew they were not because I had checked each one personally.

I went right over to handle the situation personally. She walked me down the hall to the master bedroom where the window grilles were all laying on the floor in pieces. I told her I wanted to see the other rooms, but she said she just wanted new grilles. I had noticed one of the bedroom doors was closed so I opened it to check the grilles in that room. When I did, I apparently scared the dog that was hiding in there. He was at least half my size. Before I could run from him, he ran from me. He ran right to the front window and leaped up on it, tearing the window grille to pieces. When I turn to look at the lady, she just lowered her head and said, "I'm sorry." I left and never went back.

My favorite touch up story occurred while I was still in college. Dad had built a house in one of the neighboring cities for a university dean. About six months after they moved in, the dean's wife brought Max a touch up list, just as we had instructed her to do. Max went through the list one item at a time and discussed with her how we would handle each thing on the list. The last item on the list was a request to lower the water level in the commode. Max explained to her that the water level was set at the factory and there was no way to remedy that. She kept on insisting that he do something about the water level. Finally, Max asked her why this issue was so important. She said "When Huns sits on the commode, Huns hangs in the water." I saw this man on television many times after that, and each time I quietly chuckled inside.

⊷⊶

There is one dark side of society that the building business is definitely not immune to and that is theft. Actually stealing from builders is much easier for the thief than stealing from regular folks, because no one is home, yet. There were three types of thieves that plagued our industry. The first was your friendly neighborhood do-it-yourselfer. Just like the guy who backed the station wagon to the front door in an earlier chapter, there were folks who thought they had the right to shop at your construction site, in lieu of going to the lumberyard.

The college summer that I worked on the Greensboro crew produced a strange incident. We were always losing shovels full of sand from the mason's sand pile. We had the sand delivered by the truck load, and it left after work by a little red wagon. We topped out a lot of sand boxes. This really never upset me since the sand box had a special place in my heart. My last official task one afternoon on the job was to help the sand truck driver back in the driveway and dump the sand at just the right spot. Once that was done, we went home. When we arrived on the job site the next day, the sand pile was gone. I mean it was really gone. You could not even prove that it had ever been there. It had to be a neighborhood job because no one else would have meticulously swept up each grain. I hope they all enjoyed the sand.

The next kind of thief was the malicious kid or kids who were more interested in vandalism than stealing things. Vandals never seemed to forget to take anything that was not nailed down. We arrived on a nearly completed job site one Monday morning to discover one of the worst cases of vandalism I had ever seen. They had painted obscenities on the walls and cut gashes in all of the cabinet doors. They even took a caulking gun and filled every door lock in the house with caulk. They must have exited through the front door, because on the foyer wall, they wrote, "By the way, you build a damn good house." They would not have liked us so much had we ever caught them.

We caught our share of vandals over the years. One of our projects was being hit on a fairly regular basis. The vandals were mostly destroying equipment. All of our subcontractors were angry because any piece of equipment that they left on the job overnight would get messed up. We finally decided to hire an off duty police officer. I picked him up and delivered him to the job site at just about dark one evening. No one would be suspicious of my car making a late afternoon visit to the house. He had been hiding in the attic for less than an hour when the vandals showed up with a new recruit. They bragged to their new recruit, and to the listening ears of the officer, about everything they had done. He pounced down from the attic and arrested all of them.

The officer called me right away, and I met him at the police station. The parents of the kids were summoned, also. It was a gathering of the who's who of doctors and lawyers in our town. Every single parent claimed the police officer was lying, and they were all mad at me for hiding him in the attic. We had obtained the permission of our client, who also happened to be a respected lawyer himself. That fact, more than any other, helped to eventually calm the distressed parents. Some days you just cannot win.

The third kind of thief was the hardened criminal, who stole things to sell to a fence for money. This type of thievery cycles with the economy. The tougher the times, the more they steal. Their most common target when I was building was appliances. We would wait until the last minute to install the appliances. Sometimes, even that was not waiting long enough. During the recession of the late 1970's, copper prices rose rapidly and our water lines became targets. The worst thing about a copper thief was that they would cut off the pipes hanging down under the floor so close to the under side of the floor, that a plumber could not attach a new joint to the old pipe, making it extremely expensive to repair and replace what been stolen.

—⟶⟵—

Not everyone you hire works out. Sometimes when you get real busy, you need additional labor. I hired one guy because he was big and strong and seemed intelligent enough to be trainable. So, I was wrong. My least favorite thing was firing people. My second least favorite thing was haggling over wage demands. This young man decided to challenge me one day concerning the amount I was paying him. He had not been working with us too long, but he thought he deserved a big raise. I did not think so. It was the way he presented it that was his downfall. He approached me as soon as I drove up to the job site. He said he wanted a two-dollar an hour raise or he would quit. This sounded like the perfect opportunity to get rid of him, so I said that I accepted his resignation. He was dumb-founded, with an emphasis on dumb. I turned and walked away as I told him he could pick up his paycheck on Friday when everyone else got paid.

We both left the job site, but he made a big mistake. He went to my house and rang the front doorbell. One of my daughters answered the door. He told her that he was coming back in an hour, and I had better have his paycheck. She was really scared and called me immediately. I went home, wrote his paycheck and waited for him to arrive. When the doorbell rang, I answered it very cautiously. He was standing alone on the front porch, so I joined him there. As he demanded his paycheck, he slid open his shirt to reveal a gun. I was never a boy scout, but I believed in being prepared. I pushed back my shirt and my gun was bigger than his gun. I tossed him the paycheck. He grabbed it and left. Oh yes, as he left, I did mention something about him never setting foot on my property again. I hated labor negotiations.

The economy always cycles. At least it always has cycled. I have enough experience behind me now to know not to predict the future. About every six to nine years building would suffer a slump. This meant layoffs and downsizing. Six or eight months later you were wondering where your carpenters were, and would they come back to work. During the Carter years when mortgage interest rates reached 16-18% I got down to one employee. Then the Reagan years came along and we hit our high of 34. One day I was sitting alone in my office when it struck me that 34 families relied on me to be able to make a payroll every week. That was one of the scariest moments of my career. After that thought sunk in, I scaled the crew back.

The building business is like steering an ocean liner. You cannot stop it on a dime. The types of houses we built averaged six to eight months in construction time. Some of the really big ones took longer than that. By the time you realized you were in a recession, it was half over. Just when you had scaled back to a size geared to ride out the slow times, things were cranking up again.

We usually built a mix of custom and spec houses. The trouble with the market was that it was impossible to keep the right mix. The best way to advertise your product was to build spec houses. Realtors™ and prospects would spend their weekends roaming through your houses and writing down your name. As a result, you became loaded with custom work. Custom work was great because you knew you were going to get paid when the job was finished.

By the time you cycled through your list of custom homes, there were no more contracts to be signed. Your spec homes had not appeared on the open market for months, meaning you had been without your best marketing tool. Your only choice was to load up on spec homes. The up side to that part of the cycle was that there was no client to occupy all of your spare time. The down side was wondering if the right prospect was going to appear just at the right time and buy the house. The worst thing that could happen was for a down cycle in the economy to occur while you were loaded with spec houses. Years of profits could be wiped out with months of interest payments on unsold inventory.

The longer I remained in the building business, the more I realized that you had to be a little nuts to risk that much money producing a very expensive product that took a long time to turn over. Dad used to say when times were good, folks would claim that houses were selling like hotcakes. He proclaimed that if that were so, we would be better off selling hotcakes, because the investment needed was so much smaller.

I will never forget sitting on one particular spec house for a long time. I had long since spent my profit on interest payments to the bank. I was delighted when the real estate agent finally brought me a contract. I had to settle for less than what I was asking, and the contract required me to invest some more money into a number of changes. Nonetheless, the prospect of finally ending the interest payments made me grin between the grimaces. When closing day came, I added up the numbers and realized I had to bring several thousand dollars to the closing. A year and a half of work and I did not take home a dime. The Realtor™ got her full commission. It did not take me long to realize it was time to get out of the building business and do real estate full time.

≋ 11 ≋

TRIALS ......

You always want and expect to be paid for the work you do. On a number of occasions, people hired me to design their house and to create a set of plans and specifications, even though they intended to have their cousin Fred actually construct the house. This was all right with me as long as I knew their intentions up front. Most of the time, however, I used my ability to design as a way to obtain the final building contract. I always informed the client that if for some reason I did not get the bid for the construction job, they would still owe me for the plans.

This policy had always worked well until I met the Smiths. Egos play interesting roles in events. I was a little skeptical about working with these folks, but they had bragged for months that they were going to build the biggest house in town. I was flattered when they came to see me to discuss designing their house. I will never forget standing in my foyer discussing with her how big she wanted her foyer to be. She said she wanted double front doors with a big brass doorknocker on each door. She was an attractive, well built young lady, but when she stood there and proclaimed that she wanted to have the biggest pair of knockers in town, I should have realized that this couple was a prescription for disaster.

The proposed house was so big that I had to purchase a special size of drafting paper on which to do the drawings. We worked for months. Several times through the process, she would arrive at my home office with a new stack of plan magazines, and a completely new style of house in her mind. After a while I felt like we were going around in circles. One day she called and said that they had decided to work with another designer. I told them that was just fine and that I would send them a bill for my time. They agreed and the parting was cordial. I had kept a running total of my time and added it all up. It came to three thousand dollars. I had never billed anyone that much for design services before, but I had never spent that much time with a client before, either. I had the beginning drawings for three entirely different styles of house.

Feeling justified in my claim for compensation, I dropped the bill in the mail. After 30 days I sent them a second bill, thinking and hoping that it had gotten lost in the delivery process. Thirty more days went by and I sent another bill. After 90 days, the next bill had a little note attached saying that if they did not pay me, I would turn the collection of the bill over to my attorney. A couple of days later I got a check in the mail for two hundred dollars and a note from their attorney saying that cashing the check would certify that I had been paid in full. I sent the check back.

I wanted my money, but they had also stepped on my principles. The next day I ran into my attorney at a Rotary Club meeting and we discussed the situation at length. He said that he would gladly write them a letter but we both agreed that it would probably do very little good. The obvious next step would be to sue. My attorney said he would sue them but it would cost me twenty-five hundred dollars, and if it went to a jury trial, it would cost five thousand dollars. Both of those scenarios were appealing to me until he told me that in North Carolina, you could not sue for your attorney fees. The last thing that I wanted to do was to go to all of that trouble and have my attorney end up with all of my money. An even worse scenario would be for his bill to be bigger than mine. As we finished the conversation, he turned back toward me and said, "You can always sue them yourself." I asked him how to do that, but he told me he could not ethically get involved in that process.

I think what he really meant was that there was no money in it for him. Determined to get my plan fee, I discussed the situation that evening with my wife. She was teaching some courses at the local community college at the time. She said she would drop by the school library the next day and see if they had any books on civil procedure. They did.

The local courthouse is a scary place to most non-attorney types. Most folks would be content to live their entire life and never go in the place. It is actually a building full of some pretty decent folks. Having spent my career in the building business, I was used to dealing with "public servants." The first thing that you must remember when dealing with these people, is that technically, they work for you. The second thing to remember is never to let them know that you know they work for you. Most county employees, however, take their jobs seriously and have a real sense of civic duty.

Working with building inspectors for years prepared me for dealing with public servants. Building inspectors take themselves seriously because they have a tremendous responsibility to protect the public. Obviously, this great responsibility comes with great power, including the power to shut you down. When dealing with a new inspector, I would always ask them about a technique I wanted to use. By asking for their opinion up front, they knew I respected what they had to say, and I usually learned something I did not know. Still, after our conversation, we usually would get along pretty well.

Folks in the local courthouse are much the same way. They each have their field of expertise and are eager for someone to come in and ask for their help. If you are nice and treat them with respect, they will guide you through any process you might want to undertake. This technique proved to be invaluable when we decided to file our lawsuit. In fact, from time to time during the entire process, I would detect an eagerness on their part to help the "little guy" use the system without the aid of an attorney. I think some of them were having as much fun as I was.

I was hoping that simply filing the lawsuit would make my clients pay me, and the whole thing would just go away. Evidently, they assumed just the opposite. They assumed that a terse response from their lawyer, threatening to go to trial, would scare me off. We both underestimated our opponent. Their attorney, J. Paul was one of the highest priced attorneys in town. It gave me a great deal of satisfaction to know that they were spending money at a much faster rate than I was. I do not know why most attorneys choose to use their first initial and their middle name as a means to be identified. I wonder if their parents took that into consideration when they were born.

J. Paul informed me that they intended to fight my suit as far as it took. He also informed me that they had been very insulted when the sheriff came to their house and served them with the lawsuit papers. Good.

According to our guidebook, the next step in the process was to conduct interrogatories. Evidently, J. Paul was using the same guidebook. He scheduled the interrogatories. We met in a small room in the courthouse and he even had a stenographer present. This meeting was to act as a mini hearing without a judge. The object was to ask questions of your opponent and get their statements on the record. I did not take it nearly as seriously as J. Paul did. I think this irritated him just a bit.

With all of that behind us, the next step was to schedule a hearing before a judge for the sole purpose of setting a court date. I went into each of these sessions not really knowing what to expect. I had a lot of experience learning to play things by ear, and that turned out to be quite helpful. The first hearing was quick. The judge asked if both parties were present. I told the judge that I was there, and J. Paul told the judge that he represented the Smiths. He said they were out of town. He informed the judge that he was, therefore, asking for a delay. The judge granted his motion and we all went home. I did not think anything about what happened until I found out that the next hearing would not be for another 30 days.

Two more hearings passed and the Smiths were always out of town or had some other excuse. I realized that I was being played. The distinguished Mr. J. Paul always seemed to get whatever he wanted. When the fourth hearing rolled around, I had planned to speak my mind. I walked into the small courtroom and to my surprise, the presiding judge was the former attorney that had so graciously paid me for that garage which I had failed to include on his bill. When it was our turn, I let J. Paul go first. He proclaimed that the Smiths were out of the country, and therefore, were unable to go to trial at this time. I had to give this attorney credit for coming up with a new excuse each time. This one was very creative.

I stood up and told the judge that I was just an ordinary citizen trying to collect a debt. I said the system made it impractical for me to hire an attorney, so I was doing it myself. I also told him that this was the fourth hearing of this type that I had attended, and each time they had an excuse. I could tell the judge was actually listening to what I had to say. So, I said that as a private citizen, I just wanted to know if I had the right to have my case heard. Well that struck a nerve with the judge. He pounded his gavel, and I jumped. He then looked at J. Paul, checked his calendar, and proclaimed a date for the trial. He even went a bit further and told J. Paul that he would accept no further delays from the Smiths. At last I was going to have my day in court.

A couple of days before the trial was scheduled to begin, I wandered into the courthouse to make friends. In the Clerk of Court's office, I approached a friendly face and explained what was about to happen with my case. I wanted to know which courtroom we would be in and who would be the judge. To my dismay, I learned that the trial would take place in the main courtroom and the judge was someone of whom I had never heard. I wondered what happened to my friend, the judge that had scheduled the trial. In the long run, however, I felt that I would be better off with a stranger. My new friend in the Clerk's office told me all about the judge. She said he was fairly young and extremely fair. That was all I could ask.

I had watched a lot of Perry Mason shows and read the book from the local community college, but I really had no idea what I was doing. My new friend from the Clerk's office just told me that when I had a question, ask the judge. That turned out to be good advice. On the first day of the trial, the large courtroom felt like an empty gymnasium. The only folks there were Cathy and me, J. Paul, Mr. Smith, and those folks that collectively make up the "court costs" when you lose.

They brought in 13 jury prospects and seated them in the jury box. The extra one was to be an alternate in case one of them became ill, or just got too bored with my case to hang around. Cathy and I sat at the table reserved for the plaintiff. It was in front of the rail that separated the spectators from the participants. We were on the right side and J. Paul had a similar seat on the left side. He was not very interested in exchanging glances. He was all business.

The only other folks in attendance that day were the rest of the jury pool. These were the folks who were anxiously awaiting someone else to be selected so they could go home. The judge explained to the jury that I would be representing myself. Then, he told me to proceed with questioning the jury for the selection process. I stood up and thanked the judge. I had learned from watching TV that you thank the judge for everything, whether he deserves it or not. I gave the jury pool a brief accounting of what the case was about. Then I asked them if anyone had a problem with my intentions. One lady spoke up and said her husband was a builder, and he had clients in the past that would not pay him, too. J. Paul frowned. I turned to the judge and said, "They will all do just fine."

J. Paul was not nearly as confident about this particular group as I was. He went into great detail questioning each juror. He dismissed the one whose husband had not been paid. I had liked her. I just sat still and watched their facial expressions. The longer he questioned them, the better he made me look.

Lunchtime arrived and J. Paul was still questioning the jury pool. I asked him where Mrs. Smith was, and he told me that she was not going to attend the trial. This revelation really disappointed me because I was looking forward to cross-examining her. With her on the stand, the jury might get to hear about her brass knockers. I was sure that J. Paul knew her well enough to keep her far away from the courthouse. Since she disliked being served with the lawsuit papers so much, I wondered how she would react to being subpoenaed. I was off to see my friends in the Clerk's office. They helped me fill out the necessary papers. Then the sheriff's deputy headed out to find Mrs. Smith.

J. Paul spent the rest of the afternoon picking a jury. By the time he finished, I felt really good about my chances. The judge decided we had had enough for the first day and said we would resume in the morning. To this day, I have not figured out what judges do with all of the time that remains when the trial is not going on. I really had not planned on this taking a second day. The first thing I had to do was figure out what I wanted my crews to do the next day. Then I went home and had a good laugh. It was time to prep my star witness, me.

The second day started with a bunch of jurors that could not believe we were still there, either. I explained to the judge that I wanted to call myself as my first witness. He nodded his approval. I walked up to the witness chair and was sworn in. I told the jury that I did not know how to question myself, so I would just tell them the story of what had transpired. They chuckled, the judge smiled, and J. Paul looked quite displeased. I started with our first meeting. No, I did not mention her desire to have the biggest pair of knockers in town. I did tell them about my efforts to collect the bill and the part about J. Paul sending me two hundred dollars. That brought some grimaces on a couple of jurors' faces.

After telling the entire story to the jury, I decided to lay out all of my work in front of them as well. I had brought a large roll of sketches and drawings with me. I laid them out, side by side, on the courtroom floor. They covered the entire area from the front rail to the judge's throne. The jury was impressed. Somewhere during the process, J. Paul objected to my laying out of the papers, but the judge denied the objection. I was on a roll then. When I was finished testifying, J. Paul only asked me one question in his cross-examination. How much did I charge per hour? I answered the question and stepped down.

Mrs. Smith was in attendance, dressed very conservatively. I think J. Paul had gone over to her house and picked out the wardrobe. She did not look happy to be there. It was time to call her as my witness.

After the bailiff swore her in, I asked her to recall her version of the events that I had presented to the jury. Her mouth opened, she began to talk, and I just sat back and listened. She explained how they had carefully selected the property. I knew how much they had paid for the land because it was a local joke in the real estate community. No one had ever paid that much for a building site in our area. The jury did not know how much they paid, so I was determined for them to find out. I interrupted her at one point to ask her what they paid for the land. She said that she could not remember. I told her the amount, and asked if I was correct. She said yes. I could tell the jury was paying close attention now. Her ego started to take over at this point. Before she was through, she had made the perfect witness for me. J. Paul did not cross-examine her. The jury seemed quite entertained and so did the audience in the courtroom. It was the first time that I had noticed that the courtroom was about half filled. I had no idea why, or who they were. I rested my case.

J. Paul called a local architect named Arnold. I had known Arnold for a long time and there was a lot of mutual respect between Arnold, myself, and my Dad. Dad and I had designed a lot of large homes over the years that Arnold would have gotten to design if Dad and I had not been around. Despite the mutual respect, he did not mind being forced to stick it to me just a little.

The line of questioning to Arnold mainly centered on what he had done for the Smiths. He carefully never referred to any work that I had done before they employed him. A couple of times during the questioning, Cathy would nudge me and point to her legal pad where she had scribbled the word "objection." I would quickly stand and object hoping that she was writing the reason for my objection on her pad. She was always one step ahead of me and would hand the reason for my objection. I would glance down and then tell the judge why I had objected. I learned that sometimes the sweetest words can be "Objection sustained." Wow, move over Perry Mason.

Then, J. Paul asked Arnold how much he paid his draftsmen. At this point I realized where J. Paul was headed with his questioning. He wanted to equate my work to that of Arnold's draftsmen. J. Paul was finished with Arnold. It was my turn to cross-examine the witness. I asked Arnold if his draftsmen did the designing or did they finish the ideas that he had developed. I did not want to imply that they were "cross-hatchers", but we all had to start somewhere. He verified that he did the design work. Then I asked him how much he charged per hour. He hemmed and hawed and said that it varied with each job. After asking several different ways I finally got Arnold to give the jury a general idea of what his services ran. My cost per hour just happened to fall gently between what Arnold charged and what he paid his draftsmen. Being quite satisfied, I ended my cross-examination. J. Paul, with a slightly arrogant tone, rested his defense.

By this time, the judge had once again decided it was too late in the day to continue, so court was adjourned for the day. He said we would resume the next morning with closing arguments. Once again we headed home to prep for closing arguments and do a collective chuckle. We could not believe the trial was headed into a third day.

They let us enter the courtroom by a side door which gave us direct access to the plaintiff's table. I put all of my papers down, took my customary deep breath, and glanced around the courtroom. It was packed. There was not an empty seat. Almost every young lawyer that I knew in town was there, but I still did not know why. "All rise." The judge came in and he immediately called on me to present my closing argument.

I stood up and, of course, thanked the judge. Then I thanked the jury for sitting there for three days. I told them that I was just someone like them, that had done some work for a client, and the client had refused to pay me. I said that all I really wanted was to have a neutral third party listen to my story and decide what was best. I started to tell them how long it had taken me to get my case to trial, but J. Paul objected. This time the judge granted his objection. I reminded them of the volumes of work I had shown them. Then I thanked them again and told them I was satisfied. Short and simple was my motto. Then it was J. Paul's turn.

You would have thought he was auditioning for a Broadway play. He went on and on about how evil I was for first not satisfying the Smiths, and secondly, for dragging them through this trial. It was during these statements that he lost the jury, because it made the Smiths appear to be extremely arrogant for not permitting me to have my day in court.

Once J. Paul finally sat down, the judge instructed the jury about what they needed to do in the jury room. He pointed out how the law was designed to deal with such civil matters. Then he asked the jury if they had any questions of him. One juror spoke up and asked if they were limited in what they could award the plaintiff. That brought a widespread low rumble throughout the courtroom. The jury went out to deliberate, and we went in search of the nearest vending machines. After hanging around the hallways for less than an hour, we were told that the jury was coming back. The courtroom immediately filled back up and we quickly took our place at the front table just before those famous words, "All rise."

The jury foreman announced that the jury had awarded me the entire amount that I had requested. J. Paul stood and filed notice of appeal. The judge rolled his eyes, but he really did not plan for anyone to see that gesture. He then instructed me to proceed with filing the necessary papers to allow me to receive my judgment. I had no idea what that meant. Before I could ask the gavel came thundering down and my day in court was over, or so I thought. Someone tapped me on the shoulder. It was a nice young lawyer from a neighboring town who had witnessed the sold-out proceedings. He said he admired what I had done and that he would walk me through the final paper work. On the way out of the courtroom, a court clerk told me that the judge wanted to see J. Paul and me in his chambers in 30 minutes.

After filling out the closing paperwork in the Clerk's office I headed down to the judge's chambers, having no idea what to expect. There we sat. J. Paul and I were across the desk from the judge. He looked almost human without his fancy robe. He asked J. Paul if he was really going to appeal the decision to the state supreme court in Raleigh. J. Paul said that was exactly what he intended to do. He turned to me and asked me what I thought of that. I simply said that I guessed they had a book about that procedure too.

He then asked me what my thoughts were, as a private citizen, about the entire process. I told him that I was relieved to finally be able to tell my story. I said the entire process was slow and cumbersome. Also I told him that the idea of this case going to another level was absurd, but that I would see it through.

The judge suddenly changed the tone of his voice and said that we needed to settle this whole thing right then. What amount of money would I settle for right now, he asked. I told him I had always been willing to take half. He seemed startled and instructed J. Paul to tell his clients to write me a check for fifteen hundred dollars. He said he would agree to that. I told the judge that I would not agree. The judge was stunned and asked why I would not agree. I told him that I did not trust the Smiths. I told him I wanted the check from J. Paul and I wanted to pick it up at four o'clock at J. Paul's office. The judge did not give J. Paul a chance to respond. He just told him to do it and showed us out. Justice had been done.

About eight months later, I spotted the judge attending one of our Rotary Club meetings as a guest. I quickly got my food and sat down across from him. As I started to introduce myself, he interrupted me saying that he knew exactly who I was. We had a great conversation that day. He told me how much it had pleased him to see a citizen using the system in the correct way. Then he started chuckling and told me that I had no idea what had been going on during the trial. He said that he had never witnessed anything like it. It seems that after the first day, word had gotten out that J. Paul might be losing to an ordinary citizen. The local lawyers started dropping by the courtroom to check it out. He said by the third day, the courtroom was full because they all had wagers on who would win and how much I would get. He said that he did not know how much J. Paul got paid, but it could not have been enough to cover the grief he took for losing to me. J. Paul never did speak to me after that.

≋ 12 ≋

......AND TRIBULATIONS

I was ten years old when Hurricane Hazel struck the North and South Carolina coast in 1954. As I explained earlier, we had gone to Cherry Grove Beach every summer, always staying at the Cherry Grove Manor. It was a large three-story frame hotel that sat right on the oceanfront. A few days after the storm moved on up the coast, Dad decided that we were going to go to the beach and see the damage for ourselves. I still have the home movies we took that day, but the images in my brain are much more vivid. Besides, those images in my brain are in color.

We stood on the beach in amazement. The back half of the top two floors of the Cherry Grove Manor sat majestically on the wide strand of sand. This area of the coast is called the Grand Strand because at low tide the beach was well over a hundred yards wide. Somehow the hurricane had lifted up the hotel, removed the entire bottom floor as well as the front half, and gently placed the top half on the wide beach. There was absolutely nothing left on the foundation but a view. The hotel had been divided right down the middle as if it was designed that way in a very neat fashion. On what used to be the third floor, the division had gone right through a bathroom. The half of the bathroom that remained contained the lavatory and medicine cabinet. The most startling thing about the entire sight was a lone drinking glass sitting on a shelf in the open medicine cabinet.

When you gazed up and down the beach, there was only one house left standing on the oceanfront for 15 miles in either direction. The same could be said for the second and third row of houses as well. Some of the original beachfront houses could be found about a quarter of a mile inland. I learned that day that some things do not float away. Everywhere you looked on the beach, there were commodes and bathtubs. They were not attached to bathrooms anymore. It was too bad that we did not know how to recycle porcelain in those days. At the tender age of ten, I learned an early lesson that you do not mess with Mother Nature.

I never thought that I would see or experience anything like that again, but I did. The worst damage I ever saw was along the Gulf Coast six months after Camille came ashore. Cathy and I were driving to Houston to a National Homebuilder's Show. There was a lot of irony to that trip. We were going to study how to build better and stronger houses. None of those techniques would have mattered, however, if Mother Nature had taken aim at your project.

In 1989 Hurricane Hugo made landfall in Charleston, South Carolina and proceeded to track north/northwest. That path took it directly over our house near Winston-Salem, over 250 miles from Charleston. Luckily for us it was downgraded to non-hurricane status as it passed through Charlotte, some sixty miles to the south. Our house suffered no damage but we lost a lot of trees. We lived deep in the woods, where you could not see your neighbor's house, even in the winter. It was an eerie feeling, standing outside and listening to the near hurricane force winds howling through the trees. At first the wind was out of the east, then the south, and finally the west. That told me we were on the eastern edge of the former eye of the storm. Every few minutes, we would hear a strange tangling of branches, followed by a ground-shaking thud. We were constantly looking up and hoping that the sounds were not coming from a tree within arms length of our house.

Dad owned some beach property at that time in his life, and he was anxiously awaiting a chance to go to the coast and check on his property. The authorities had closed the beaches to prevent looting. They were requiring you to bring your deed with you if you wanted to get by their checkpoints. We all piled in one car and headed to the coast. It was exciting in a strange way. I felt like we had to go through Check Point Charlie just to see the ocean.

Years before, Hazel had actually done the Grand Strand a huge favor by tearing down all of the crummy old turn of the century wooden beach houses. They were replaced by a far superior product. Hugo had been as powerful as Hazel but the damage was much less severe. Dad was part owner of a beachfront motel that was three stories tall. Each suite of rooms was separated by concrete filled block walls that ran front to back throughout the structure. All of the first floor suites were destroyed. As the ocean surge hit the front of the motel, it pushed the front wall of each suite, and all of the interior walls, up against the back wall, filling each unit with sand. The concrete partitions held and the upper units were undamaged. When I looked at the damage that was there, my mind wandered back to that lone glass in the medicine cabinet, and of course, the commodes on the beach.

<hr />

Few hurricanes ever come inland, at least as far inland as Charlotte or Durham. When I got out of the building business, I sold or gave away most of my larger pieces of equipment, including my chain saws. That was a big mistake. In 1996 Hurricane Fran had been churning off of the coast of North Carolina for a couple of days. It was only entertaining the weather folks on TV. Then it gathered strength and headed inland at Wilmington. I remember standing in the lobby of the real estate office about five o'clock that afternoon talking to another agent. He asked me where I thought Fran was going to go. I drew a line in the carpet with my foot and said, "Right through the front door." I was right. Fran was not downgraded to tropical storm strength of sustained winds less than 70 miles per hour until 30 miles north of our home in Durham.

The lights went out about ten o'clock that evening. The first tree hit the house about two o'clock in the morning. We leaped out of bed. Using a flashlight, we could see the tree had hit the house right above the front master bedroom window. Within minutes we were dragging our mattress down the stairs and putting it in the kitchen near the center wall. I am not sure why we did that because there was no way we were going to get any more sleep that night.

About four o'clock in the morning the eye wall of the hurricane passed over the house. The sounds of the night went from the constant thuds of falling trees and wind to dead silence. Fourteen minutes later all hell broke loose again. I could tell, throughout the night, that we were losing a lot of trees in our back yard. However, every time I tried to shine the flashlight out the back door, all I could see was darkness. When dawn started to arrive, everyone on our street emerged from their houses to check out the damage. There were trees down all along our block, but the real show place was my back yard. We had lost 21 trees in the backyard and luckily all of them had fallen away from the house to the South. We were not so lucky with the one tree we lost in the front yard, but I will take those odds any day.

These trees were in excess of 80 feet high and some were much taller. I quickly discovered why all I could see out the back door had been darkness. The largest tree in the yard, a triple trunk white oak, had fallen over. The bottom of the stump was all you could see when you looked out the back door. The upended base of the root system was easily ten or twelve feet tall. This tree alone was responsible for taking out at least eight other trees in our yard. It also took out my deck and ripped the electric meter off of the back of the house.

It was nice to see all of the neighbors at one time, but we all agreed an old-fashioned block party would have been a simpler way to do it. The straight-line winds that blew down all of those trees in my yard, did not take a single tree in the yard on either side of my house. You could, however, follow a line of damage, similar to the damage in my yard, directly south for about one half of a mile.

I needed a chain saw. Cathy and I jumped into the Jeep and set out to find someone, anyone, who might own a business that was open that morning. We drove over fallen trees, around fallen trees, and through floodwaters that we probably should not have attempted to cross. We stopped at every open gas station we passed and asked who would have a chain saw to sell. Country folks can be real helpful in situations like this. Each one to whom we talked, sent us a little further out into the country. Finally we hit pay dirt. About 18 miles out of town we found the guy we were looking for. It was a little country store with one gas pump and a shelf full of chain saws that was destined to be empty by nightfall. Luckily the owner took plastic and I headed back toward the house. I called my son Jeff, who was a student at Duke at the time, and he rounded up four or five friends who would volunteer to help us in exchange for all the pizza they could eat. Mark was in Divinity School at Duke so Amy and Mark helped us every day also, making a down payment on that room I would add on to their house years later.

By early afternoon, I could hear the sound of chain saws all over the neighborhood. I could even detect the sound of dump trucks, and yes, a crane. Back to the Jeep I went to search for the crane. The tree from the front yard, the one that landed on the house, was so tall that 60 feet of it was hanging over into the back yard. As experienced as I was with a chain saw, I knew that I wanted no part of the task of removing that tree. We were lucky in that the only actual damage to the structure of our house was a crushed cornice that overhung at the front edge of the roof. I wanted to keep it that way and a crane was the only answer.

I found the crane and talked with its operator. Unfortunately, I was not the first one to meet with him that morning. He had already begun to accumulate a long client list. He did agree to come by the house when he took a break that afternoon to evaluate my situation. About four o'clock, he pulled up in front of my house in the large cab of his truck, having left the crane behind. He got out, leaving his partner in the cab. He and I studied the giant tree hanging over my house and discussed the various options we could use. Then I walked with him around to the back yard so he could see how much of the tree was actually hanging over the house. He took one look at my back yard and turned to the guy in the cab of the truck. He hollered, "Hey, Harry, you've got to come look at this yard." It was at that point that I knew we had a special mess. Harry was impressed, too.

This revelation was further confirmed when the insurance adjuster came to check out the damage. I had called my insurance agent the morning of the storm and the next day he had an adjuster on site. After discussing our needs and writing us a check for some startup incidentals, he asked if he could take some pictures of my back yard to show his kids when he got back home to South Carolina. It was at times like this that you realize that the people you do business with are far more important than the company they represent. Our homeowner's insurance was with a big national company, but the agent we used was the same agent we had dealt with in Winston-Salem, before we moved to Durham. He had always taken good personal care of us and continued to do so in this special time of need. I was glad he was not a computer on the other end of some on-line Internet insurance site.

What a tangled web Mother Nature can weave. Our back yard was like a big pile of pick-up-sticks. The biggest challenge we had was to know which tree limb to cut first. Where the inexperienced homeowner gets into trouble is cutting the limbs in the wrong sequence. I was so grateful for everything Slim had taught me. The trees had fallen with such force that there was a tremendous amount of energy stored up in the twisted limbs. We saw and heard some interesting twists and pops the next few days. We even had to duck a few times. I did all of the cutting while Jeff and his fellow Duke classmates hauled limbs, and hauled limbs, and hauled limbs until the street in front of our house could hold no more.

⸻◦⸻

Unfortunately, Fran was not the only tree problem I had with my current house. I love trees. Before we moved to Durham, our house was located deep in the woods. The driveway followed a winding path because I did not want to cut down any significant trees. Not everyone feels that way. One of my neighbors recently cut down every tree in his yard. I guess he did not want to be bothered with the little things trees do. Personally, I like the reflected sunlight in winter and the shade the trees provide in the summer. I also like the lower air-conditioning bills, but as they say, "to each his own."

One afternoon my next-door neighbor called me at my office and asked if I was sitting down. This is never a good start to a phone call. He said a tree had snapped off and the top part had landed on my roof. He said I should come home right away. This was disturbing news on several levels. One level was that it was cloudy and the forecast was for rain by nightfall. When I pulled into the driveway I was amazed to see a 40 foot section of tree trunk, at least 12 inches in diameter, sprawled across the roof of my house. About one-half of the front section of the roof on the two-story main part of the house was crushed. I immediately called two friends who were in the remodeling business and begged for their help. I do not know what I would have done without them. They came right over and climbed up on the roof. After sawing the treetop into sections and rolling it off of the roof, they spread a tarp over the damaged section. At least we were dry. That whole event prompted another call to my insurance agent.

There are a number of lessons that every homeowner should take away from this story. First of all, always know a crew you can call in an emergency. Secondly, as I have mentioned before, have a good relationship with your insurance agent. My current home was built with those 2 x 4 factory engineered trusses that I talked about in an earlier chapter. When you damage one of those, you must have a licensed engineer describe the solution in writing. To use that solution to repair the damage, you must buy a building permit from the proper governing authority. Then, your remodeling buddies can go to work. It is absolutely necessary to keep all of the aforementioned records, because when you decide to sell the house, you will be required to produce documents saying that you did everything the correct way. And we wonder why everything costs so much!

Another interesting sidebar to this story is the insurance angle. The base of the tree was located about three feet onto our neighbor's property. It was, therefore, his tree. It had been dead for several years and I had notified him of that fact. He had chosen to ignore my warning. At that point, the liability for the damage caused by his tree, shifted directly to him. Your insurance company will usually cover a justifiable claim, unless they can blame it on someone else. When my agent pursued the neighbor's insurance company, he discovered that it was the same company as mine. This meant of course, that the insurance company was going to have to foot the bill either way.

Insurance companies are not just about paying the claim. They are also about placing the blame. The house next door happened to be rented temporarily to a family who were in the process of building a new home in the area at the time this event occurred. So in this case, the landlord's insurance bore the brunt of the claim. What most folks do not realize is that insurance claims, especially ones like this one, where the owner had been warned, count against the Clue rating. The Clue rating is a score you have, which, like your credit score, can affect your ability to purchase reasonably priced insurance in the future. This particular landlord did not like me very much after the insurance placed the claim against his account. A couple of years later he tried to buy a vacation home in the mountains and was denied insurance altogether. He really did not like me then. Luckily for me, he sold the house next door.

<hr />

Weather can be far more subtle than hurricanes and tornados. I spent 28 years in the construction business. The most important thing I had to do each day was to listen to the weather forecast for the next day. The weather had total control over every thing that we did. We always tried to have an alternative work site for the crews. Sometimes it was too cold to work, and sometimes it was too hot. Rain and ice disrupted our masons, our bulldozer, and our roofers. The fall was our most consistent working weather. One year, I was trying to get a house finished on my own street by Christmas so that the new neighbors could move in before the holidays. It had been a busy time in the building business and our regular masons had accepted more work than they could finish. This left me with no choice but to find an additional mason crew. November was approaching and there were about 30 days worth of brick work to be finished on the house. The inside of the house was nearly completed and that part of the process should make it on time. We had often put off landscaping until springtime, but we at least had to have all of the concrete work in place before the folks could move in. The grading for the walks and driveway could not take place until after the masons were through. It rained every day that November except for three. Weather's impact on housing can be significant because of its unpredictability.

Most North Carolina communities have snow removal equipment that consists of a large bright yellow ball that rises and sets every day. For the most part, this works well. The influx of northerners in recent years would beg to differ. Timing is a critical factor in the construction process. I remember one particular house with a complicated roof system. We were well into the fall when we started the construction phase. That was bad timing. The basement was in and the walls were up by Christmas. The goal was always to "dry it in" as quickly as possible for obvious reasons. The roof system, itself, was going to take several weeks to build in perfect weather. Our problems started with an ice storm, followed by a week of sub-freezing weather. That was followed by another ice storm. All in all, what should have taken two weeks, took six weeks to complete. All of the wood framing was exposed to the weather for a long time. I hope there was no long-term damage to the house, but I bet that some day their floors might squeak.

There is a long standing joke in the real estate business that says that if it was not for the high divorce rate, agents would not have nearly as much business. In the building side of the business, the shiny new home is often the result of attempts to save a marriage. There was one particular couple for whom we had built a house shortly after they got married. Years later we were building them a new large home. It had become difficult to get them to agree on decisions that needed to be made in order to move the project toward completion. Our goal had been to finish the house by Thanksgiving, but they had reached an impasse on appliances and light fixtures. They drew a line in the sand with each other. We turned out to be the victims in this case. He decided it would be cheaper to stay in his small house through the winter and pay small utility bills than to move into the big house before winter. With the house nearly done, we were forced to keep it heated all winter and pay the extra interest on the construction loan. This incident caused several pages in our contract to be revised.

≋ 13 ≋

CONTACTS AND CAMERON

There is a well-known saying that declares that it is not what you know, but who you know. I believe this to be true in most areas of life. Whether you are in the building business or the real estate business, there are times when you not only need to know people who can help you, you also have to be able to win them over in order to be credible. Winning them over is usually done by entertaining them in some way or another. For 28 years I had tickets to Cameron Indoor Stadium to watch the Duke University men's basketball team, the Blue Devils, play basketball. A recent publication ranking the top 25 sports venues in the world, ranked Cameron number five over all. I always felt it was number one. So did most of the contacts and clients that I took to ball games. This was how I entertained folks. I was able to close many deals, secure many construction contracts, entice numerous investors, and keep a lot of employees happy by taking them on a little road trip to Cameron.

Sometimes I was not trying to win a new customer, but I was trying to reward an old customer with whom I had already done business. In the real estate and custom construction business, having happy clients means getting referrals. There is no amount of advertising one can do that comes anywhere close to the results you achieve from a good referral. When someone personally tells a friend or acquaintance that you will do them the best job, the chance of your actually getting their business is probably 90 per cent or better. I found that once I had taken a client to Cameron getting the referral was almost a lock.

Cameron Indoor Stadium was opened in 1940 and was, at that time, the largest arena south of the Palestra in Philadelphia. Today, its cozy 9,300-plus seats comprise one of the smallest basketball arenas on the major college basketball circuit. This fact also makes it one of the loudest, most intense, and yes, craziest sports venues in the world. The gothic stone exterior blends right in with the other gothic stone buildings that make up the original part of Duke's West Campus. When I give potential new customers tours of the Durham area, they will inevitably ask, "Where is Cameron?" Some will want to know where Coach K lives or where Dean Smith lives, but they all want to know where Cameron is located.

When I point it out, I usually hear "Really?" in disbelief. It is a beautiful, but non-imposing building, and in no way looks like the grand landmark they had envisioned. Then I take them inside. The intimate size of the place is striking. The raised panel oak trim and the brass rails throughout are overwhelming. When I walk them out onto the playing floor, they look up and see all of the scenes that they have been watching on television from their couch while at home on a Saturday night. Hanging from the rafters are the championship banners and the retired jerseys. We stand there in silence, and I know each one of those clients is hearing the roar of the crowds and the cheers for their heroes echoing through the silence. I remember one client taking out his cell phone as soon as we emerged back into the sunlight in front of Cameron. He called a relative back home and said, "I just got to visit the shrine!"

The lower half of the arena is reserved for the students. For years it was the only major arena where the students sat courtside for 360 degrees around the court. The sound of their cheers bouncing off of the steel beams holding up the roof, made playing on Cameron's court the most intimidating experience in college basketball. The upper part of the arena, above the brass rail, is where the old folks sit. Some of them can get extremely enthusiastic as well. The students are referred to as "Cameron Crazies." It is a well-deserved title, but not one that has been recently earned, as the last couple of decades of Duke students would have you believe. The title has been crafted over the last 50 years.

I was a student back in the 1960's when Coach Vic Bubus led Duke to prominence on a national level. We were ranked somewhere in the top five every year I was there, and occasionally number one. We would wait in line for hours to get in to our seats. Just like today, all you needed to gain access to Cameron was your student ID. The lines would stretch from the doors of Cameron, all the way into the residential quadrangles. As soon as the doors opened, everyone who had patiently waited in an orderly line for hours would break and run. There were times when my feet did not touch the ground for the last 50 yards thanks to the rush of the mob.

There have been so many funny things happen in Cameron over the years. One of the best of those memories occurred when I was a student. The Vietnam War was getting under way and the ROTC program was in full bloom. During the half-time ceremony of one of the biggest games of the year, the ROTC drill team put on a splendid display of precision rifle drills. I do not know how many students were involved, but the uniformed young soldiers-to-be completely surrounded the perimeter of the court.

Their final drill ended with each participant holding their rifles up at a 45-degree angle and firing a blank. What a tremendously loud noise that was, and none of us was prepared for it. One student knew it was coming, however. About two or three seconds after the rifle blast, that student, standing on the back row, heaved a real dead goose onto the basketball floor. It landed in the center jump circle like a bag of wet cement. The timing was perfect. Shortly after the splat, the future soldiers were lying on the floor in the fetal position, laughing so hard that they were unable to get up. Thus began the modern era of Cameron Crazies and 50 years of funny, clever, creative, and sometimes gross events in Cameron.

Duke basketball fell on hard times after Coach Bubas retired. The wins came less often, but the students were always there. Their "Crazy" reputation became greatly enhanced during this period. When losing bored them, they turned to other antics. No matter what they did, however, it was well researched. They knew their basketball, and they knew their opponent. A few days after a North Carolina State player had been accused of stealing pizzas from the pizza delivery guy on their campus, the State team appeared in Cameron. When the suspected player was introduced, the entire floor was peppered with pizza boxes as the students tossed them from the stands. A couple of years later, another NC State player was accused of receiving a special deal on a car purchase. When he was introduced, virtually every student tossed their car keys onto the floor. I have always wondered how long it took the students to get back the correct set of keys.

Things got a little out of hand one night. Maryland had always been a conference rival. That rivalry was enhanced by their colorful and bald coach, Lefty Driesell. One year, the week before Maryland was scheduled to play in Cameron, one of their players was accused of raping a girl on campus. The Duke students were not completely sure this player would make an appearance that night. They were ready, nonetheless. When the player was introduced, they littered the floor with condoms. The press declared that they had gone too far. So did the University President, who threatened to ban the students from future games. This incident, more than any other, was responsible for the "Crazies" gaining a nasty reputation, rather than the clever reputation that they had earned for years.

The press would not let it go. Before all of the future games that year, sports writers would interview the upcoming opposing coach about what his thoughts were concerning the Cameron crowd. Before the final game that year with UNC, their dreaded and respected coach, Dean Smith, had expressed some disgust during an interview with a newspaper reporter about the Cameron antics. Coach Smith took the reporter's question as an opportunity to say that the Duke students were mean and that they always complained about the referees' calls. The day of the game arrived and every student in Cameron on that day had not only read about the comments, but they could quote them exactly. Virtually every student below the brass rail that afternoon was wearing a halo on top of their head. When the UNC players were introduced one at a time, instead of booing, the Crazies chanted in unison, "Hi Joe" or "Hi Bill." When officials whistled Duke for a foul, they would all chant together, "We beg to differ, we beg to differ." This clever response and recognition of their need to stay appropriate (and not nasty) was classic Cameron.

⸺◦⸺

I was at a Christmas party at a large real estate office one year during the basketball season. I had been especially eager to meet, and become friends with, a particular attorney who was related to a couple with whom I had done a lot of business. Cathy and I had been talking to his wife for a while when the conversation turned to potential Christmas gifts. The attorney's wife said that the thing her husband wanted most for Christmas was the opportunity to see a basketball game in Cameron. I told her that I could take care of that the next evening. Rarely have I seen a dignified businessperson get as excited as he did when she called him over and broke the news. After that, we were friends for a long time.

I may have made as many enemies as friends with my Cameron trips. I had a list of businessmen who wanted to be on my waiting list. After making the trip once, they would tell me that if I ever had an extra ticket, they would go with absolutely no advanced warning. They were not kidding. It was their wives that became the "enemies".

The best thing about using Cameron as my trump card was that I could never over sell it. Occasionally I would talk people into going who were not really sports fans, but they would agree to go just to humor me. It never failed. After their first trip, Cameron would always come up in future conversations.

When Mike Krzyzewski (Coach K) became head coach about 1980, it even took him a few years to right the ship. Now in 2011 he has become the winningest college coach of all time. Things evolved with the Crazies during this period as well. Coach K let it be known from the beginning that he would not put up with any nastiness from the students. He cleverly cultivated them into the best "Sixth Man" in sports. I went to a Duke vs. Wake Forest game in Winston-Salem one night and had to laugh when the public address announcer asked, just before tip off, if the crowd would remain standing until the first basket was scored. In Cameron, the students consider it their obligation to stand and honor the team at all times when the team is on the floor or are in the gym. The students stand when they first come out to warm up and only sit down during half time. I get tired just watching them standing for both halves of the entire game.

Right before the opening tip off, the Crazies all start jumping up and down in unison. Many a guest has turned to me in trepidation and asked, "What are they doing? The whole building is shaking." I would explain that it was time for the jump ball, so they were jumping. Their most misunderstood ritual occurs during the singing of every National Anthem. Near the end of the song is the phrase "Oh say does that….." When the "Oh" is sung by whoever is the guest soloist or choral group, the entire student section raises their arms above their head, forming a circle, and shouts "Oh." This is when I would always glance over at my guest to see if they were laughing or showing a look of disgust. Often it was a look of disgust until I told them that as the "Sixth Man", the students just liked to participate in the singing of the National Anthem. Once that tradition started several decades back, I can only remember one time the students did not sing the "OH." That was the night the first Gulf War started, and they had just finished a tribute and prayer for the troops. Another touching moment was the night a pretty young 16-year old girl was the guest soloist. She was doing a beautiful job with the song until she had a case of brain freeze about half way through it. Not three notes went by in silence before the entire student body instantly started singing the rest of the song. She was so relieved to have the help. Oh yes, they did the "Oh."

Not all opposing coaches or players were intimidated by the students. Some of them were real fans. Jim Valvano at N.C State always said it was his favorite place to coach. I remember one night he was vigorously complaining to the officials about a call. This argument was ongoing for quite a while so the students started chanting "Sit, Sit, Sit." So he did, right down on the basketball floor. So impressed by his wit were the students, that they gave him a rousing ovation. He waved, laughed and ended the argument.

There were a couple of rules for the road trips to Cameron. One was never to take a client to see Duke play the client's favorite team. One reason for that was that Duke usually won and that would have defeated my purpose of making it a memorable occasion. Another reason was that you were never quite sure how the client would react to such orchestrated antics. Some folks had a better sense of humor than others. Another rule was never to be late. I always liked to get there in time to show my guest around the place and let them settle in. If it was a really big game, we would get there with a little extra time to spare.

One Saturday afternoon we were playing Georgia Tech. Both teams were ranked in the top five in the country, so we arrived earlier than usual. I was really glad we did. The year before, Georgia Tech coach, Bobby Cremins, had recruited a tall kid from New York with a terrific outside shot. He had a really good freshman year, but he needed to shed a few pounds to improve his quickness. In May of his freshman year there had been an obscure article in one of the Atlanta papers saying that Coach Cremins had told this young man that if he would lay off the Twinkies and donuts, he could be national player of the year the next season. Every Crazy read the article.

About an hour or so before each game, the members of each team come out onto the court, often one or two at a time, as their team was dressing and getting taped back in the locker room, for a shoot around. When this particular young man emerged from the locker room onto the floor, he was met by two Duke students dressed in tuxedo splendor. With white cloths draped over their arms, they escorted the player to the center jump circle where a table awaited him. The table was covered with a white formal tablecloth and it featured an elaborate candelabra. Piled on the table were boxes and boxes of donuts and Twinkies.

One of the students pulled out the chair and offered him a seat. I had seen many a player come into Cameron with an attitude that would have let them be offended by this whole scene. The students were actually showing great respect for this particular player, and he realized it. He high-fived the two waiters and proceed over to the students and applauded them. He spent the rest of the warm up time challenging various students to shots from wherever they happened to be seated in the stands. He was a great sport and later that year was named national player of the year. He did not eat a single donut or Twinkie that night.

Sometimes you get a front row seat to witness history being made. It was a Saturday afternoon and UNC was in town for the continuation of the greatest rivalry in sports. This particular year, Duke was having the better season. Which team was sporting the better record rarely had an effect on the outcome of the game. Since the shot clock had not yet been invented for college basketball, and UNC's Coach Smith felt a little undermanned, he decide to slow the game down. That is an overstatement. He decided not to shoot at all. My guest and I witnessed nearly 16 minutes of the first half of a game in which UNC did not take a shot. Duke had managed to force a couple of turnovers and converted them into seven points. Then, with four minutes left in the half, a big, tall young man from UNC named Rich, stepped into the far corner of the court, received a pass, and shot the ball. It missed. No, it really missed. It missed by about four feet. The half ended. The Crazies were stunned. Then, out of the blue, in unison, they began to chant, "Air ball. Air ball. Air ball." That became a chant heard around the basketball world and in almost every college game played since that Saturday afternoon.

I have only seen someone get the best of the Crazies on two occasions. The first time occurred one night when Duke was playing Harvard. First, I will give you a little background. Lefty Driesell, who was a major winner during his days as coach at Maryland and Davidson, was a Duke graduate. Often, when Maryland came to town, the entire student section would wear scull caps to mimic Lefty's bald head. That was quite a sight. I think they were, at least, partly honoring ol' Lefty. Also, the Duke students had been known to say things like Duke was the Harvard of the South or Duke was Harvard with big time sports.

What made this night special was the fact that Duke was locked in a major recruiting battle with UNC and several other schools for the services of Danny Ferry. Danny was not only one of the best high school players in America that year, but his dad had been a famous NBA star, and his big brother played for Harvard. Never had the Crazies treated an opposing team, or one of its players, so royally. At half time, two Harvard students walked down to the side of the court and unrolled a giant scroll. It was made of two bed sheets sewn together with a long pole on each end. Once unrolled, the two young Harvard men walked slowly around the perimeter of the court so everyone in Cameron could read the scroll. There was a line drawn down the middle forming two columns. The title of the left hand column was "Famous Harvard Graduates." Among those listed were Plato, Aristotle, Jesus, Leonardo de Vinci, etc... The right hand column was titled "Famous Duke Graduates." One name appeared: Lefty Driesell. The Crazies were not offended. In fact, they thought it was one of the funniest things they had ever seen. The two guys from Harvard got a standing ovation from the crowd.

The other incident was more of a battle of wits between Coach K and the Crazies for the supremacy of Cameron. After Coach K's first couple of years, Duke has either had good teams or great teams. In this particular year, it was simply a good team and the Crazies knew it was not going to be a championship season. They were becoming a little restless and protective of the squad. An article appeared in the school newspaper, and subsequently, in all of the major papers around the state, discussing which officials had presided over the most Duke losses. To no Duke fan's surprise, the leading whistle-tooter in Duke's losses, by a wide margin, was an official named Dick P. As fate would have it, Dick was calling the Saturday night game that week. On the drive down I had briefed my guest on the rituals of Cameron. The most amazing thing about the Cameron Crazies has always been their ability to all start a chant or cheer at the same time. They are paying such close attention to what is going on that when someone starts a chant, by the first time it is repeated, everyone is participating. I had also shared the article about the officials, not knowing until we arrived in Cameron, that Dick P. was calling the game.

It was hot in Cameron that night, and the natives were more restless than usual. Dick was holding up his end of the bargain by making a series of some of the worst calls I had ever seen. They were so bad that I thought some of the Duke players might get injured. Sometimes a no call is worse than a bad call. Finally, the Crazies had experienced enough. They started a chant, "You suck…(pause)….Dick." A very sweet, elderly lady always sat in the row in front of me. She turned to me and asked what they were chanting. I told her I did not know. I lied!

I am sure Coach K was not too fond of our favorite official either, but he was not going to tolerate that kind of behavior from the students. He leapt up off of the bench and headed for the scorer's table, calling a time out on the way. He grabbed the stadium microphone out of the announcer's hand, and, in order to be heard above the crowd noise, started yelling as loud as he could. As good as the Crazies were at picking up a chant, they proved to be even quicker at stopping one. Just as coach K started to yell, the whole place became as quiet as a tomb. His declaration echoed off the rafters, "I will not tolerate you yelling, you suck Dick." We were stunned. He was stunned that it was so quiet when he yelled his proclamation. The little old lady in front of me said, "Oh my!" Coach K turned around and walked back to the bench and for a few minutes, there seemed to be a strange spell over the crowd. Then our friend Dick made the worst call of the night. Instantly the entire student body chanted, "You suck……Richard." Coach K was half way out of his chair when the word "Richard" resonated throughout the building. With a slight smile on his face he sat back down. The crowd did not respond to another call for the rest of the game. Both Coach K and the Crazies had made their point. The rest of us laughed for hours.

The kind of loyalty the Duke students have for Coach K and their basketball team is rarely found anywhere in today's world. If those of us in the real estate business could cultivate just a piece of that loyalty and devotion with our clients, we would not have to work so hard. But that is the secret–if you do not work that hard, you cannot maintain the loyalty. The student section in Cameron will only hold about half of the undergraduate student body and an even smaller percentage of the graduate student population. A few decades ago the demand for a seat in Cameron became so intense that the students started pitching tents and camping out the night before a big game. That idea caught on so quickly that an overnight campout became weeks, and sometime months. The process become so elaborate that the student government organization created rules about being in line, tent checks, and how many could occupy a tent. The tent city became known as Krzyzewskiville and now sports a permanent sign marking its location. Duke did its part by wiring the area with electricity and Internet access so the students could study in their tents. About two months into my son's freshman year, he called home and asked for some money to buy a tent. It seems that the purchase of a tent shared equal status with tuition and books.

⸺

A trip to Cameron has always been on many men's bucket list. A bucket list is a list of things you want to do or places you want to go before you "Kick the Bucket." Tops on my list for years had been to make a trip to the Masters at Augusta National Golf Club in Augusta, Georgia. A ticket to the Masters is as hard to obtain as a ticket to the Duke vs. UNC game in Cameron. I am not a golfer, but I play golf. I learned early in my business career that the old saying, declaring that more business is done on the golf course than in the office, is more truthful than you might think.

When my son turned eleven, I decided it was time to teach him to play golf. We started with par three courses and worked our way up. He loved it and could not seem to get enough of it. His three sisters were tennis players like me, and despite being a good tennis player himself, he decided early on that golf had captured his heart. One reason he told me that golf appealed to him was that the ball stood still!

I paid for a lot of lessons–all but one was for Jeff, and the lessons paid off. He would in turn teach me what he had learned. My entire interest in golf was two-fold. One was to beat Jeff as long as I could. That goal ended fairly early. My second goal was to become a good enough golfer to not embarrass myself on business golf outings. I learned that if you could consistently break a hundred, you could play socially with most anyone.

I remember playing with my lawyer and some clients at a pretty course located at the foot of Pilot Mountain. I was not a betting man, so when the other three started talking about double or nothing, "sandies", and two dollar putts, I just told them to tell me what I owed them when we finished. I played fairly well that day, but nothing too special. I am still not sure whether it was the fact that they spent the entire round discussing the bets, or whether it was the moderate amount of alcohol they consumed, but when we finished, they all paid me.

—————

Another memorable outing took place on the golf course at Tanglewood Park outside of Winston-Salem, during a golf tournament for builders and Realtors™. A fellow builder and I were playing with two bankers with whom we had both been doing business for several years. In my case, I had a million dollar line of credit for construction loans with these particular bankers. That was enough money to fund about a half a dozen spec houses at a time. Just as I was about to hit my drive on the fourteenth tee, they informed us that they were going out of the construction loan business, and were recalling our loans. My drive went deep into the woods. Needless to say, the balance of that round was a disaster.

When my oldest daughter, Carrie, was in college, her future husband, Rick, would, of course, come over every time she was home. Trouble started to brew when Rick arrived home from college and immediately went to play golf with Jeff. After hearing enough complaining from Carrie, her mother and I told her that there was only one thing to do—learn to play golf. She did, and now she is quite an accomplished golfer. I tell folks that when you are the father of three daughters, there are three times in your life when your daughter calls home and says to Mom, "Put Dad on the phone, too." The first time is to tell us she is engaged. The second time is to tell us that she is pregnant. The third time is to tell us that she had a hole in one. Carrie has made all three calls!

—————

This gets me back to the bucket list. On Palm Sunday in 2009, Cathy and I were on the way home from church after having heard another marvelous sermon from our son-in-law, Mark. The cell phone rang and it was my son Jeff, who now resides in Missouri. His birthday and mine are the same week in July, and that year we were going to be a combined 100 years old. He started the conversation with "Dad, I have an early birthday present for you since this is a special year. Next Sunday I am taking you to the Masters." I handed the phone to my wife because I was unable to speak. Wow, this was a dream come true. Jeff was in charge of a business trip to the Masters on behalf of his company, and he saved a ticket for me.

I could not wait for the big day. I had to get up at four o'clock in the morning in order to drive to Augusta in time to meet their plane. It was a little past seven o'clock in the morning, and I had just crossed into South Carolina on I-95 when the cell phone rang. It was Jeff. He said that due to a last minute cancellation he had an extra ticket. I told him it was too bad he had not called me earlier, because I could have brought one of his siblings with me. Having three sisters, what he really wanted, was for me to choose which one he should call in order for him to offer them a ticket.

I told him that he could call his sister Ginny, but she did not play much golf. Her husband Steve was an avid golfer, but his parents had just arrived for the Easter weekend. I did not think that asking Steve would be such a good idea. Then I said that he could call his sister Amy, but she did not play golf at all. Her husband, Mark, was also an avid golfer, but it was, after all, Easter Sunday, and he is a preacher. I also knew he would want to go, and that would probably not sit too well with the congregation!!

That left Carrie and Rick. I told him to call them and let the two of them work it out. Carrie always thrived on spur-of-the-moment decisions which served her well in a house full of budding teenagers. Further complicating things that morning was that each of their three kids had a role in the Easter service. I also knew that in their household at that hour, no one was up yet. Exactly twenty minutes after I hung up with Jeff, the phone rang again. It was Carrie. She said, "Dad, I'm on the interstate. Which way is Augusta?" I will always wonder what we could have accomplished, if our employees had been so dedicated.

It was the perfect golf day—72 degrees, clear sky, and a slight breeze. Tiger and Phil were paired together and both of them were in contention. The azaleas were at their peak, God was in his Heaven, and all was right with the world. What does this have to do with building and the real estate business, you ask? To this day, I will declare that the Augusta National Golf Club is the most beautiful piece of fully developed real estate in the United States. The number one slot on my bucket list has been permanently retired.

⚬

I will always cherish the contacts I made while building houses, developing land, and selling real estate. We built houses for a lot of well-known people. Some were famous sports heroes. Another client was on the plane that dropped the atomic bombs on Japan in World War II. Another client wrote some famous commercial songs. My favorite contact, however, was Woodrow. Woodrow was a generation older than my Dad, but they were great friends and had developed hundreds of lots together. Woodrow was the perfect southern gentleman. He was tall and handsome, had wavy white hair, and he had better manners than anyone I had ever met.

I had always thought of Woodrow as just a "grandfather type" figure and an all around nice guy, until I heard him speak at our Rotary Club luncheon one day. Woodrow had written a book about his life experiences before moving to our small town. What experiences they were! In his younger days, Woodrow had been the personal secretary for Henry Ford. He told us that his first job had been working for the Ford dealer in Charlotte. At the morning sales meeting one day, the manager came in and said that Henry Ford, who was in Asheville visiting his old friend George Vanderbilt, had a special request. Mr. Ford wanted someone to bring him five gallons of the finest moonshine North Carolina could produce. Ford was experimenting with converting various homegrown products into tractor fuel for farmers.

The manager declared that he had no idea where to get moonshine. This is where an industrious young Woodrow spoke up and said he knew where to get it. His only condition was that he be allowed to deliver the moonshine to Mr. Ford personally. With permission granted, Woodrow was off to Wilkes County where he purchased his brew before heading to Asheville. He said that when he got to the Grove Park Inn, an aide to Mr. Ford wanted to take his bounty. Woodrow refused to give it up

164

and said that he would sit there all night if necessary, if that is what it would take, to meet Mr. Ford. Mr. Ford, it seems, always preferred to stay at the Grove Park Inn in lieu of being a guest at Vanderbilt's magnificent Biltmore House. When Mr. Ford came down to breakfast the next morning, Woodrow was still there. Ford invited Woodrow to join him for breakfast, and later to work for him as a career. The story always made me admire Woodrow's stamina and determination.

Over his career with Mr. Ford, Woodrow said he sat in on many meetings with many famous people. For example, he said he wrote the check that Mr. Ford signed, and then presented to Thomas Edison to rebuild his laboratories after they burned to the ground. After years of meeting Presidents, purchasing gifts and real estate for Mrs. Ford, Woodrow decided to marry a girl from my hometown and settle down. Naturally, he started off as a Ford dealer and later got into real estate development. That is when Woodrow and Dad became partners in developing many subdivisions. One of the highlights of my career was getting to develop one tract of land with Woodrow before he died.

Woodrow told a story that will always be my favorite of all of his stories. He swore it was true and even included it in a short book he wrote about his experiences. He said that on one warm summer weekend, he and the Fords were visiting their rural retreat in the Massachusetts countryside, known as Hathaway House. Mr. Ford had two houseguests, Harvey Firestone and Calvin Coolidge. After summoning Woodrow to bring the car around to the front, Mr. Ford and his two guests headed out for a pleasant afternoon drive with Woodrow behind the wheel. Upon cresting a small hill, they came across a Model T Ford stopped beside the road with its hood up. Its driver, dressed in bib overalls, was staring hopelessly at the steam rising from under the hood. Mr. Ford instructed Woodrow to stop so he could try to help the farmer with his car trouble. Upon approaching the farmer, he said "I'm Henry Ford. I built this car. Let me see if I can help you fix it." Ever being the hands-on mechanic, Mr. Ford rolled up his sleeves and went to work.

It did not take long for Mr. Firestone to follow Mr. Ford's lead. He approached the farmer and declared, "I'm Harvey Firestone. I made these tires. How are they doing?" While the farmer explained the good and bad points concerning the tires, Mr. Coolidge decided that it would be cooler under a nearby shade tree. Woodrow stood patiently next to the driver's side of the car. Soon the farmer wandered over to Woodrow and asked where he picked up this group of men. He doubtingly explained that the guy under his hood claimed to be Henry Ford, and that the man kicking his tires claimed to be Harvey Firestone. Then he said that he expected the guy resting under the tree to claim he was President of the United States.

DESIGN FEATURES

THE MAIN FEATURE ON MANY OF OUR DESIGNS WAS THE FRONT DOOR FRAME.

SPECIAL WINDOWS CAN DOMINATE A DESIGN

IN CENTRAL NORTH CAROLINA THE ABUNDANCE OF BRICK PRODUCED BEAUTIFUL WORKMANSHIP AND TALL CHIMNEYS

NOT EVERY HOUSE WAS BRICK. WE SOMETIMES
USED SIDING OR A BLEND OF MATERIALS.

JUST AS THE HOUSING INDUSTRY HAS EVOLVED OVER THE YEARS, SO CAN THE INDIVIDUAL HOUSE ADAPT TO THE NEEDS OF THE FAMILIES THAT OCCUPY IT. I ALWAYS SAID THAT ADDITIONS TO A HOUSE SHOULD NEVER LOOK LIKE AN ADDITION. THE HOUSE THAT MY GRANDFATHER BUILT FOR TOOTS HAS EVOLVED OVER NEARLY A CENTURY. MY GRANDFATHER WOULD BE PROUD OF THE WAY IT LOOKS TODAY AND I'LL BET TOOTS WOULD NOT RECOGNIZE IT.

≋ 14 ≋

SELLING IN THE EARLY DAYS

Dad was a smart man. He made me study for my real estate license within six months of graduating from Duke. He knew that after four years of grinding it out in college, studying for and taking the real estate exam would seem like a piece of cake. He was right. That was when I first realized that there were no young people in real estate. My real estate preparation classes and my exam class were full of middle aged and older folks. They had forgotten what it was like to study and they were all struggling with the prep work for the exam.

When I joined my local Board of Realtors™, it consisted of a little more than a dozen aging white men. My, how real estate has changed since those days! Dad hired the first female agent in our town. I did not realize at the time that he had recognized the future. He had always liked being first when it came to new things. We had the first home central air-conditioning system in town. He thought he had bought the first color TV until he found out that his barber had beaten him to it. But his instincts about the future of real estate were exactly right.

Only a few years had gone by when the local Board of Realtors™ decided to make me president. I think their motto was to "Let the new guy do the work." Never being satisfied with maintaining the status quo, I thought that the board should take on a big community project. One of our members had just given a report on a new government-financing program for new construction homes for minorities. Since Realtors™ around the country were leading the way in those days for equal housing opportunities, I thought it would be a good idea for our group to get into the act as well. We formed a non-profit company made up of our board members and decided to build two houses through this new program. I drew the plans for free and wrote the specs. With Dad's permission, I bid the jobs at cost just to prove how cheaply we could do it. We won the bid. I do not think any of the others were unhappy that they did not get the job.

One of their biggest concerns was the potential for theft. We had selected a nice, neat neighborhood, but the reputation for materials and tools relocating in the middle of the night was fairly high. The first day on the job, I decided to be pro-active. I spotted two young boys sitting on their bicycles. They had watched us intently for most of the day. I finally went over to them and they asked what we were doing. They seemed excited at the prospect of getting to watch the two houses being built. I told them I only had one problem. I said that we could not finish the houses if anything got stolen, so I needed to deputize someone to guard the houses. Both of their hands went up instantly, so I swore them in. To this day, those were the only two houses I ever built where absolutely nothing disappeared from the job.

⟞⟝

At first, I was not sure what to expect from my new license to sell houses. I worked all day, either on the job site or in the office, on the construction side of the business. There were only a couple of folks in our town who actually considered themselves as being in the real estate business full time. It was more like being in the housing business than the real estate business. Every office offered a mixed bag of services. Most offices relied on the building side of the business to provide the bulk of their income. A couple of local firms emphasized the art of auctioneering for a major piece of their business.

We handled our real estate clients from our offices at the shop. A couple of weeks after I obtained my license, Dad listed a house for sale that I had helped build during my early college days. I had done most of the plan work for this house, and I had spent a large part of my first college summer at this house on the paint crew. A lady walked in the door one afternoon and wanted to see Dad about buying a house. Since he was not in, I eagerly offered to help her. I had no idea what I was doing since this was my first real customer. I did know enough to ask her to sit down and to have her tell me what type of house she would like.

She unknowingly described the house we had just listed. After quickly arranging to show her the only house in our inventory of listings that I knew anything about, we headed over to the property. I think that she was impressed at the degree of knowledge I displayed about the product. When we went back to the office, I wrote my first offer. When I got to the financial part of the offer, I asked her how much of the sale price she intended to borrow. She informed me that she was recently widowed, and she would be paying cash. The deal closed without a hitch, and I was mistakenly thinking that I had stumbled into the easiest profession on earth.

This misconception was further enhanced a month later when Dad asked me to accompany him on a listing appointment. On the way to the house he told me we were being asked to list a very strange house. It really was not that strange, it was just different. There were few homes in our area that were designed with a contemporary flair. This house had flair in every direction. Dad wanted me to see it. He also wanted me to hold the dumb end of the tape while he measured the house. On the way back to the office, Dad told me that he did not think the property had any chance of selling.

A week later, a young doctor from California walked into our office and asked me if we had any California style houses. I told him that we had just what he wanted. I was right. He loved it the moment we walked in. There probably was not another person that moved to our town in the next five years that would have bought that house. I was further reinforced with the thought that real estate was an easy job. Then at least 18 months went by without a single nibble. Real estate reality had set it.

—◁◦▷—

Real estate promotions do not always turn out as advertised. I remember a local brick company running a promotional contest when I was in high school and still working as a cross-hatcher on the drawing table. The whole town was excited because no one had ever offered such a large prize in a local contest. The prize the winner would receive was to have their house completely bricked on the exterior. All you had to do was enter your name. The buzz built for weeks and then the winner was announced. As I look back on the contest results, I wonder what the odds were of the winning house being a small, less than one thousand square foot, four-sided house on the busiest street in town, across from the busiest restaurant. It was like the brick company's advertising sign announcing the winner had been made for that location.

Dad and Woodrow had been quite successful developing one very large neighborhood in particular. One of their biggest rivals decided that the time had come for one of their own developments to become the biggest one attempted on the local scene. It was an ambitious project, and they advertised their project heavily. When the time came to have a grand opening, the rivals announced that they were going to raffle off a new station wagon. It was to be presented to the contest winner the following day on the courthouse steps. The lucky recipient would also have their picture featured on the front page of the local paper. Anyone present at the grand opening was eligible to buy a chance on the new car for ten dollars.

Dad never missed an opportunity to see first hand what the competition was doing, so he went to the grand opening and bought a ticket. He stood next to another one of his competitors who had mustered up the same degree of curiosity as Dad. The contest was a reverse drawing, meaning they eliminated tickets one at a time. When they got down to five contestants, Dad was still in contention. He turned to his friendly competitor standing next to him and offered to sell him his ticket for twenty dollars. Dad figured a ten-dollar profit at this point was better than nothing. His rival said no, so Dad stayed a little while longer.

There is nothing worse in the real estate promotion business than to have your biggest competitor spoil your day. Dad won the car. The next day, our whole family was eagerly awaiting the arrival of our new station wagon at the courthouse steps. High noon had struck on the big bell in the clock tower, but there was no car in sight. Then we noticed one of the local newspaper reporters waving to us and asking us to come around to the backside of the courthouse. When we got back there, he presented us with the keys to the car on behalf of the developers. They chose not to show up. The photographer took our picture and started to leave. As he walked away, Dad asked him if he could have a copy of the picture to keep. The reporter said that he had been instructed not to put any film in the camera. Despite our missing out on becoming media hounds, we really enjoyed the car.

—◦—

I had a favorite uncle named Alan who was a Colonel in the army. While he was stationed at Fort Bragg, he would take me hunting on post. My fondest memory of Fort Bragg was when he sneaked me on to the post the day President Kennedy came to announce the forma-tion of the Special Forces. I liked just about everything about Uncle Alan except the way he played tennis. He had the worst looking game I had ever seen. He chopped, sliced, spun and retrieved you to death. Despite my ranking on the junior tennis circuit in the state, he practi-cally always beat me. He was tougher than I was. He taught me some great lessons through the years. In the early days of integration, he asked me if I would wear an "equal" pin to symbolize equal rights. He could not understand my telling him that I preferred to treat people the same, rather than wearing a symbol. He did not know the lessons that I had learned from having Slim as a friend.

Sometimes, trying to do the right thing can get you into a lot of trouble. The real estate business had historically been full of whispers in the old days as agents thought they were protecting the integrity of neighborhoods. Proudly, as social conditions began to change in the South, the real estate industry helped lead the way. We as real estate agents were subject to a lot of test cases in those days. When a black couple came into your office, you were never sure if they really wanted to buy, or if they just wanted to find out if you would sell to them. Dad had taught me always to put the customer first, and Slim had taught me that all folks are OK.

In the door one day, came a black couple who wanted to buy a house in a previously all white rural neighborhood in the southern part of our county. Luckily for them, I was the agent available. Off we went to see the property. This area did not have the most sophisticated group of neighbors. After surveying some of the surroundings and the occasional Confederate flag, I was secretly hoping that they would decide to buy somewhere else more hospitable. They did not. I wrote the offer and got it accepted, thus breaking new social ground in our county.

Not long after they moved in, I got several threatening phone calls from men identifying themselves as members of the KKK. Shortly after receiving one of those calls in the early evening, I was playing with the kids in the basement playroom when a stranger appeared outside of the back door. That scared me. I called Dad and he came over and brought me a gun. The next morning Dad brought the sheriff over to my house. He gave me instructions on how to protect my family and myself. He taught me to look behind the bushes when I went outside and always to check out the back seat before I got into the car. I still do both of those things today. I was not going to tell him about my new pistol but he already knew about it. He instructed me on when to carry it and how to use it. He said after a while all of this trouble would die down, and I would not have to carry it any more. In the meantime, he said for me to not shoot the paperboy. I think wearing the equal pin would have been easier.

There were other lessons to be learned the hard way. We were building our first spec house in the Clemmons area, and it was getting far enough along to make me real eager for a client. We were trimming out the family room one afternoon when an agent brought what appeared to be a very pregnant lady to see the property. As an agent myself, I was trying to do everything I could to entice her into buying it. Just when I thought I had made the deal, I asked her when her baby was due. She told me that she had given birth four months earlier, as she turned and walked out the door. Needless to say, she did not buy the house. To this day, I have never again even remotely suggested that a woman might be pregnant.

This particular house did sell before we completed it, but not before some more disappointments. The development was literally on the edge of the suburbs. Beyond the subdivision's borders was some beautiful rolling North Carolina countryside. Unfortunately for one client, there was some of that countryside just before you got to the neighborhood. One gentleman and his agent had visited the property several times. He seemed to love the design, the floor plan, and the setting. He was from New Jersey and that was his downfall. The agent informed me that his wife decided that no matter how much he liked the house, she would not buy a house that required them to drive by a cow on their way home.

I should have learned my lesson about being too nosey when I asked the prospective client when her baby was due, but I did not. This same house was being built on the only vacant lot on a one-block long street with a cul-de-sac. You could not help but notice the neighbors and their daily habits. After all, we were on the job site all day long and most of the neighbors were in and out quite a bit, except for the house next door. These folks left early and came in late so were never got to meet or speak to them. I always tried to get to know the other folks on the street for a number of reasons. I wanted them to know our product and take an interest in finding themselves a new neighbor. I also wanted them to keep a watchful eye on our property when we were not there.

A truck from a local pest control company arrived at the house next door one day and stayed for several hours. This would not have attracted our attention except that he came back every day for the next two weeks. Our whole crew was convinced that we were building in the middle of Peyton Place and the neighbor was having an affair with the pest control guy. Finally I asked the neighbor on the other side what was going on.

It seems that one of the heat ducts in the suspicious house had become disconnected in the crawl space and the open end was lying on the ground. The crawl space door had been left ajar and a skunk wandered in to the crawl space. Seeing the open pipe was irresistible to the skunk, so in he crawled. The husband was sitting quietly in his family room reading the newspaper that evening when the skunk poked his head up from the ductwork by flipping over the floor register. They were equally surprised to see each other and neither moved for quite some time. Finally the skunk, having satisfied his curiosity, disappeared back down into the heat duct.

Thus began a two-week effort to capture a skunk without giving the skunk time to react and ruin the house forever. After many ideas were rejected, a company from Charlotte was called in because they had a mobile flash freeze machine. They lured the skunk into a predetermined section of the ductwork by using food as bait. Just as the skunk thought he was enjoying a good meal they flash froze him in a split second. This turned out to be a much more exciting incident than an affair with the bug man would have been.

Sometimes there were no classes to prepare you for what you had to do. Dad had listed a modest three-bedroom brick ranch that belonged to a prominent local doctor. It was located in a small subdivision in the southern part of the county. It had served the doctor well as rental property for a number of years. He told Dad that it was currently empty and that made it a good time to sell the house.

In those days we did not have appointment centers to arrange for showings. Besides, this house was empty so I did not need an appointment. I grabbed the key off the key board in the office where we placed all of the keys for our listings. This was in the era before lockboxes. When you wanted to show another firm's listing, you first had to call that firm to schedule the appointment. Then you were required to go to that firm and sign out the key. Immediately after showing the property, the other firm expected you to promptly return the key.

In this case it was our listing, so I piled my clients into my car and off we went. When I pulled into the driveway I noticed a pickup truck in the rear driveway. I asked the couple to wait in the car while I checked to see if anyone was there. Shortly after ringing the doorbell, the doctor answered the door wrapped in a towel. He explained to me that it was his day off and he had been mowing the grass. He asked us to wait a few minutes while he finished his shower and then he would be on his way. We sat patiently in the car for about five minutes before he backed out of the rear driveway and waved to us as he left.

When I showed a piece of property in those days, I usually entered each room ahead of my clients. After touring the living areas of the house we headed toward the bedrooms. We looked at bedroom three and then bedroom two. My clients were carefully examining each closet in every bedroom in order to determine if the closet would be large enough. I moved into the master bedroom while they were still in bedroom two. On the floor was a mattress. It was the only furnishing in the house. I thought that was a bit strange. I opened the master closet and it was full of clothes. Then I glanced down and saw two bare feet attached to what appeared to be two bare legs. They were not male feet or legs, either. I quickly closed the closet door and stood in front of it, obstructing its access. When the clients came into the room they commented about the mattress and I said I had no idea why it was there. They asked about the closet and I told them it was just a standard-size closet. I did not budge so they moved on to the master bath. We soon finished the tour and got into the car. As we drove away I spotted the doctor's pickup truck parked at the first intersection we passed. I guess he was waiting for us to leave so he could go back to the house and pick up his friend.

⸺◦⸺

There is a well-known saying in real estate that the three most important factors in selling a house are location, location, and location. In my personal opinion, that old saying only applies in a good market. In a prolonged bad market the three most important factors are price, price and price. I am constantly amazed at what folks will buy if they think they got a good deal. In good times, when making money is easier, the buying public is less interested in what they pay than they are in what and where they are buying.

Dealing with another real estate agent can be an interesting experience. I had a spec house nearing completion in Winston-Salem. It had a list price of $200,000. New construction spec houses were generally subject to a different set of negotiating rules in a good real estate market. Few builders would bargain with their price in a hot market. They would always use the excuse that they could add up the costs of the bricks, mortar and labor and get an accurate cost. The value of a resale house was always more subjective and therefore rarely sold for the asking price. The market played a huge factor in both scenarios. The builder would negotiate a lower price only if he had too much inventory, or needed to start more projects to keep his crews together. The bargaining factors on a resale house are a little more complicated. In a booming market, the price can actually go up instead of down if there are multiple offers on a house. Another key factor is how much does the seller need or want to sell. The combinations of these factors are endless.

I received an offer on my $200,000 spec house just as it neared completion. A couple of months earlier I would not have been willing to bargain, but it was time to move on to the next project. The offer was for $190,000. The agent who brought me the offer disclosed that she was representing herself. I can negotiate with the best of them, but in reality, I always preferred to go directly to the point. I discussed with the agent the fact that we were both in the real estate business; so in order not to waste each other's time, let's just split the difference at $195,000. She said no. So I formally countered her offer at $199,000. After a few days, she upped her offer to $191,000. I came down another thousand dollars. She went up the same amount. After a period of three weeks, we met at $195,000. She was real proud of herself for negotiating with me so well. I was thoroughly puzzled.

Many young first-time homebuyers will ask me if I think the cost of the house is too high. I chuckle and tell them I remember when I was a kid that the average cost of your final dream house was $25,000. My Grandfather used to price the houses he built at $200 per room, plus the outhouse. When I first went to work officially for my Dad, we were pricing houses between eight and ten dollars per square foot. So yes, I tell them houses do cost too much. But then, so does everything else.

The one thing I have always been able to count on during my career in housing was that the price and value of a house would always go up. The rule has been that if you take care of your home and keep it updated, it will increase in value. I have seen a few flat cycles, but never a down cycle as far as price was concerned until the last several years. The housing industry, which makes up one third of the US economy, is currently on a downward cycle. Discussing that situation will have to be left for another, less humorous book.

Not all of my negotiating for homes has been for my own spec houses or listings. I have four adult children and they all own a home. In fact, they have all bought at least two homes already in their young careers. The first to buy was my oldest, Carrie. After selling the townhouse we helped her buy while Rick was in medical school, they were off to Asheville for a four-year residency in OB-GYN.

I sent a referral to an agency in Asheville that had an excellent reputation. Referrals can be icing on the real estate agent's cake, when they work well. Sometimes a simple phone call to someone you know in another city will earn you a referral. Of course, you need the permission of the client to place the referral. The agent placing the phone call can usually earn about 25 per cent of the commission to be earned by the agent on the other end, who is doing all of the work. Most good agents will gladly yield that 25 per cent for what normally turns out to be a sure thing. When corporate relocation companies place a referral, the charge to the agent doing the work is usually at least 35 per cent or more. When the slice of the pie gets that small, the veteran agents will often say no thanks to that deal. This often leaves the referred client in the hands of a rookie.

Since I did not know any active agents in Asheville at the time, I asked the company for whom I was working to place the referral. We got a rookie. He was a nice young man, eager to please. Cathy and I met Carrie and Rick at the real estate office in Asheville and the five of us piled into a car that would have been crowded with four people in it. Cathy and I introduced ourselves to the agent as Mom and Dad while we were still at the office. From the back seat I calmly told the nice young agent that Cathy and I were his worst nightmare. I told him we were both licensed real estate agents. I was only kidding about the nightmare part of the story, but I wanted to see how he would react. Being seated directly behind him, I was able to observe the redness and swelling in his neck quite clearly. Then I laughed, but he didn't. I know that I did not put too much pressure on him because he did a nice job that day.

I had been in that agent's situation many times with parents and their children and usually hated it. I was determined only to be helpful that day, but I was not going to tell that to the agent. He probably would not have believed me anyway! By the end of the day Carrie and Rick had found a house they wanted to buy. Before the final decision they had narrowed it to three houses. When we returned to each house for a second look, I urged them to walk with me to the back corner of the lot. There I would ask them if it looked like their house from that view. Only one did and that is the one they bought.

This house would become the source of several interesting stories. One of them happened to include golf. In fact, they may have stayed in the Asheville area permanently if it had not been for their desire for a better golf climate year round. Anyway, one weekend while Carrie was a few weeks pregnant with our first grandchild, she and Rick decided to go on a weekend golf retreat. When they returned on Sunday evening, they saw what no homeowner wants to see. Water was running out of every part of the house that it possibly could. It was running down the front steps and it was running under the garage door and down the driveway.

By the amount of water damage, we estimated that the hot water line to the dishwasher had broken shortly after they had left on Friday. The house design was what we in the business referred to as a split foyer design. When you entered the foyer by way of the front door, you had two choices. You could go up one-half a flight of stairs to the upper level or down one-half a flight of stairs to the lower level. The upper level housed the bedrooms, the living room and the kitchen. The lower level contained a guest room, a playroom, a third bath, as well as a garage and storage area. Every thing was a mess.

We, of course, were summoned instantly and spent a few days helping to organize the mess and assess the damage. This was not a job for super Dad. Fortunately they had a good homeowner's insurance policy. The house was not livable and the repairs were going to take three or four months. The insurance company paid for them to live in a nearby hotel, just a few miles from their house, while the work was being done. On the upper level, they gutted the entire kitchen and put in new cabinets, counter tops, appliances and a new floor. The carpenters had to remove the lower four feet of all of the drywall on the upper level because it had been water logged. The carpet had to be removed and replaced, along with most of the subfloor. The lower level had to be completely replaced. Of course they lost a lot of furniture, clothes, and just plain old stuff.

About three months into this ordeal, Cathy and I went up for a quick overnight visit. Carrie was getting more pregnant by this time, and the hormones were becoming quite out of balance. The first couple of hours we were there, all I heard from her was complaining. Since this was my first experience at having a pregnant child, I did not want to add to her misery. So I sat her down and asked her a simple question. I asked her if when they bought this 30-plus year old house a year or so earlier, would they have taken the deal I was going to propose? The deal was that if she paid me $250 (the amount of their insurance deductible), and I put them up rent free in a luxury hotel, including three meals a day while I did the work, would she accept my deal. I told her I would give them a brand new kitchen complete with new appliances, and all new carpet and paint throughout the entire house. I would replace the entire lower level including the bath. In essence, I would totally update their house. A big smile came across her face and she said, "Wow, would I." Then I told her that is exactly what she was getting! She did not complain any more once she saw her situation from that perspective.

⚊⚊⚊⚊

Rick had worked for me some in the summers and had become interested in wood-working as a hobby. He had enough room in his garage for some tools and equipment. After I had helped supply him with some shop tools that I had gotten after Dad died, he was ready for a big project. He decided that he was going to build a hand made crib for our new grandson, Austin. He wanted all of the wood to be mahogany. After Dad's death I had moved all of the various woods he had collected from his basement over to the shop for storage. I picked out an abundant supply of mahogany and hauled it up the mountain one weekend.

This crib turned out to be a huge masterpiece. It was beautifully finished. It featured a pull out drawer underneath and rails that hinge down when you need to reach into the crib. By the time Austin was old enough for a crib, the S.S. Austin was ready to sail up to his room. There was only one problem. The S.S. Austin was wider than the door to Austin's room. Rick had measured the door but not the opening. The opening is smaller than the width of the door. The difference is the thickness of the lodging, or door stop, on each side of the door jamb.

We were coming up to Asheville that weekend anyway for the launching of the S.S. Austin, so I told them that I would help them remove the lodging and get the new crib into the room. Rick paid close attention to the process because he knew that someday he would have to repeat the process when they moved. After Rick finished his residency in Asheville they joined an OB-GYN practice in Burlington. The S.S. Austin also made the trip down the mountain after Rick successfully extracted it from the bedroom, by once again removing the door stop. This time it was going to be the future sleeping place for Andrew and later, Emily.

Having placed another referral to a Burlington agent, we once again went house hunting with Carrie and Rick. After looking at houses for several days and really not finding anything they liked, the agent called us with news of a brand new listing. They were going to be the first customers to get to see this particular house. We met them for lunch knowing that we had to wait until two o'clock to see the house. Before meeting the agent, we drove by the house so we could get a good look at the neighborhood. We had a good laugh when we drove by the house and saw that the owner was literally running behind his lawn mower in an effort to make the property look presentable before the two o'clock deadline.

On the day that the moving van arrived with the S.S. Austin and all of their other belongings, I got a frantic phone call from Carrie. It seems that this time the S.S. Austin was not just one-half inch too wide, it was two inches too wide for the bedroom door it needed to enter. Rick had apparently become frustrated with the whole process and was tearing down the door. I asked Carrie to put Rick on the phone. I told him to have fun tearing down the door, because it had to go anyway. This seemed to make him happier. I also had him write down exactly what to order from the local lumberyard and to call me as soon as it got there. Once it had arrived a few days later, I told him I would come over and hang the new door unit for them. It took the entire width of the rough opening to allow the S.S. Austin to sail into this particular bedroom.

A couple of days later I got the call that the new door unit had arrived. I went over immediately. Rick watched the entire operation again, and I gave him some pointers on how to set a door unit. Once it was in place, all that was remaining was to set the nails on the face of the casing. Setting the nails is a process by which you drive the head of the nail about one sixteenth of an inch below the surface of the wood. The objective is to create enough room to put some putty over the nail before you paint the casing. To set a nail, one uses a nail set, which looks somewhat like an oversized, fat nail. Holding the nail set in one hand and a hammer in the other hand, an experienced carpenter can usually set the nails with two gentle taps of the hammer. Rick seemed particularly enthralled with this process. He said to me at one point that he did not understand how I could tap every nail just right without making a mistake. I turned to Rick in amazement and said that I did not understand how he could perform a crash C-section in 37 seconds (a hospital record he held during his residency) after the anesthesiologist yelled go. If my setting nails amazed Rick, he would have been overwhelmed at the precision with which Slim could drop a tree or Peabody could fit a miter joint. That day taught me a lot about appreciating each person's individual talents.

⚒

My second oldest daughter, Ginny, and her husband Steve moved to Cleveland so Steve could do a residency at the prestigious Cleveland Clinic. This meant another referral call to the Cleveland Heights, Ohio area, and a journey all the way up I-77. The following Christmas brought a rare visit for me to the real North in the dead of winter. We had made a couple of visits to the North Shore of Chicago in the early years of our marriage. That was the first time I had been so cold that I thought my face would actually freeze. Lake Michigan already had, and the ice shapes it formed were indescribable. That is also where I witnessed workers pouring a four-foot deep footing for the first time.

Cathy's parents were adding a garage onto their house. I had never watched a concrete truck back up to a footing and empty the entire load without slowing down. Cathy's parents' home on the North Shore of the Chicago suburbs was just six blocks inland from Lake Michigan. Most mornings, when I awoke, it would be snowing. Seeing it snow was a rare and exciting experience for a young man from the South. Cathy's mother would always say, "It's not snowing, that's just a flurry."

That Christmas in Cleveland, it "flurried" about four inches worth of snow each night. Ginny and Steve had purchased an old house in Cleveland Heights for two reasons. One reason was the fact that there were no new houses in this beautifully maintained suburb. The other reason was, if there had been new houses, they would not have been able to afford them at this point in their careers. Their old house had an old kitchen which I had promised to improve in the four days I would be in Cleveland. The first night we arrived required us to make a trip to their version of Home Depot. Unfortunately, it was about eight or ten miles away. The only way we could get all of the material back to their house was to put the pieces of plywood on the luggage rack on the top of the car. There was no way to tie it all down, and we did not have time to find any other solutions since the store was about to close. I volunteered to hold the plywood on top of the car by sticking my hand out the window and gripping it the best way I could. I think four blocks was the most distance we covered at any one attempt without the plywood falling off. To this day, that night was the coldest experience of my life. The kitchen turned out beautifully, but I worked so hard those few days that I could hardly drive back down I-77. It was a good thing that it was downhill all the way home.

<hr/>

Sometimes, the most important folks in a project are the people behind the scenes. That is certainly true in a real estate transaction. In North Carolina closings are done in an attorney's office, and the key person is often not the attorney, but the paralegal. Early in my real estate career, most of the closings were done at the local savings and loan.

I remember one early sale to a young couple who was buying their first house. We arrived at the savings and loan for a two o'clock closing.

Present were the two buyers, the loan officer, the attorney and his paralegal, the listing agent, and of course, me. We had gone through most of the papers and explanations when it had finally become time to sign the note and the deed of trust. The attorney had explained each of the documents as we progressed and mentioned that these last two were the documents that meant they were actually borrowing the money to buy the house. He showed them where to sign and the young man started to affix his signature. He had to put the pen down because his hand was shaking too much. He tried again, but it started shaking even more. In an effort not to chuckle in front of my client, I excused myself from the table. One by one, the entire group left the table in an effort to calm the client. He wanted to sign the papers but just could not make his hand hold still. With all of us hidden, but sneaking a look around the corner, he finally succeeded. We all suddenly reappeared, and they lived happily ever after. Actually they lived happily ever after in several more houses that I sold to them over the years. He had finally gotten the hang of signing those papers.

Dad's favorite attorney, Frank, had a paralegal named Shirley, who was the best I have ever worked with. I remember going down to Frank's office one day to ask Shirley a question. I was surprised to see every seat in the lobby but one was taken when I entered the office. Shirley's desk was in the lobby, and there were nine of us waiting. The door to Frank's office opened, and he slowly walked into the lobby. Seeing the packed house, he started with the first potential client by asking if he could help them. They said no. They explained that they were waiting to see Shirley. He went all of the way around the room and got the same answer each time. When he got to me, I just said, "Me too." Frank dropped his head, turned around, and slowly went back into his office and closed the door

—————

Wayne became a friend after I designed and built a house for him and his wife and their growing family. At that time he was just a few years into his career of becoming the most renowned barbeque restaurant owner in the region. Later in his career, the New York Times named him the maker of the best barbeque in the country. That declaration allowed him to cook his creations for Presidents and world leaders. I am happy to say we are still friends today. That might not be the case if I had not gone the extra mile.

Wayne had decided that he wanted to buy a lake house for his family to enjoy when they were not all working at the restaurant. We looked at a number of properties and had put in a couple of offers, only to have them fall through along the way. Once we finally settled on a property, I started doing the behind the scenes leg work necessary to bring the deal to fruition. With some deals, there just seems to be a problem at each step in the process. That certainly was the case with the lake house. After a few delays, Wayne's patience was starting to wear thin, and he was about ready to give up on the whole idea.

The morning of the proposed closing, all of the necessary parties met at Frank's office. Shirley started going over the papers. When Frank came in, he said he had found a problem with the title. Wayne was ready to cancel the contract when I asked Frank what had gone wrong. Frank explained that when the current owner had been deeded the property, the clerk in the Register of Deeds office had not noticed that the deed had not been properly notarized. It seems that the notary, Jane Doe, had filled out everything correctly, but had forgotten to sign the notary portion of the deed. Frank said we could not close until we had this problem corrected. I asked him to give me the deed, and to also give me until four o'clock to find Jane Doe. Wayne agreed to wait, but said that if I did not have it corrected by four o'clock, the deal was off. Out the door I went and I headed back to my office.

All I had to go on was the name of the young lady who had failed to sign the deed eight years earlier, and the name of the county where she had only partly performed her duty. Even though the deed had been recorded in Davidson County, it had been signed and not fully notarized in Forsyth County. Since Forsyth County was our neighboring county to the north, I knew that if I could just find Jane Doe, assuming she still lived somewhere in the county, I would have time to capture her signature and return by four o'clock.

Hoping to have really good luck, I called the phone company's information line in Forsyth County. Naturally, there was no Jane Doe listed.

This required Plan B and Plan B was not yet fully developed. Then I had an idea. I called the phone company office in Forsyth County and asked the lady who answered the phone if they kept their old phone books. She said they did, but they were down in the basement in the archives. I told her it was extremely important and that I would hold while she fetched the book from eight years ago. I was playing a hunch that Jane Doe was a young notary at the time of her goof, and had since married someone other than John Doe. The hunch paid off because the nice lady at the phone company office found an eight-year-old directory. Jane Doe had been living in the town of King in the northern part of Forsyth County.

I now know what chasing a wild goose means, and all I knew about this wild goose was that eight years ago it lived in King. Deed in hand, the car and I headed to King. I had almost an hour's worth of time in the car to figure out what to do next. The only thing I could come up with was to find a local barbershop and start asking questions. There was a small shopping center on the right side of the main road into King. I pulled in and starting scanning the businesses one at a time. At the very end of the row was a striped barber pole. There were several barbers and a few customers inside. Numbers increased my odds, or so I hoped. No one, however, had heard of a Jane Doe from eight years in the past. They did suggest that I consult with the local beauty parlor. With directions in hand, I ventured further into King until I found the beauty parlor. Beauty parlor folks know everything and tell even more.

They not only knew Jane Doe, they knew her married name and her street address. After giving many thanks to the ladies, I headed into one of King's old tree lined neighborhoods. Jane Doe was now Jane Smith, and I knocked on her door. No one answered, so I knocked some more. I had come too far to run into a dead end at this point. While pondering my next move, one of the neighbors emerged from her house and inquired as to my intentions. I explained about the notary problem on the deed and that all I really needed was her signature. She explained to me that Jane was not home because she had had a baby earlier that morning, and she was recovering in Winston-Salem at Forsyth Hospital.

We had four children over the years and I was not welcomed into the delivery process until the fourth one arrived. Even then, there were vocal objections from some of the nurses. I knew that getting in to see Jane Smith was going to be a problem. Using a skill that I later used in the Clerk of Court's office during the trial, I sized up the staff at the maternity ward desk and picked the one I hoped would be the most approachable. It took a lot of talking, but I convinced the young lady that this was a legal matter of the utmost importance. She guided me down the hall to a nurse's station where she outfitted me from head to toe with surgical gown, booties, and headgear. Then she led me into what looked like a holding room for new mothers. I was afraid to do much looking around, and something told me my time in there would be limited. I got right to the point with Jane Smith. She smiled, apologized, and promptly signed the deed. No sooner had she handed me the pen when the double doors to the new mother's suite burst open, and there stood a nurse that must have been eight feet tall and weighing in at four hundred pounds. She yelled at me, "What are you doing in here?"

All of my years of playing a high caliber of tennis, including occasionally jumping the net after a victory, came into immediate use. I did not bother to answer the nurse. I was too busy running out the door and heading down the hall. It really is hard to run and undress from a hospital gown at the same time, especially with a four hundred pound nurse right behind you. I certainly hope the kind young nurse who assisted me did not get discovered and fired. There was no time to stop and thank her. I finally made it safely out of the building and into my car. There was just enough time to get back to Frank's office in time for the closing. I had a real story to tell, but I knew no one would believe me.

≋ 15 ≋

SELLING TODAY

The years have brought so many changes to the real estate business. During the early years of our marriage, we lived four houses down from the head of the local phone company. I had pestered him for years with questions about when we would be able to have a phone in our car. Finally it happened. Every builder and agent I knew had a car phone installed. It was not long before the technology allowed the phone's ringer to be wired to the horn on your vehicle. Having spent years on the job with no one having the ability to contact us at all, we all felt the necessity of answering every call. The only problem was that in a new home subdivision, the builders were in the houses and the phones were in the cars. Horns would ring all over the neighborhoods all day long. It must have been quite a sight watching builders leaping over stacks of 2 x 4's while shedding their tool belts as they bounced down the entrance ramp on the way to their trucks. My experience in the maternity ward at Forsyth Hospital had been good training for this eventuality.

Like every other phase of society, the computer changed the building and real estate industry more than any other previous innovation. Computers had become so advanced by the late 90's that a cold chill was running throughout the real estate industry. Would the real estate agent be replaced by the computer? The real estate agent had always been the owner of the information, no matter how crude the container was for that information. It had been our job to make ourselves and our multiple listing books as full of information as possible. It was also our job to convey that information to our clients. Besides, no member of the general public wanted to lug around a multiple listing book all day.

By the end of the 1990's there was an economic downturn in primarily the computer and software related industries. Our family had set up shop in Durham in the early 90's for the sole purpose of practicing only real estate as a profession. It was the best market in the country. It was the logical place to be since I had made the one and one-half hour drive to watch every Duke football and basketball game for 28 years. Now I lived eight minutes from Cameron. Cathy started working at Duke where they had all sorts of benefits such as health insurance and retirement plans. These two items were missing in the real estate industry.

As the economic downturn started to affect the Research Triangle Park area of North Carolina, literally thousands of laid off computer techies thought they could step into the real estate business. They assumed they had the jump on the future of real estate because they thought that computers would dominate the real estate industry. What most of these folks did not possess were good people skills. I would have dared any of them to talk their way into that maternity ward at Forsyth Hospital. The bottom line was that the real estate industry had advanced from a high touch business to a high touch/high tech business. I do not think the high touch factor will ever go away.

In the spirit of Dad, when computers first came out, I wanted to be one of the first to buy one. I was not sure what it was good for except as a word processor. As someone who entered his freshman year at Duke armed with just a slide rule, a manual typewriter, and an AM clock radio, I thought a word processor was pretty cool. The first TV computer game was Pong, and we had one of those, too. That occupied hours of our time. Over the next few years I kept my eye open for advances in CAD systems. CAD stands for Computer Aided Design. In other words, a cross-hatching machine.

Some folks like to go to art museums; others like to shop at the mall. I always preferred browsing in a hardware store. My hometown still has the best hardware store I have ever seen. I would go to the National Home Builders annual convention occasionally with two purposes in mind. First, the exhibit floor amounted to the biggest hardware store in the world. Second, it was the best way to keep up with advances in CAD systems. I knew deep down inside me that when I found a CAD system that drew plans the way I did, I would buy it. Timing always plays an interesting part in out lives. Six months after Dad died, we were in Atlanta at the big show and there was the system I was looking for.

It was way too expensive but Dad had left me some money. I felt that he meant for me to spend it on this particular computer and software package. It even did cross-hatching, as well as drawing each individual brick on an elevation drawing. Though expensive, it did pay for itself many times over. I got a lot of jobs because I could draw a client's house and then give them an aerial tour of the property without leaving my office. The state Home Builders magazine even did a story on me saying that I had the most advanced CAD system in the state. Dad would have been proud, I think.

Starting fresh in a new market takes some good luck and several good decisions. It also helps if the market is one of the best in the country. Even though I had never solely relied on real estate commissions for a living, I had not worked for a salary since I left Dad's construction company and started my own business some 18 years earlier. It takes an almost pioneer mentality to work as a commissioned salesperson. I admire them all for striking out on their own. It is truly in the spirit of the American way.

When I got to Durham I looked around to see which companies had a lot of signs in people's yards. Next I made a list of those companies I wanted to visit. At the first place I visited, the manager was able to see me right away. When I introduced myself, he said that he had known my Dad and had taken a GRI course under him. He wanted to know if I still had the model house. First of all, GRI stands for Graduate of the Realtors™ Institute. This was a postgraduate type professional designation that about 20 per cent of Realtors™ have, but all of them would like to have. It is like enrolling in Real Estate 101. The year after I got my GRI certification, Dad was asked to teach the construction course, which was one of many parts of the overall course structure. After completing the course that first year, he was voted the most outstanding teacher at the Institute. This got him all fired up. When he got back to town, he told me that he needed a demonstration model that he could use in the next class.

We decided on how big it needed to be to be seen by everyone in the class. We also made a list of what it needed to demonstrate. Since there were so many parts that needed to be displayed, we decided that it should be presented on a turntable to double the number of parts to be exposed to the audience. Basically, it became a two-sided cut away model featuring a basement on one side and a crawl space on the other. Half of the roof was made of trusses and half of the roof demonstrated a stick built roof system. We tried to think of everything.

Once it was designed, I told Dad that I would build it for him. The first thing I did was what I did with each house project. I made a materials list and gave it to Artis in the shop. He looked at my list and said, "What in the world is this for?" He had never seen floor joist that were one-eighth of an inch by one inch by 24 inches long. The stud sizes were even stranger looking than the sizes of the floor joists. After explaining to him what we were trying to do, he began to produce my materials list.

Many hours went into the project, but it turned out to be a thing of beauty. One problem I had to solve was how to transport the model house. Dad did not go anywhere without his Cadillac, so I had to construct the model house so it could be broken down into three parts. It had to fit into his car. After that, he never bought another Cadillac without first testing to see if the model house would fit.

After he had won the best teacher award for his second year's effort, I learned that he had taken credit for the building of his soon to be famous model. I quickly called him on it, and he agreed to let me put my name on the model as the builder. Since he died, I have had many offers from Realtors™ and builders across the state to buy the model house. I will not sell it because I now teach a Continuing Education course for the Real Estate Commission, based on Dad's old construction course. He taught at the Institute for 22 years and won the best teacher award 21 times. He came in second once. That really bothered him, and he never could quite let that go. Now the North Carolina Association of Realtors™ gives an annual best teacher award, named after Dad. I keep the model house in my storage room next to a 2 x 4 named Ray.

———

After discussing the model house and real estate in general, with the office manager at the real estate company, we both felt comfortable with each other. I signed on after working out a commission plan. Then he gave me some interesting and wise instructions. He said he knew that I knew how to sell, but he did not want to see me in the office for the next two weeks. He wanted me to ride through every neighborhood and new subdivision in town and get to know the product. For a guy whose favorite thing used to be making roads in the sandbox, getting to know the local terrain seemed like a great idea. I still pass along that advice to new agents today.

Getting started in a new market is not easy. It does not matter how much experience you have, you still must build up a client base and that takes time. I was lucky to have started in Durham right before the advent of the private phone line in each office. Every phone call and everyone who walked in the front door of our office had to go through the agent on duty. We were assigned a rotating share of phone duty in those days. The veteran agents, with an established client base, rarely accepted phone duty. I took all I could get. This was also in the days before we had an appointment center to schedule all of the showings. That task was also done by the duty agent while waiting for a paying customer to call or walk in the front door. The duty agent's position could get hectic, especially in the spring of the year, our busiest season.

I had made a few sales that first year but I was really waiting for my first big break. On the way to the office one morning to meet a client with whom I had been working for several weeks, an oncoming car ran me off the road. My car and I ended up unscathed in someone's front yard. My knees were shaking so badly that I had to just sit there for a while until all of my body parts stopped vibrating. Once I finally reached the office, I immediately got a call from my client saying that there was an emergency at his work place, and that he would be tied up all day. I did not think my real estate day could get any worse. Fortunately, it didn't.

With nothing on my schedule, I walked into the duty agent office and asked the lady on duty if she needed any help. She said that she was fine for the moment, but she appreciated the offer because she knew that it would soon get hectic. I went back to my desk and tried to make myself look busy. Just when I was about to run out of creative thoughts, the duty agent called me and asked if I could come up there and help her. Jumping at the opportunity, I was practically there before she hung up the phone. Lynn, the duty agent, said that she had two calls on hold and one prospect to call back. She asked if I could possibly take the couple that just walked in the front door. The trouble with walk-ins was that they required you to spend time with them in the conference room, and that rendered you useless at phone duty.

There was always an assigned backup phone duty agent, but they rarely showed up. Who could really blame them for not showing up? Most of the time you sat around for the five-hour shift with nothing to do, while the primary duty agent skillfully manipulated the situation so the backup agent would not get any of their business. Luckily for me the backup duty agent had failed to show, so Lynn was glad to have some help. I offered to just entertain the new walk-in couple until she was free enough to work with them. She was quite adamant that she would never have time that day to work with a walk-in. I think the duty room was starting to get to her just a little. I then offered to pay her a referral if the couple turned into a sale. By this time another phone line was ringing so she turned to me and said, "You take them, no strings attached." By that time, our walk-ins were probably wondering if anyone was going to wait on them so I hustled out into the lobby to introduce myself.

In those days the average sale was around $100,000 and a really good sale was about $250,000. Bill and Betty were now in the conference room sitting across from me, exchanging pleasantries. They explained that he had retired a little early, and since their son was working in the area, they wanted to look into buying a house here. They were so nice and sincere that they made me feel like I might actually have a real customer. Then I popped the question. "What price range are you interested in," I asked? She quickly said, "At least a half a million." He nodded his head and I silently gulped.

The first thing I told them was that we had plenty of houses in that price range, but it would take me a few minutes to do some research. They said that would be fine since they needed to go to the driver's license bureau and have their licenses switched to North Carolina. After promising to be back in an hour, out the front door they went. I was convinced they meant to really move here since they were already getting new driver's licenses.

I quickly went into the computer room and started doing research. It was not long before Lynn stuck her head in the door and commented that the walk-ins did not stay long. I told her they were coming back in an hour after they switched their driver's licenses. She asked what price range they were in, and I told her that she did not want to know. She asked again and I said nothing. Then she looked over my shoulder at my search parameters on the computer screen and said, "Damn."

We spent a number of days looking at some really fabulous houses. The more they saw of our area, the more they liked it. They still had an extremely large house to sell in the northeast. After a few days of looking at everything that we had to offer, they decided that the best move for them would be to buy a lot. Later, they could build the house they really wanted when their house up north finally sold. So I found them a lot that was almost as expensive as their original house budget. They settled into a rental while they waited for progress to occur on the house in the northeast. I did give Lynn a referral fee on the lot sale.

⟨⟨⟨⟩⟩⟩

Their newly purchased lot was about 20 minutes south of our office, but their rental was just blocks away. Over the next year of waiting, Cathy and I became good friends with Bill and Betty. We went to a lot of fun restaurants and movies together. As that first year ended, Bill and Betty were rethinking their desire to be so far south of town and away from all of the fun places of entertainment they had become used to visiting. One day Bill called me and said he had a favor to ask. I told him that of course I would be happy to help him any way I could. Then he told me that he had received an offer on his house up north. After explaining that he felt that the agent back home would not have his best interest at heart, because she could only see dollar signs resulting from a potential closing, he asked me if I would negotiate the sale on his behalf. Of course he meant for me to stay in the background. I also realized that I was not going to get paid anything either. I really did not mind that part because he was my friend, and the only risk I had was to my negotiating reputation. This was when I learned that real estate experiences could be ironic. This was going to be the largest deal I would ever put together and I was not going to get a penny.

After telling me the asking price and the offer price, Bill said he thought it could be worked out. After all, they were only eight hundred thousand dollars apart. The first thing I did was ask him to have his other agent send me a copy of all of the documents. I never did know if the other agent actually knew I existed. The stack of papers and credentials was nearly an inch thick. After I read all of the materials, Bill made a counter offer. All of the offers back and forth were presented in decimals. By that I mean, for example 3.1 million or 3.4 million. I had certainly never negotiated anything in decimals before. It was quite exciting, even if I was not getting paid. Finally a bad thing happened. When you are negotiating, the one thing you do not want to have happen, is for your clients to draw a line in the sand. The line this buyer and seller had drawn happened to be two hundred thousand dollars apart.

As the saying goes, I felt like I was flying blind at this point in the negotiations. It really helps to listen to the tone of the agent representing the other side in any negotiation. I did not have that luxury. I advised Bill to hold firm and see if we could bluff them up. Bill was real adamant that he had yielded enough and would not go down on his price one more dime. It was a Monday and Bill told the agent up north that he was going to stand firm. The bluff did not work like we had hoped. The buyer's agent informed us that if we did not accept his offer by noon on Friday, the deal was off.

I could detect a little bit of worry in Bill's voice when he gave me the news. Negotiating skills mainly come from experience and intuition and not from a textbook. I basically have two rules when negotiating.

The first rule is to always put yourself honestly in the other party's shoes and ask yourself what you would do. The second rule applies only if the other party does not do what you thought they would do. Rule number two was simply to ask yourself why did they do what they did. Rule number two applied in this situation.

I asked Bill how many times the buyers had visited the house. He told me that they had been there six times with their agent and one time with a designer and remodeler. Hearing this information, I was convinced that the buyers really wanted the house, so the deadline date must have something to do with their proposal. I told Bill to tell the buyer's agent that he needed until the following Monday to make that kind of decision. We were hoping to flush them out. It worked.

Their agent reported back to us that they were leaving Friday afternoon on a sailing trip in the Caribbean and would be incommunicado for two weeks. I told Bill that I thought that we had them over a barrel. My gut told me that they were too emotionally invested in the house, and would not risk getting on that sailboat without owning Bill's estate. Bill agreed. He stood firm on his price, and he and I paced the floor for two days. Thursday evening Bill called me to tell me the buyers had accepted his price. I sure was glad to hear that news, because my advice had sounded more confident than it really was. I did not get paid for that deal but Betty and Bill sold their lot and bought a large house using me as their agent on both occasions. Over the next few years Bill sent me a lot of customers after he came out of retirement. Most importantly, however, was that the four of us became good friends for life.

You would be amazed at the role animals play in real estate. Dog owners and smokers are basically the same breed. Neither group believes that their house actually stinks. Of course they make every effort to clean up and they often apply huge amounts of air freshener. Sometimes the result is the same odor you get from using too much cologne in lieu of a shower after a trip to the gym.

The dog owners honestly love their dogs, because they are conditioned to having Fluffy around. Fluffy does not often scare away a potential client, especially if she is in a cage. Bruno, however, needs to be somewhere in the next county when the house is being shown. I have tried to show many properties when the first thing you heard after ringing the door bell was Bruno rushing to greet you. Almost every time the clients simply decide they will skip that house. I took a couple to a house out in the country north of Raleigh one Saturday afternoon. They, like so many others, dreamed of living in the country on a couple of acres of land. Our showing instructions included that dreaded phrase, "Beware of the Dog!" It further instructed us not to go into the fenced back yard or onto the deck. I was hoping that meant that Bruno was tucked away safely within a fenced enclosure.

When we got out of the car, we heard a bark that any large dog would be proud of, but the dog was nowhere in sight. While we were touring the inside of the house, Bruno was studying us from the back deck. Bruno was big. The note pinned to the kitchen door that led to the garage said definitely not to open it because the dog had access to the garage. My client was dying to see the inside of the garage. The plan I offered him was that I would try to entertain Bruno from the safe side of the sliding class doors while he took a quick peep into the garage. I emphasized the word quick. Bruno was quite content trying to figure out how to eat me through the glass doors, until he heard the kitchen door open. He evidently knew that sound very well. In a split second Bruno had disappeared around the back corner of the house. I was yelling to my client to get back into the kitchen as I leaped over a chair to get to the door. The client got back into the kitchen just as Bruno entered an open door from the garage to the back yard. I think Bruno made it across the floor of the double garage in one giant stride. He hit the garage side of the kitchen door at the same instant that the client and I threw ourselves against the kitchen side of the door. I thought the door was coming off the hinges, but it did not. They had really liked the house and property, but all they, and I, wanted to do was to get out of there.

My favorite set of showing instructions said, "If the snake is not in the glass case in the foyer, do not show the house." It also said that under no circumstances were you to go into the back yard. Well, the snake was in the case. It was a big case. I do not know how big the Boa was but the tour of the house made me a little uncomfortable. When one of my clients wondered out loud if the Boa in the case had any relatives living in the house, we left. To this day I wonder what in the world was living in the back yard.

We had a dog and a couple of cats as pets while the kids were growing up, but they lived outside. I can't understand the silliness in the showing instructions that state, "Don't let the cat out." You can talk to a dog sometimes, but you cannot talk to a cat. If the cat wants to get out badly enough, it will find a way. I have spent a number of hours over the years trying to herd a cat back into a house. They do not co-operate until they are darn well ready. There is a story that was told to me by several different agents who swore it was true. It has now become urban legend in these parts. It may, however, have been an urban legend before it spun its way into local real estate folklore.

It seems that one morning an agent in Raleigh was showing a potential buyer a house that was tagged with the infamous instructions about not letting the cat out. As they toured the inside of the house the cat followed them everywhere. This particular cat was black with distinctive white markings. When it was time to leave, they locked the front door and started across the porch. Sitting on the porch swing was the cat. They had no idea how the cat got out without them noticing, but there it was. Efforts to negotiate with the cat were non-productive so they tried surrounding it. For the next four hours, the agent and the young couple chased that cat all over the neighborhood. Finally they captured the creature and tossed it in the front door. As it turned out, the cat on the swing was the twin to the cat in the house. The cat on the swing lived next door and rarely got to socialize with its twin. By the time the owners got home the two cats had done thousands of dollars of damage to the house. For the cats, it was an afternoon to remember.

—◦◦◦—

Not too many years after our move to Durham, I was showing a nice couple houses surrounded by several acres of land. When you sell in the Durham area, you often sell in the entire Triangle area of North Carolina. The Triangle consisted originally of Raleigh, Durham, and

Chapel Hill. The shape formed when you connected the main frames of the computers at Duke, UNC, and NC State in the early days looked a lot like a triangle. Today, of course there are many other communities in the Triangle such as Cary, Wake Forest, Hillsborough, and many more. To find a home sitting in the middle of several acres required you to venture away from the heart of the major cities and explore the countryside.

After looking at a number of prospective listings, we arrived at a home on five acres, several miles south of the town of Apex. The house was sitting fairly far off the road and appeared to have a riding rink of some sort in the front yard. The house was kind of plain looking but the setting was nice. Once inside we toured the first floor and ended up in the master bedroom on the second floor. A balcony off the master bedroom overlooked a fabulous pool and an expansive back yard.

The owners were out of town but had left the responsibility of house-sitting to a young couple who acted as our tour guides. After admiring the beautiful pool I noticed what appeared to be a large fenced enclosure all the way at the back of the property. I asked the couple what was back there and they asked us if we had a few extra minutes to go back there. My clients nodded that it was OK, so off we went.

When we got closer, we could see that the fenced area actually had two ten-foot high heavy duty chain linked fences surrounding the area, one fence being three feet outside of the other one. I could not imagine what required such a high degree of security. Inside of the fences was the biggest dog house I had ever seen. In the play yard just beyond the doghouse was a bowling ball and a railroad tie. Our guide picked up a garden hose and said, "Watch this."

Out popped the biggest male lion I had ever seen. At least he looked like the biggest because he was ten feet away from me. Luckily, between the lion and me were two rows of strong looking fence. The young man continued to spray the lion until he stood on his hind legs, at which point I slowly started to back up. After being assured it was safe, I stuck around for the show. The lion started to roar. Our guide said, "Does that roar sound familiar?" Then he informed us the animal was a show lion, and his roar was used for the character Chewbacca in the first Star Wars movie. The three of us said things like "thanks" and "bye" as we headed for the car, being grateful not to have been dinner for Chewbacca. By the way, we were told that the bowling ball and the railroad tie were simply the lion's toys. Who said showing houses was not full of surprises?

———

Despite all of the animal stories that could be told, people cause more problems than dogs, cats, or snakes ever could. The worst closing I ever had lasted over five hours. Luckily, it had been scheduled for the late afternoon in the conference room at our office. After months of showings and deliberations, we were finally at the closing table. The trailing spouse, man or woman, is usually the problem when doubt creeps into the equation. Just like the wife who refused to drive by a cow, I had one wife decide that she did not like the pine trees in the South. Her real motive was not to have to give up her handy beach house at the Jersey shore. The primary spouse is usually more interested in getting on with the new job than they are with house details. Many trailing spouses have greatly altered their partner's careers by being inflexible.

There we all sat around the closing table. I represented the buyer and they had chosen a lawyer that I had never met before, or heard of, for that matter. The seller's agent was present, but not the seller. That turned out to be a good thing. Everything was going just fine until it was time to sign the note and deed of trust. The wife balked, and said that she was not going to sign. She said that her husband and I had picked out this house and she did not want it. The truth was that she had chosen this particular house from dozens of similar houses I had shown them. The bottom line was she wanted to move back to the northeast. I still do not know why. The husband and wife started a multi-hour argument about the house. Sometimes they argued in front of everyone and sometimes the rest of us excused ourselves. Their teenage kids were present and at one point they were forced to take sides. They wanted the house.

The attorney's husband was a psychiatrist, and at one point she stepped out and called him for advice. The husband was adamant about purchasing the property. I have witnessed both buyers or both sellers want to back out at the closing table. Usually those situations work themselves out as long as a little money changes hands. This case was a real mess. What finally solved the delay was a threat by the seller to sue for non-performance. The husband also promised to put the house back on the market in six months if she was not happy there. Needless to say, I did not get, nor did I want, that listing.

⬤

The most gratifying closing I ever had involved an elderly widow. She had inherited a piece of junk from her parents. The old sayings about, "to each his own" and "everyone's home is their castle", certainly applied in this case. I don't even remember why she called me to list the property. The house had been empty since the recent death of her parents. She did not live there because she was renting a little place on the edge of town. Getting comps for this piece of property was difficult because it was located in an old residential area on the east side of town where it faced a busy road. There was no potential for selling the property for commercial use since the zoning was all residential for blocks around. The only prospects available to us would be slumlords that were scooping up property at ridiculously low prices.

I listed the property in the mid to upper thirties. After doing all of the real estate commission math, my share was only going to be in the hundreds of dollars at best case scenario. Dad always taught me that the customer came first, so I felt this little old lady deserved the same service that Bill and Betty had gotten. A number of agents back at the office wondered why I even took the listing. I told them that if they had to ask the question, they would not understand the answer.

In its day, early 20th century, it was a nice house in a nice neighborhood. All of those factors had declined over the years and now it was a piece of junk. But it was the only junk she had and she attached a great deal of sentimental value to the property. Early in the listing period there were a few showings but nothing more than you would expect. My client did not understand the pace of real estate. All she wanted was her cash to live on. I decided to become proactive. I shopped the house to several agents I knew that worked with investors. I got a bite. The investor making us an offer had a reputation for not always performing in a timely manner. He had offered a cash sale for around thirty thousand dollars with a fairly short closing. I encouraged her to take it because I felt it was the best we were going to do.

Since it was a cash sale, I added one caveat to the contract. For every day the closing was delayed, I got the buyer to agree to pay the seller two hundred dollars. When it came time to close the buyer was unavailable. I approached his agent and he laughed at the penalty clause, saying I would not dare enforce it. Four days later, we met at the attorney's office and the buyer presented his check. The eight hundred dollars was not included. I told them to produce the other eight hundred dollars or we would walk away from the deal. I may have discussed other potential consequences. After a little deliberation with his agent, the buyer added the extra eight hundred dollars. I have never had a more satisfied or happier client. It was not much money but it was more than she had. I added up the number of hours I spent on this deal and divided them into my commission. I made less than four dollars an hour, but the look on her face was priceless.

⟞⟝

Durham's cultural make-up makes it an interesting city. No ethnic group has a majority of the population. Any time I am given a referral by an individual or a corporate group, the first thing I do is call them at their home and find out what they would be looking for when they came here for an exploratory visit. I always love it when I find out they have never been here before. That gives me the opportunity to have clients with an open mind. People are strange. They usually listen to everyone's opinion about an area except the experts'. This particular doctor, I was told, was world renowned, and he was coming to work for my biggest corporate client. I was eager to please.

During my interview phone call, I learned that their plan was to sell their highly marketable high-rise condo in the big city, to keep their beach property, and to invest most of their condo earnings in the stock market. This left what they called a modest housing budget. I called it a very nice housing budget. Our prices around here are higher than the rest of the South and the Midwest, but we always look cheap to folks from the Northeast and the West Coast.

I never try to guess a client's race over the phone. First of all, I do not care and secondly, I am often wrong when I do guess. After informing my new clients that I considered their budget to be "high end", I asked her what they liked to do for their personal entertainment. She said her husband was an avid golfer. I told her there was an ample supply of houses available here in golf course communities. She indicated that she did not want to be on a golf course, and that they only wanted to look at new housing.

Then she said something which I found most interesting. She said they were both interested in pursuing black history studies. I quickly told her they were coming to the right place. I described some of the opportunities for black studies available in Durham. She seemed pleased and excited with the potential. Then she said that they appreciated my suggesting such a great variety of neighborhoods, but they also wanted to look at high-end all black neighborhoods. I told her we did not have any high-end all black neighborhoods.

The next sound I heard from her was a low-keyed, disappointing "Oh." It took a few seconds for me to realize that she had misunderstood what I had meant. In as cheerful a voice as I could muster, I explained to her that this was the South and we had solved those issues years ago. I told her that in Durham, you lived where you could afford to live, and joined whatever church and country club you desired. I had forgotten that the big cities might not be as progressive as they think they are.

Probably half of the clients with whom you work, end up buying the opposite style house from the one they originally describe to you. For several days I showed them new houses and none of them seemed to suit. After the first day of riding them around and listening carefully to what they had to say, I did a little more research. I came up with what I thought would be the perfect house for them. It was older than what they wanted, and it was on a golf course. On the second day I could not get them interested in viewing my new selection. By the third day, he finally said that he wanted to at least look at the house on the golf course.

It was a large, beautiful house on a lake as well as a golf course. I figured that I had struck out with this house since he did not spend more than five minutes looking inside the property. She toured the house for at least a half an hour. When she started her second trip around the inside of the house, I felt it was time to find out where he had gone. Just off one of the several decks was a tee box. He was standing there watching each group of golfers tee off over the lake. That is when I knew he was going to buy the house.

I suggested that we ride around to the clubhouse and check on the availability of memberships. She wondered out loud if they would be welcomed there. I chuckled inside and took them over to the club. When we entered the business office of the club, I introduced them to the lady in charge as potential members. The manager jumped up, gave each of them a hug, and took them on a tour. Welcome to the South.

<hr />

Sometimes the problem with spouses is just a lack of communication. I have a good friend who has bought several properties through me. For several years he had been looking for the perfect large tract on which to build a retirement home. His other requirement was that the property be suitable for development by his heirs. Having located what seemed like the perfect piece of property, we proceeded with writing an offer and getting it accepted. Part of the terms of the deal included a $500 option fee, paid to the seller, for the buyer to have the right to do his due diligence on the property. Once we worked out the final numbers, the seller took the papers home and secured his wife's signatures in all of the appropriate places. The next morning he met the buyer and me to present the signed offer, at which point we handed him the $500 option fee check. If at the end of the 90 day due diligence period everything met the satisfaction of the buyer, then we would proceed to closing. If there was a problem, then the buyer had the right to withdraw from the offer and get his earnest money deposit back. In either case, the seller kept the option fee.

This was truly one of the most beautiful pieces of property I had ever seen. I was crushed when the buyer told me that the environmental engineers had found soil contamination on the property. Regretfully, my buyer withdrew from the deal. About two months later my buyer called me and said that he had drawn up a new proposal for the property and needed me to present it to the sellers. This time the offer contained a 90-day remediation period during which the environmental engineers would clean up the contaminated soil. The cost was to be split 50/50 between the buyer and the seller. The seller's part of the cost was to be deducted from the previously agreed upon sale price. Furthermore, there would be a cap on how much the seller had to pay. This all sounded reasonable to me and I was convinced that I could get the sellers to accept this proposal.

Armed with the new offer and the check for the new $500 option fee, I scheduled an appointment with the sellers at their house located on the property. It was shortly after the evening meal, and we all sat around the kitchen table. When you have presented as many deals as I have over the years you can sense when you think you are winning. I was sure I had them ready to accept the offer. Then I pulled out the $500 option fee check and said, "Here is the $500 option fee check for you to keep, just like the last one." The wife hesitated a moment and said, "What last check?" At that point I knew there was trouble in River City, as the saying goes. It seems he had bought a camper for the back of his truck, or something to that effect, with the first option fee check and never mentioned it to her. Forget about the environmental engineers, this deal blew up on social issues.

⊸⊸⊸

Sometimes you cannot trust your own clients to tell you the entire truth. One client with whom I had worked on several occasions asked me to list his house. It was a nice piece of property in a marketable price range located in a rural subdivision. The seller prepped the house for sale by doing all of the things that I suggested he do. There was no reason to think anything was wrong. In the 1990's, neither our listing agreements nor our list of questions for sellers were as personal or invasive as they are now. After a few weeks on the market, we received an acceptable offer.

The closing process was going to take about six weeks. With about two weeks left until the closing date the seller called me one morning to tell me he had filed for bankruptcy. I said, "You did what?" I asked him why he did not wait two more weeks until the house was closed.

He said a friend told him he thought it would be a good idea to go on and do it, so he did. The only good news to come out of this story was that the buyers were not pressed for time. It took an additional nine weeks for the court appointed bankruptcy trustee to release the house for the closing.

Some clients are not clients at all, but professional lookers. When you are trying to build a client base in a new city, you tend to ignore this fact quite often. I was starting to come to that conclusion with one particular lady. Besides the obvious clue of looking for houses over far too long a period of time, there were some other hints. One being, the husband rarely came along, and when he did, he would quickly veto the suggested house. She did, however, unknowingly do me one favor.

When you have been in the housing business as long as I have, all of the houses start to look alike. I am convinced that there are just seven house plans in the whole country and every house is a version of one of them. Most lookers want you to leave them alone but be available to answer questions. Professional lookers just want you to open the front door. One of my favorite things to do while clients are looking at a house is to study the homeowner's collection of photos and memorabilia. Since I had already decided that this was the last Saturday afternoon that I was going to devote to this particular professional looker, I told her to look around all she wanted. I headed for the recreation room where most of the family photos are usually displayed. This was a large, beautiful house on several acres, but it was the pictures on the wall that started to intrigue me.

Most folks hang their diploma on the wall somewhere and this guy was no exception. After reading that document, I had established that his name was John. As I walked into the recreation room, the first photo to catch my eye was one of The Duke, John Wayne. Since he is still enjoying the number one ranking on my movie heroes list, I went right up to the photo. To my surprise there was a personal note to John and it was signed by The Duke himself. I found similar photos with personal notes signed by Charlton Heston, Ronald Reagan, and many others. I was definitely wondering who this guy was?

On the far wall was an extra large framed photo of Marine One with President Reagan and Nancy climbing down from the famous helicopter.

I will always remember the note: "Thanks for eight great years!" It was signed by Ron and Nancy. I glanced out of the upstairs window of the recreation room and saw that the owner was in the driveway washing his car. I did remember to tell my professional looker that I would meet her outside if she had any questions. I got to spend a few minutes with the pilot of Marine One that flew the Reagan's around for eight years. Sometimes this business has special and unpredictable rewards.

⚍〜⚎

Often, the problems in real estate are not caused by animals, buyers, or sellers. They are caused by the other real estate agents. Early in my Durham real estate career, before the appointment center was established, agents had to personally call the listing company to schedule their showings. Agents were to assume when they gave you a lock box combination, that it would be all right to proceed with the showing. Normally if a house was occupied, the agent at the listing company would set the appointment and call you back. For three consecutive Saturdays I had different clients that wanted to look at the same home in one of Durham's finest neighborhoods. At two o'clock on the first Saturday I pulled into the circle driveway. Before I get the key out of the lock box of any house, I ring the doorbell to see if anyone is inside, even if I think the house is empty. Remember the house with the naked lady in the closet?

To my surprise, someone answered the door and asked who I was. I told them I had an appointment to show the house at two o'clock. They explained to me that no one from the listing company's office had called them. They wanted us to wait about five minutes so they could gather up everyone and leave. We waited. One week later I had another two o'clock appointment, or so I thought, to show the same property. This time when the owners answered the door, they said that I looked familiar. Once again no appointment had been conveyed to the sellers. And once again we waited in the car until all of the occupants had left.

Finally, when week three rolled around, I approached the front door with uncertainty, even though I was positive I had scheduled the showing correctly. Once again one of the owners opened the door and said, "Oh, it's you again." The wife hollered into the den that the same agent was here again. The husband responded by saying it was OK to let us in. She said they were not going to bother to leave this time. As we circled through the den, there sat the husband in his boxer shorts watching a football game. Needless to say, we did not linger. The agent in this case had really dropped the ball.

Sometimes agents are not as smart as they think they are. One of the most successful agents in Durham once sent out a flyer promoting one of his listings. He listed all of the wonderful features of the house. My favorite item was his description of the dining room's Wayne's Coating. For those of you who did not laugh, the term is wainscoting. I still use that flyer in my Continuing Education classes as a reference for being sure that you know your terms in developing marketing materials.

One of the houses I showed Bill and Betty that first year was in Chapel Hill. It was an expensive house which required that the listing agent had to be there for showings. I hate it when agents say that. I put on a fake smile and met the agent at the door. She took us around and carefully pointed out which room was a bathroom and which room was the kitchen. Bill and Betty would look at me with an expression that said they were smart enough to tell which room was the kitchen and which the bath. When we went into the equipment room the listing agent proudly pointed out the large gas water heater. I looked at the water heater and then I glanced at Bill. His face had a look of disbelief. I could instantly tell that Bill knew the difference between a gas water heater and an electric water heater. I calmly told the agent that the water heater was not operated by gas, because there was no flue running from the top of the unit to the outside. The embarrassed agent decided it was time to move on to the next room.

I do not think Bill and Betty would have bought the house even if they had liked it because they no longer judged the listing agent to be competent. Just as in the case of the reference to the Wayne's Coating, once the client thinks they are more knowledgeable than the agent, the agent does not stand a chance of being successful.

The majority of the time, everything eventually works out in a real estate deal. If it were not for the things that do not go well, I would not have anything to write about. The one group that we can count on consistently to screw something up is, of course, the government. My first experience with how local governments tended to ruin things goes back to our first house. Toots the bootlegger had sold the house to the local golf pro, who lived there for several decades. When the house was constructed in 1928 there was no golf course. The original nine holes of the course were built as a WPA project during the Great Depression. Years later, when the back nine was constructed, the house found itself adjacent to the sixteenth green. It was probably the only house on the course in the beginning. I certainly do not know of an older one in the vicinity. The house originally had a well which was located in the cellar. It was another place where old Toots stored his product.

It must have been some kind of civic miracle that just about the time the back nine of the golf course was built and a water system installed, this house ended up attached to the water line for the sixteenth green. Our water pressure was just fine except when the golf course superintendent decided to water the sixteenth green. The shower would go from a healthy spray to a slow drip. Many times I was forced to put on a bathrobe while I was dripping wet and walk over to the green to cut off their sprinkler. Often, this was at night, especially in the summer when it would be too hot to water the greens in the daylight.

I was always a little bit curious about the fact that our water bill was always the same, no matter how much water we used. Our City owned the utility department so we were buying water from them. They also owned the local golf course. There were plans in the works by some local developers to build a large subdivision just down the road from our house. The developers wanted their new land annexed into the city so the city could provide water and sewer. The proposed water line to supply the neighborhood was to pass right in front of our house. The sewer was to come from a different direction since it was solely based on gravity flow. I saw this event as my liberation from the slow drip shower experience.

The only catch was that my house was not in the city limits. After doing some research I discovered that in the past, the city had furnished water to houses that were not in the city limits. For these select few houses the monthly minimum charge was double the standard monthly minimum charge for an inside the city residence. I also discovered that we had always been charged the minimum inside the city rate because that is what the local golf pro had been paying. After all, he was a City employee.

We petitioned the City to be annexed. The City denied our request, and instead of annexing us, they sent us a large bill for an unusually high water usage for one month. I was not happy. After doing a little math, I realized the bill amounted to the difference between the inside the city rate and the out of the city rate times the number of months we had lived in the house. I demanded that they come read my meter because I had no idea where it was located. I waited for the meter reader to show up one morning and when he arrived, he could not find the meter either. After a quick call from his truck's two-way radio, he paced off some steps and looked some more. Following another call back to his office, he got out a shovel and started to dig. Three feet further toward the core of the earth, he struck a water meter. It took considerable digging to clean out around the meter so that it could be removed. It was obvious that this meter had not been read since it had been installed decades earlier. Once he pulled it out of the ground we could see that the glass cover was broken and the needle indicators were also missing. The meter reader took a new meter from his truck and installed it. Then he looked at it and said that it showed I owed every penny. I was not born yesterday!

Dad told me that you could not fight City Hall, but I thought it was time to start practicing. After enough trips uptown to complain about the sham, they agreed to cut my trumped up charge in half. I paid the balance of the bill, but decided that it was time I started attending city council meetings on a regular basis. It is amazing what you can get accomplished when they know you are watching. Having attended all of those council meetings came in handy a few years later when it was time to build the addition to our house. The new wing I described in an earlier chapter needed to be built where the septic tank was located. I needed city sewer. For that to happen, I needed to be annexed into the city. Luckily for me, the golf pro who had left town when he sold me the house, had decided to move back. He owned the land next to mine and wanted to build a new house. I made sure they did not extend any favors to him that they were not willing to extend to me. We both got new water lines with excellent water pressure and sewer hookups.

⟞⟋⟍⟍⟋⟍⟞

When Dad died in 1990, his estate included an old service station. Do you remember the house on Main Street where Mom slid down the stair rail as a child? After Dad bought the property for the purpose of using the handrail for the foyer staircase, he tore the house down. He leased the property to a major oil company so they could build a service station. It was on the opposite corner from where Dad and his buddies solved the world's problems on Sunday afternoons. Eventually there turned out to be a station on all four of those corners. When the lease expired, the oil company moved on to greener pastures, and Dad leased the building they left behind to a cab company.

By the time the estate got the property, the only activity on the site was the growing of weeds behind the old service station building. As vacant land the property was appraised at fifty thousand dollars. This was not as much as it should have been worth, had it contained a thriving business, but it was more than we had. The environmental movement had taken control of all of the rules that governed sites that contained current under-ground oil tanks, as well as any former sites. We were not allowed to sell the property, or do anything else with it for that matter, without the approval of the EPA.

The first order of business was to have the property tested so that the EPA could give the property a numerical ranking from one to ten. A high number meant you must immediately remediate the soil and a low rank meant action was not necessarily required. Of course the property owner was required to hire an EPA certified firm to do the original testing at the property owner's expense. The testing firm found only minor evidence of any problem from the soil on the property itself. In fact they required us to repeat the test several times just to get those results. They did however drill test holes in the middle of the intersection and determined that there was a leak somewhere. Since we were the only one of the four corners being tested at the time, the EPA decided that we must be to blame. We received a ten.

Once you receive a ten, you are required to remediate the soil. Each state has a Super Fund for such problems, but the Catch 22 was that you did not qualify for the Super Fund until you had spent fifty thousand dollars trying to remediate the problem. Of course, you had to use an EPA approved contractor to do the work. I am quite sure that each of these firms contributed mightily to the re-election campaigns of their local Congressmen. Each phase of the soil work would cost approximately ten thousand dollars. At the conclusion of each phase would be a new round of tests. We were still a ten.

Once we finally reached the magic number of $50,000 in expenditures, we carefully applied to the Super Fund by documenting all of our expenses. They accepted our report and the State of North Carolina took over the remediation process. The first thing they did was re-classify the property, giving it a number two ranking. They said it did not need any more work. We sold the property for fifty thousand dollars. So much for inheriting that corner! You will have to forgive me if I seem a little skeptical of some of the environmental movement's intentions.

I sold an historic old house to a young doctor who was doing her residency at Duke. There was a vacant lot next door that she could have purchased, but chose not to. All she was looking for was a place to live while doing her medical studies. When her work was nearly done, she called me to come out and list the property for sale. The marketing process proceeded normally and, not surprisingly, another agent brought us an offer from an incoming medical resident.

The day before the closing was to occur, the buyer's lawyer called me and said there was a problem with the property taxes. While verifying the payoffs on the property, the local tax office had decided that thousands of dollars in property taxes were due. I knew this could not be correct because the mortgage my client had obtained required her to make tax escrow payments as part of her monthly mortgage installment. I verified with my client that her payment structure had not changed since she had been living in the house, so I knew the money had to be somewhere.

After a week of delays and investigation, the lawyer and I discovered what had happened. When my client bought the property, the tax office mistakenly wrote down the number of the vacant lot next door as her residence. The assessor rode out to check the house and found only a vacant lot. The tax office, for four years, had billed the company managing the escrow account for only an amount of taxes to cover a vacant lot. Having discovered their mistake when the lawyer checked for tax payoffs, the county wanted their back taxes. I questioned the county's right to go back against an individual for the county's mistake. The county claimed the law gave them the right to correct their mistakes as far back as six years. Luckily for my client, all of the extra escrow money was sitting in her escrow account. No one had ever wondered why the account contained such a large amount. I still do not think they figured it correctly because when the taxes got paid, she left with a pretty fat check. All is well that ends well.

I had always thought the escrow management business was run well until stories like this next one started to happen. We were part owners of a small investment company that owned a few rental properties. As typically happens, the loans on the property were sold to a new lender and the escrow accounts were taken over by another large national escrow management company. The first of the following year we received a notice from the county tax department that the taxes had not been paid on one of our units. After weeks of investigations and dozens of phone calls and trips to the tax office, it boiled down to the escrow company simply mixing up their account numbers with the wrong mortgages.

Of course the county would not use the overpayment on one account to pay what was owed on the other. I asked the county to just write a check back to the escrow company for the overage on the one account, so the escrow company could send the county what was owed on the other account. That turned out to be way too simple a request. The county tax folks finally explained to me that that the escrow company alone had made over seventy-eight thousand dollars worth of mistakes just in our county that one month. They would not write an individual check to clear up just one account. Eventually it all got straightened out, but I cringe at the thought of how the whole system operates.

I do not know what the future holds for the real estate business. My crystal ball is broken. The industry is under attack politically, but that is nothing new. Housing has always been the bull in the china shop as far as the national economy is concerned, and it has been able to take care of itself. The key to real estate in the past has been that home values have always increased as long as you took proper care of your property. A prolonged recession is the only thing that can interfere with the confidence of the American people to pursue their dream of home ownership.

Technology has been both a help and a hindrance. Today's younger generations especially, seem eager to Tweet and Twitter every movement made during the house selling process. There are many things that are better left unsaid. Personal safety becomes an issue when you talk about your every movement on the Internet and post pictures of your possessions on You Tube. Technology may be able to streamline and facilitate how customers gain knowledge about property, but it cannot take the place of professional and experienced guidance that gets the buyer and seller to a satisfactory closing.

The real estate industry has always spawned cottage industries. Not that issues such as radon gas and mold are not important to discover, but companies that test and remediate these issues have sprung up faster than taco stands. Not every area has the same degree of problems with these maladies, but the possibility of them being in your house is spread through scare tactics. I always wondered how the world grew to over six billion people before they discovered that your house may have mold. The newest craze is that everything must be green. I believe in protecting the environment, but part of our problem is who is protecting us from the environmentalists. I was in a new green certified house recently, and they bragged about how they used the new two-button style commode. Push button one if you did the old number one and push button two if you did a number two. It reminded me of my kindergarten teacher. Most of these things just add to the cost of a house, costs that will never be recouped and will ultimately do little for the environment. Adding to the cost of houses does a lot to slow down the housing industry and makes it increasingly more difficult for the industry as a whole to survive. I do not think the folks who sat on the corner on Main Street on Sunday afternoons in my hometown solving the world's problems, are one bit safer from oil pollution now than they once were; but I know a group of folks that have made a lot of money without evaluating whether they have made any difference in the environment—and I wonder where my fifty thousand dollars went.

≋ 16 ≋

LEAVING A MARK

I really do love trees. I loved placing a house where we could take advantage of a special tree or grouping of trees. When I built our house in the country, we had a winding driveway because I wanted to disturb as few trees as possible. On the other hand, there is nothing quite like cutting down a large tree and hearing that unforgettable thud it makes when it crashes to the ground. Trees are a wonderfully diverse commodity. The things we can make out of wood are endless. We plant more trees each year in this country than we cut down. They are probably our most renewable resource. That is why I do not get all bent out of shape when I get a thrill out of cutting one down. But there was one tree.

During all of those years we lived in Toots' old house, I would ride by this one spectacular tree every day as I went to work, or just rode into town, for that matter. It was the largest, most beautifully shaped tree in town. Eventually, as I rode by that tree, I made a promise to myself that some day I would own that tree.

Timing has a way of affecting just about everything we do. I used to think that timing set off a chain of events. Now I understand that an entirely new set of timing events can alter the path taken by a previous set of events. We will discuss this some more later, but I want to get back to my favorite tree.

Things were going well in business and I was getting an itch that I needed to scratch. I wanted to do a big project of some kind. I wanted to leave a mark. We were in our mid thirties and our youngest of four children was around five years old. With no more babies to be raised, we wanted to set our sights forward. Our good friends with the Williamsburg chimney had invited us to their mountain house for the weekend. It turned into one of those brainstorming weekends. They had the same itch.

Here is where the timing kicked in. My favorite tree was for sale. Attached to the tree was an historic old house and about 20 acres of property with commercial potential, facing one of the two main thoroughfares in our town. We decided that we needed to do some research on the property to figure out how we could both develop it and preserve the history of the property.

After the weekend was over, the research began. We learned that the historic old house, known as the Eanes house, was possibly one of the three oldest houses left standing in our town. One of the other two oldest houses was Woodrow's stately mansion on Main Street. It was thought by many to be the oldest remaining house, but the records were unclear, thanks to a fire that had destroyed the original court house over a hundred years earlier.

The third of the three oldest houses was the Craven house located one block off of Main Street, next to the First Presbyterian Church. As timing would have it, the church was undertaking a building campaign and the Craven house was in the way. After some late night discussions, the four of us decided that it would be neat if we saved the Craven house from a certain terrible fate by moving it to the Eanes property. We immediately came up with the idea of moving other old buildings to the site and forming a shopping village.

As the resident designer of the group, I was called upon to create some quick sketches of the property showing our proposed little village, complete with parking lots. The sketches just made us more eager to continue. First we tried to estimate the proposed cost of the project. Next, we determined how many square feet of rental space we needed in order to provide enough income to make the payments. With those numbers in hand, we immediately realized that we needed a bigger boat, as they say. Timing was going to be critical. The church was ready to demolish the Craven house. The Eanes house was still on the for sale market and we did not want to chance losing it. We needed at least two more investors with deeper pockets than ours, and we needed a loan. Those were busy days but we got all of those goals accomplished.

—◁▦◁◟◞▦▷—

Our first objective was to move the Craven house so that the church could proceed with their expansion. The church agreed to donate the Craven house to us if we could move it quickly. After interviewing three moving companies and getting bids, we chose our house-moving contractor. That is when I found out that getting a moving company was the easy part. The journey from its present location to the Eanes property covered a little more than a mile, if you took the short cut. The short cut involved crossing Main Street, going next to the town's largest industry, crossing the main line of the Southern Railway at a grade crossing where there was no road, and passing an elementary school. All of this needed to be done in the middle of a workday.

The Craven house was a large two and one-half story house with high ceilings and two central masonry chimneys. The moving company told us that the two chimneys weighed more than the rest of the house, so they had to go. We carefully measured the width and height of the house to determine if we had room to use the route that we needed to take. There were a number of overhead power lines that would need to be temporarily removed as the house went by. Since the City owned the local utility company, I had to first sell the city fathers on our project. They were surprisingly enthusiastic at City Hall. Their cooperation helped us co-ordinate the entire event. I do remember having only six inches of clearance between two very permanent looking power poles located on either side of the street in the first block of the journey. I hoped that this spot would not give us trouble.

We had received some good publicity in the local newspaper leading up to the big moving day. There was a parade like atmosphere. Many groups of school children took field trips up town to witness the event.

I had been both fascinated and puzzled by the design of the Craven house. It had appeared to have two fronts. The back of the house was as eloquently designed as the front, yet the back did not face anything but a simple back yard. This mystery would soon be resolved. Our most prominent spectator that day was my old friend Woodrow. He stood proudly on the corner of Third and Main on the front lawn of the old Post Office building. As the house came up the street Woodrow told me that it was the second time he had watched the same house go up Third Avenue.

That is when we learned that the Craven house, like Woodrow's house, had been part of a long line of antebellum mansions lining that side of Main Street in the early years. Woodrow explained that when he was little he watched teams of mules pull the Craven house by rolling it over logs. It was moved from its original location on Main Street to make room for the Post Office. It stood for many years just a block away on Third Avenue, where all of us, who were younger than Woodrow, had always thought it had been originally built. Woodrow further explained that the house was pulled sideways off the lot on Main and down Third to its new resting place on the opposite side of the street. Thus the front of the house became the back. Mystery solved.

Everything went well for the first block. Then we came to the six-inch spread between the two power poles. As it turned out, I had only measured the space between the two poles near the bottom. They leaned toward each other at the top. As the house moved between them, it got stuck. Delays were not going to be our friends that day. We had to pass the furniture factory before the day shift ended. Furthermore, we had a specific time window to cross the railroad tracks before the 5:30 PM freight train was scheduled to come through. It had been hard enough to get permission to cross the tracks, but there was no way the railroad was going to stop the afternoon freight train.

After a frantic call from me, the City utility office quickly dispatched two boom trucks to the scene. The linemen in each bucket on top of the boom trucks lassoed the tops of the poles and started to pull them apart. The local superintendent for the utility company was kind enough to wait until after the house passed freely by to tell me how worried he had been that the two poles would snap. Our trials, however, were just beginning.

After crossing Main Street, it was a downhill run for a couple of blocks as we headed toward the largest of the local furniture factories. The power line that needed to be moved looked a little larger to me than the other ones that the utility folks were taking down and putting back up. As it turned out, the reason that line was so large in diameter was that it provided the main power feed to the factory. Despite one of our new partners being the son of one of the owners, we could not send a thousand people home from work early that day. So we sat there in the street, patiently waiting for the 4:30 whistle to blow. Our partner had secured permission for us to cut the power to the plant the moment the whistle finished blowing. That, unfortunately, was not the whistle I was worried about the most. It was the 5:30 whistle on the afternoon freight that was making me sweat.

While we waited for the furniture factory shift to end, a number of us went two blocks ahead to prepare the tracks for the all-important crossing. There was a bridge over the tracks a block to the north, but the state highway department would not give us permission to use it. I think they feared the weight of the house would bring it down. That would have been a big problem. The Southern Railway said we could cross their tracks on the condition that we did not physically touch them. This meant we had to lay a wooden road using crossties on both sides of the rails as well as in the middle, between the two rails. Once this step was completed, we went back to the house and awaited the 4:30 PM whistle.

When the last sound of the whistle finished, the utility crew had that line down in a record amount of time. The house immediately started moving toward the old railway station and our makeshift road. Just past the old station the house had to make a hard right turn and line up with our wooden pathway. This was harder to do than it looked. A 40 ton house does not turn on a dime, nor does it let you make adjustments back and forth. The moving company knew what they were doing and hit our wooden road dead center.

We started across the tracks about 5:15 PM which was a good hour behind schedule. What a difference there was between pulling the house on pavement and trying to pull it across wooden ties that were laid on the soft ground. The house started to shake and sway. All of a sudden, I was less concerned about the afternoon freight than I was about getting the house successfully across the railroad tracks. We were exactly half way across the tracks when my heart stopped. A train whistle blew. All I could think of was a Hollywood crew filming the freight train engine plowing through the middle of the Craven House. It would have been spectacular. The sound of the whistle made the moving crew step on the gas and the house lunged to the far side of the tracks. We were safe at last. I found out later that the whistle came from a switch engine moving some cars on to a siding about a half-mile to the south.

As we passed by the elementary school, we did pause and watch the afternoon freight train go by. Yep, that would have made a big mess. Even though school had been out for several hours by this time, the schoolyard was packed with kids watching the giant house creep by. Our destination was within sight. The house spent the night in the back parking lot of the drug store next to our property, before being placed on the site the next morning.

⊷ⅉⅉⅉↄ⊶

The Craven House was the biggest parcel we moved but it was not the only one to present a challenge. We combed the history books and the archives for records of old school buildings in our county. We found what we thought to be the oldest school but it was in no condition to travel. We spoke to the owners anyway about the property, and to our surprise, they had no idea of the significance of their inheritance.

We focused on the third oldest school building in the county, according to all of the records we researched. It was located about 26 miles south of the project on the far side of High Rock Lake. When we rode down to the site where it was suppose to be, it took several passes by the property before we spotted it. It was rather far off the road and it was almost completely hidden by weeds. With caution, we hacked our way through the jungle feeling a lot like Indiana Jones on a quest. Once we got to the school building we found it to be in surprisingly good condition. We also found it to be surprisingly large. The tin roof had protected it through the years, serving to preserve the structure's soundness well. But how do you move something that large, that far?

The answer was a chain saw. We literally cut it into four house trailer size pieces. We dismantled the roof structure and labeled the parts so we could easily reassemble the roof system on site. The moving company had no troubles hauling the remaining four sections, just like they were pulling a camping trailer. Once the four pieces arrived on our site, our second challenge arose. Since the school was the last of the big pieces to be moved, the movers were getting eager to go home. They claimed that there was no way to pull or back the pieces to their final resting spot atop the footing we had poured for the future foundation.

Setting up old houses on a new site was just the opposite process from building a new structure. Once the footings were poured, the next step was to drag the old structure over the footings and leave it propped up on railroad ties at a height just inches above the height of its future foundation. Laying the foundation was always a little tricky because the masons had to crawl under the house to build the interior support piers. Once the outside walls of the foundation were complete, the crew would ease the structure down to the foundation using huge hydraulic jacks.

There were several reasons we did not have enough room to pull the four pieces of the schoolhouse into place. One reason was the existence of a beautiful tree and hedge line that separated our property from the bank next door. The tree line was what distinguished our quaint old setting from the modern world that lay beyond. Another reason was the fact that we had already placed structures on both sides of the schoolhouse site. As a result, we parked the four parts of the school in the parking lot behind the bank, and I got on the phone. We needed to find a crane operator. We needed a crane big enough to lift each piece approximately 80 feet in the air, swing it over the tree line, and place it on a foundation. Since we were dropping (oh, I hope not) the pieces from above, we decided to build this foundation first.

The first crane operator met me at the site and immediately said we needed a bigger crane than his. That is what the second crane operator said, and the third. I was having visions of a late night bonfire in the back parking lot of the bank when the fourth crane operator looked at the project and said, "Piece of cake." Of all of the things we had to do to move the various buildings, watching the crane swing the school sections over the tree line was certainly the most amazing.

The smallest parcel we moved was an old log smoke house that sat behind an old tavern that dated back to the 1700's. George Washington had once spent the night at the tavern that was sitting on the banks of the Yadkin River at an old ferry-crossing site. For a few dollars we purchased the structure and hauled it to our site. Even though there were no remaining eyewitnesses, we had to assume that George Washington once ate meat that had been hung in the smokehouse. It sounded good, anyway.

Our project had some early success. Our U. S. Senator even showed up and gave a speech at the dedication. A restaurant, that was the main tenant in the Eanes house, had some early success too, but as often happens to restaurants, patronage waned. I was there one night in the restaurant dining room during a huge thunderstorm, staring out the front window at my favorite tree. God must have had a different opinion of my tree, because a large bolt of lightening struck the tree dead center. The shock of the sight almost knocked me down. It took about a year, but the grand old tree died. Eventually, so did our dream of an historic shopping village.

<hr>

Sometimes we think too big when it is the smaller marks that add up over time. I remember pulling through a drive up bank window one day. I handed the teller my deposit. After looking at the name, she said, "Are you the guy who tore down the old house on the 16th green and built a new one?" I simply nodded my head to indicate a yes. We had not torn down the old house. It was right there in the middle of all of the additions we had made to the original structure. My philosophy of adding on additions to a house has always been to make the addition look like it was part of the original structure. The bank teller had just verified my philosophical success as it applied to Toots's old house. I was smiling as I drove away.

Another small but memorable moment occurred while building the addition onto Amy's and Mark's house. The two rooms were under roof and the windows were in. It was time to cut the hole through their former exterior wall so the utility room would have access to the rest of the house. I said to her, "Here is where we find out if we measured right." What I did not tell her was that I was never totally confident that we had. Out came the trusty old chain saw and the cutting began. I had more than my professional reputation at stake this time; I had my family to impress. We were not off as much as an eighth of an inch. I was extremely proud.

There are some really beautiful houses scattered around central North Carolina that make up the many marks I have left behind. None of them would have been created had it not been for Dad making me recite the parts of a house before I went to bed at night or his making me spend endless hours learning to cross-hatch. They are also a result of folks like Slim and Artis and Peabody, and so many more. These guys were the true craftsmen that made it all happen. Sometimes I feel that I was just along for the ride, but it was a good ride.

The real marks I leave behind are the ones I created with my wife, Cathy. Our four wonderful children, that led to our ten super grand-children, are the finest marks anyone could leave. I can only imagine the marks they will make before they are through.

≋ 17 ≋

LOOKING BACK

Other than the lessons taught to you by your parents and those other folks who are in a position of influence, timing and events tend to shape the course of our lives. Given the way I was raised, I had always planned to go to NC State University to study architecture. State, at the time, did not require you to have any foreign language courses in high school, so I happily maintained that standard. I did take two years of Latin my freshman and sophomore years in high school because that is what everyone did who planned to go to college. I did not learn much Latin, and though I did not like the teacher very well she did like me. After my sophomore year, the teacher had planned a trip to the national Junior Classical League convention in Albuquerque, New Mexico. She wanted to take an exhibit to display at the convention. Since I was better at building things than I was at Latin, I volunteered.

Did I mention that I did not like the teacher that much? I built the most beautiful model Roman house she had ever seen. It had a center atrium that was open to the sky. The walls were built out of real concrete which made it look extra authentic. She gave me an A for the year. She was planning to take a bus all the way to Albuquerque. I knew that if the Roman house was to survive the vibrations of the trip, it would have to be extra strong and properly reinforced. It wasn't. I used a very weak mixture for concrete that had a high sand content. There were no reinforcing wires in the walls at all. When she got off of the bus in Albuquerque and opened up her travel box, there was nothing there but a pile of grey sand. Did I mention that I did not like the teacher much?

My senior year in high school brought a number of defining moments that made me want to go to Duke University and study something more philosophical than architecture. Luckily for me, Duke let me in despite the fact that I was one of only a handful of freshmen without their modern language requirement. I had evidently spent too much time building that Roman house. However, unluckily for me, Duke let me in without my modern language requirement. On my first day of French class the professor came into class and said something I could not understand. After asking the person sitting next to me what he said, I knew I was in trouble. He said, "Je ne parle que francais dans cette classe" (translation: I am only going to speak French in this class). Since everyone else in the class had taken at least two years of high school French, I felt any objections I had would have fallen on deaf ears. Life is, after all, full of challenges.

⚊⚍⚌⚍⚊

My French 1/French 2 professor was a nice man. Unfortunately, he felt sorry for me. He respected my futile efforts and passed me along to the next level. The professors for French 63 and French 64 actually expected me to learn enough French to pass the course. Passing the course also happened to be a requirement for graduation. I could read it. I could write it and I could speak it. I just could not hear it or understand the oral word. Unfortunately for me, all of the exams in French 63 and 64 were given orally. Today I think they would say I was language challenged.

While at home on Christmas break during my junior year, I had one of those all night jam sessions with Dad that started with "Son!" That beginning was a sure sign of trouble. Dad told me that he did not care what it took, how hard I had to work, or how much it would cost, but I was to hire a tutor and pass French. Upon arriving back at school after the holidays, I immediately discussed Dad's new mandate with my roommate, who like me, was also on the varsity tennis team. He told me that he had been dating a girl for a few weeks that was a French major. Since exams were only two weeks away, I asked him to see if she would help me. Later that afternoon, he told me that she would meet me in the library at eight o'clock that night at the table where I usually studied.

French was not the only thing on my mind that night. Immediately following exam week was fraternity rush week. This was a weeklong series of parties designed to impress unsuspecting freshman about the benefits of joining a fraternity. The best thing about rush week was that it was a chance to impress some unsuspecting young co-ed by asking her to be your date for the week. This was often done by bringing in a ringer from another campus.

Talking to Dad was not the only thing I had done over the holidays. I had also rekindled a relationship with two former girlfriends in an effort to decide which one I wanted to ask to come down for rush. On the way to the library that night I stopped in the student union to use the pay phone. I flipped a coin to see which one I would call first. When the decision was made, I rang the number for her dorm, only to find out that she had just left to go to the library. Since it literally was a toss up, I immediately dialed the other girl. I missed her by five minutes. I thought, oh well, I'll just head on over to the library and learn some French.

At eight o'clock, I looked up from my French book and walking toward me was a young co-ed named Cathy. After introductions, we headed over to the Divinity School next door where I knew some classrooms were left unlocked at night. After two hours of studying French, I suggested we head down to Maola's Bar and Grille to get something to eat. I desperately wanted to distract her from realizing just how bad I was at French. The dance floor was empty, and I had a quarter in my pocket. I suggested we dance. I punched the same song five times and my life changed forever. We now have four children and ten grandchildren.

⁓

I am satisfied that the timing of those two phone calls did more to shape my life than any other event, but there was a runner up. Twenty years ago I got a 24 hour bug one afternoon. It was the kind of bug you get that lets you know that sooner or later you are going to lose your cookies. Well, that happened in the middle of the night and the contents alarmed me. After an early morning call to my doctor describing what turned out to be dried blood, he met me at the hospital for some tests. As it turned out, I had a grapefruit size malignant tumor that was destined to rupture my stomach lining within a few days, usually resulting in instant death. The doctor assured me that the dried blood did not cause my twenty-four hour bug. It was just good luck and good timing that we found the tumor before it became an emergency.

To me, all other timing stories pale in comparison, but they were important to those people in the stories. I remember early in my career the insurance industry came out with a product called mortgage insurance. If either spouse died, the mortgage was paid in full. The savings and loans were selling these products to the new homeowners at the closing table. It sounded like a good product at the time. The first time I heard it presented to one of my clients, I really encouraged the couple to purchase the policy. They bought the insurance and the husband died two weeks later. She owned the house debt free, and I felt really good.

Early in the book I described unloading a truck full of concrete blocks by hand during one of my college summer experiences on the job. The house was being built for a member of the crew of the Enola Gay that dropped one of the atomic bombs on Japan. He seemed like a real nice guy. One day while we were building the house on a hilltop outside of Greensboro, the future owner came out and set up his skeet shooting equipment. He practiced for several hours. Of course I was curious about skeet shooting, and he offered to help me learn a few things about it. When we were through that afternoon, he gave me his skeet launching equipment. I did not know what to say but I accepted the gift. It brought me many hours of pleasure over the years. Approximately two months after we finished his house, he committed suicide. His friends said he never completely adjusted to dropping the bomb. I never hit a clay pigeon without thinking of him.

At one point in my career I had built ten rental units over a period of four years. There were three duplexes and one-four unit apartment building. After several years of managing the units, chasing the monthly rent, and mowing the grass, I decided that the effort was not worth the investment. I sold them all to a local doctor who was looking to enhance his investment portfolio. Six months later one of the kids in the four-unit building accidentally set the apartment on fire. The child lived but was horribly disfigured. Never had I been so glad not to own a piece of property, even though the owner at the time was not to blame at all.

One of the most enjoyable parts of the day on a construction site was lunch. The whole crew would sit around and eat whatever our wives had packed in our lunch bags. We would also solve all of the world's problems. We were in the process of building a house for some good friends, which was to be located on a several acre tract next to his brother's house. While we sat under a huge shade tree one day, we had a great view of the back of the brother's house. One of us noticed some smoke starting to billow out of the basement window. We knew that the occupants were gone for the day, and the only people that had a view of the back of the property were us. One of the crew members ran to a neighbor's house to call the fire department and the rest of us headed for the brother's house. Part of this story proves that things actually got done before the invention of the cell phone. Had we decided to eat lunch in any other location on the property, the six thousand square foot house next door would have burned to the ground. It turned out that the owner of the house had cleaned out what he thought to be cold ashes from his fireplace. He had put them in a cardboard box, of all things, and placed them next to the basement door. Time took care of the rest.

Not everything is based on timing. Some things I get to blame on Murphy's Law for the way they worked out. We brokered a tract of land for a Seller. While we were waiting for the contract to close, the Seller died. Then we had to wait for the will to be probated and the heirs to be established. Once that was completed we scheduled another closing. During that waiting period, one of the heirs died. Naturally it was the heir that was in charge of the estate. All six of the remaining heirs had been declared wards of the state, so getting it all sorted out took quite some time. Once that was finally completed, we set another closing date. During this period, the husband of the couple purchasing the property died. The wife indicated that she wanted to continue with the purchase once the estate was settled. I was not sure it would ever close, unless we sold it to Murphy himself.

⟨⟨⟩⟩

As I look back, there is a list of events that really shaped my life. One of the biggest was a trip a friend and I took across the country after high school. I had a 1958 Corvette, which I am still convinced was the greatest car ever built. One of the most popular shows on television back then was Route 66. I wanted desperately to make that trip, but I knew I had to be able to pay for it first.

During my senior year in high school I had taken on several industrious projects. One project involved spending months mapping out every building and house in our town for a senior project. This project had no chance of turning to dust like the Roman house did. In fact, I sold the maps all over town and even presented one to the city council, which they hung in the council room. I also strung tennis rackets, which was a good business in our tennis crazy town. I was saving this money for college and also for what I hoped would be a trip down Route 66.

To this day, I still cannot believe my Dad let me go. I know it was a more innocent time back then, but I really cannot believe we went. Dad had driven a group of friends to California in 1938 to see Duke play in the Rose Bowl. He said he drove all the way out and all the way back because he was the only one that did not drink. He wanted me to learn the things that he had learned, and to experience things that he had experienced. It was years later, after all of the excitement had worn off, when I actually realized just how much that experience helped me mature. He wanted me to be ready for my college days that were about to come. I remember him saying that it would be much easier to get to know the people you met in college, if you knew first hand something about where they came from. He was right, of course. As for the things that happened on the trip, they could become a future book.

Dad did not always make the right decision. On one of those Sunday afternoons when I was little and Dad was sitting with Woodrow, Charlie and another friend from Salisbury on the bench in front of Charlie's service station on Main Street, an opportunity presented itself to him. He was asked to be one of the original one hundred investors in the company that eventually became Food Lion. I do remember the whole family being somewhat amazed that he did not invest with his friend. He said that he did not know anything about the grocery business and wanted to spend whatever money he had on real estate. Those one hundred investors became fabulously wealthy, and I am stuck here writing a book!

———

Another thing Dad had always said was that once Carol and I finished college, he wanted to buy a beach house. I was not sure I believed him but I always kept that thought in the back of my mind. The beach was his favorite place, and he had taken us there for a week in June since we were little kids. One of my goals after getting married was to take our first trip to the beach as a couple. It happened that first spring, nine months after the wedding day. After work one Friday, Cathy and I headed to the coast. There was one particular motel where we had always dreamed of staying. It was going to be a great weekend. It was well after dark when we arrived to the beach area. While driving down what was then a two-lane road through the swamp between Cherry Grove Beach and Myrtle Beach, we had a flat tire. I was tired to begin with and when I finished fixing the flat, I was tired and dirty. Upon arriving at the motel of our dreams, the rude desk clerk treated us like runaway kids and said they were full.

We drove more than twenty miles back to Cherry Grove to stay in the place where the family had stayed every June. The next morning it was off to Charleston to further exercise our independence. After a terrific day we headed back to our motel. While slowly cruising up the beach front road in Ocean Drive Beach, we spotted a "For Sale" sign in front of a neat looking white house with pink trim. It surely looked like a great family beach house. The next morning we could not wait to eat breakfast and ride back to that beach house we had spotted the night before. We walked all around it since no one appeared to be there. Then we decided to call the agent and ask her some questions. Her name was Peggy and she was a hoot. Peggy insisted on showing us the property after I convinced her that we were looking for property for my Dad. It was the perfect beach house and came fully furnished.

When we got back to the motel, it was time to check out. But first I wanted to call Dad and tell him what we had seen. After I finished describing the property and the price, which even included owner financing, there was a period of silence. Cathy asked what was going on and I just shrugged my shoulders. Then I hung up the phone and told her that Mom and Dad would be arriving at the beach in four hours. It was a four-hour trip, and they arrived exactly four hours later. Mom later told me that when they pulled up to the house for the first time, Dad turned to her and said that they had just bought a beach house. Dad bought and sold a number of beach properties after that, but the Pink House was always a special place for the family. It became the family retreat. And I thought he was kidding about buying a beach house.

⁂

I cannot write this book without telling at least one tennis story. Few things influenced my life in a more positive way than tennis. There were many good times to be had playing the junior tennis circuit all over North and South Carolina. I still hold my varsity letter from Duke on the same level as my diploma. I made many friends over the years playing tennis. Some of them became friends because we got along so well, and some became friends because we started off as intense rivals.

One of my biggest rivals was a multi-star athlete named Jim from one of the neighboring towns. We played long, grueling matches against each other during high school. Some of these matches would end with rackets being thrown at each other and the Coaches saying, "Now boys!" Despite all of the rivalry, we became friends over the years.

While I was learning the building and real estate business, he was becoming a well-known athlete throughout the South. When I was about 30 years old, I was playing the best tennis of my career. Dad and I had built an indoor tennis center in our town. I taught tennis lessons there for several hours, four nights a week, just after work. Therefore I always had my tennis gear in the car. I was having a late lunch at the counter at Wayne's barbeque restaurant one day when Jim came in and sat next to me. He was an assistant football coach at the time at a major university and was also the reigning state men's singles champion in tennis. I told him about our new indoor tennis facility and asked him if he had his racket with him. He said, "Always." After finishing lunch we headed over to the indoor courts to play. It was empty that time of day and no one was due until my first lesson at five o'clock.

Once we warmed up, it was just as intense as the old days. By this ripe old age of 30, thank goodness, we were way too mature to throw any rackets. He won the first set in a struggle and I won the second. The third set seemed to go on forever with neither of us giving an inch or taking a break. It was a friendly test of wills. By the time I hit the last winner and took the third set, it was all I could do to stroll up to the net and shake his hand. I was desperately trying not to show how exhausted I really was. Jim shook hands saying he was late for an appointment. He left the court quickly and headed up the stairs to the lobby. The moment I heard the outside door slam shut I sat down on the court. I was so tired that I was not convinced that I would ever move again.

About 15 minutes later my three teenage pupils arrived for their lesson. After walking out on to the court, they immediately asked what was wrong with me. I told them I had just beaten the reigning state champion, and I was not sure that I would ever move again. One of the kids laughed and said that my exhausted condition probably explained why there was a guy lying on his back in the parking lot. I peeped out the door and there was Jim, staring at the sky. He had not been about to admit to me how tired he was also. It seems we had both given our all. The whole incident reminds me of the big house I negotiated for Bill and Betty. It was the largest deal I ever put together, and I did not get paid a dime. I had just played the best tennis of my entire life and no one saw it. At least for a few minutes, in my mind, I was state champ.

<hr />

When I look back over a long career, sometimes I just chuckle at the silly things. We had two dump trucks while we were building houses. I bought them from Dad when he retired from the construction business. One truck was red and the other was green. As soon as I bought them I had them painted Duke Blue. The steering wheels were still green and red respectively, and for the rest of my building career everyone on the crews referred to the two dark blue trucks as either the green truck or the red truck. We confused a lot of our clients.

I once had clients who wanted an old English design on the exterior of their house. They particularly wanted a mortar joint on the brick-work where the mortar appeared to ooze out, as opposed to being cut off cleanly. I did some research and could not come up with a proper name for the look they wanted. They had showed me a house in Winston-Salem that had the very look they wanted. After days of trying to explain the type of joint to the masons, I finally put one of them in my car and drove him by the house. He took one look at it and said, "Why didn't you tell me you wanted a slobber joint?"

There were other slang names that the guys in the crews used as their everyday language. Floor joist were called sleepers. The cornice at the bottom of the roofline was called the boxing. Boxing was a big deal with Dad. I rode with him to interview a new carpenter foreman who was interested in subcontracting the framing on some spec houses. As we walked on to the property where he was building a house, Dad took a close look at his boxing. He turned to me and said he had seen all he needed to know. The boxing was as straight as an arrow. That showed Dad that the man knew what he was doing.

This carpenter was limited to simple straightforward houses, however. Once, Artis made a fancy doorframe for the front door of one of his houses. The frame had fluted pilasters on each side of the door. These pilasters were supposed to sit on top of a chamfered flint block, which was to be the bottom piece of the doorframe. Instead of standing the flint blocks up like they were supposed to be, he had laid them down so the frame looked like a big shoe. We had to keep it simple after that.

⸺✦⸺

It is still the people I meet over the years that made my work inter-esting and worth while. Two comments have always stuck with me. One came from an old friend of Dad's who ran that best ever hardware store I mentioned earlier. I was in his store one holiday when there was just a skeleton staff working. I went up to Ardell, the owner, to ask where something was. Of course, he knew where every item in the store was located. Then I said, "Ardell, do you ever go home?" He looked up at me over his glasses and said, "I am home."

A similar incident happened with my old friend Lewis. He was the one who got me started in the Winston-Salem market. We were having lunch together one Saturday after spending several hours looking at potential lots on which I could build spec houses. During lunch, just out of curiosity, I looked at Lewis and asked him if he ever quit working. His reply was from the bottom of his heart. He said, "I love what I do and I don't feel like I have ever worked a day in my life." These types of dedicated men and women are hard to find anymore. The loss of these members of the Greatest Generation makes me really miss the old days.

A couple of other quotes that have stuck with me over the years involved politics. After the bout with City Hall over our water meter, I decided that I should at least get involved with what was going on at City Hall. For years, Dad had made a habit of attending the city council meetings. I started to tag along and found out that I really enjoyed them. There were nights when I was the only one in the audience. Interestingly, after several years of attending meetings, the council members actually asked my opinion on occasion. Eventually they appointed me to the Planning and Zoning Board where I served 11 years; the last seven as chairman. At one point along the way the Mayor of our town had to resign because his real job was moving him to Atlanta. I called him one night after I learned he was leaving to tell him how much everyone in town would miss him. He chuckled and said I was kind to say that but the truth was, as he put it, " Five per cent of the people will miss me, five per cent of the people will be glad to see me go, and 90 per cent of the people won't give a damn."

A couple of years later I decided to dabble in politics myself by running for city council against an incumbent that I thought could be beaten. As soon as I announced, I went by the local savings and loan where we did a lot of business. I wanted to talk with the man in charge who was a good friend. I had always respected his advice and considered him to be quite wise. I thought he would be pleased, but he looked at me and said, "Why did you do that? Now you have forced all of your friends to make a choice."

I learned more than that bit of wisdom with my short flirtation with politics. Being somewhat of an idealist at the time, I truly thought that some of the poor segments of the community would appreciate having a councilman that would treat everyone fairly. Not long after I announced I was running, some of the leaders of the black community came to visit me at the office. They immediately told me how many votes they could deliver, and how much it was going to cost me. They seemed shocked when I told them I was not going to buy any votes, but instead, I was going to be fair and represent everybody equally. They laughed and said it had always been done the other way, and if I did not pay them, I would not have a chance of winning. They were right. I lost after a third candidate appeared in the field right before the filing deadline. He mysteriously got all of their votes. I was out of politics forever.

When Dad first started in the business, he opened a draftsman's office on the second floor of one of the buildings downtown. Dad's big break came when one of his longtime friends, who had made that trip to California with him to see Duke play, hired Dad to build a new wing on his family's textile plant. Dad hired a carpenter crew, and Dad and the foreman of that crew became partners in the construction business for decades. Later in life, after the textile plants had all closed and Dad had retired from the building part of the business, Dad made room for his old friend at the real estate office. He was basically retired and did not do much, but it gave him a place to go, and a ton of respect. I always thought it was one of the neatest things Dad ever did.

I tried to follow that example on a number of occasions. Helping Ray buy his house was one example. Another young man who had worked for me during his high school summers, called me one day from jail. He was there for non-support. His life had turned south at the moment, but I knew his potential. I bailed him out of jail and gave him a job. He later went back to school and became a success. There were others, but the numbers do not matter. Helping folks when they are down can certainly be more rewarding than making a big sale.

Sometimes when you look back, you wonder how you survived. Cathy was a year behind me at Duke, but she took one set of summer school classes at Wake Forest and graduated in three years near the top of her class. Did I mention that she was smarter than me, too? That happened to be the summer I was assigned to the Greensboro crew. Remember the crew that left Slim up on the roof with the snake? The daily schedule involved meeting the crew at the shop at 6:30 in the morning and driving to Greensboro. After arriving back at the shop around 6:00 each evening, I would rush home to bathe and eat. Then it was off to Winston-Salem to see Cathy at Wake Forest. The 45 minute drive back home from Wake Forest around eleven o'clock at night was a torture. I cannot even guess how many times I ran off the road after falling asleep. It is amazing what young love will make you do.

⸻

The memory that probably best describes how our whole family navigated the building and real estate business together took place on an evening in May. Jeff was six years old, the girls were eight, ten and twelve, and it was dress rehearsal night for the annual ballet recital. I always claimed to have paid for more tutus than any man alive, since Cathy also danced as much as the three girls. Jeff and I had a lot of good "guy time" together, especially during the month of May. That night Jeff and I were headed to the courts where I was playing a tennis match.

Jeff and I had carefully stayed out of the way while the girls prepared for the big night by putting on their tutus and tights and coating their hair with some kind of gel. All six of us were gathered in the master bedroom and bath putting finishing touches on makeup and hair, changing clothes, and getting ready to leave the house. It was a really hot May day and the air-conditioning was working overtime. Right before we were ready to leave, the lights flickered, the air-conditioning stopped running and the lights went out. I asked Jeff to go check the electrical panel in the basement to see if the breaker had flipped. I would not have let him reset it, but I knew he knew what to look for. After all, he also grew up knowing the parts of a house. I will never forget his call from the basement door to tell us that the basement was on fire. Cathy and I looked at each other assuming he was exaggerating—he was six after all—and we decided I had better go check out what he saw. I walked to the basement door and looked in. To my horror, he was right. I called from the basement to Cathy to call the fire department. She shouted back: should I get the kids out of the house? I said yes, and she and the kids went out the front door to the front yard after calling the fire department.

Meanwhile, I was in the basement frantically searching for a flashlight. Unfortunately, it only enabled me to see the smoke better. For just such an occasion, I kept a new hose and spray nozzle already attached to a spigot in the basement. After cutting on the water and grabbing the nozzle, I pushed toward the far end of the workshop where the flames were fairly intense. I could see that the electrical panel was the source of the fire which meant that I could not throw water in that direction and chance a larger electrical fire or worse, electrocution. The flames were extending out about ten feet from the panel and heating up the bottom of the 50-plus year old floor joists that my Grandfather had carefully installed. I was determined to save the house, although, looking back, it seems like a very foolish idea. I concentrated the water on the floor joists in hope of keeping them from becoming kindling for a much bigger fire.

All of a sudden, I tripped over something in the dark. I dropped the flashlight and it broke upon impact. Panic was not all that far away because by this time I had no idea which way was out, and I was doubting my ability to stop the progression of the flames. Then I heard a sound far lovelier than any of the music scheduled for the ballet recital that night. I heard the sirens on the fire trucks speeding down our street. Moments later the firemen had set up smoke extraction devices, killed the power to the main panel from the outside, and escorted one frazzled, smoke-smudged Dad to fresh air and daylight. Later they told me that the main breaker on the outside panel had become loosened over time, arcing the full voltage from the street side power source into the panel and melting the main cable. They also said that this type of incident was the suspected cause of many house fires that totally destroyed houses because no one was home to call the fire department. We almost made that category of burned down houses.

There we were, standing in front of our beloved home. There were three young girls in full ballet dress, one little brother, a Mom and a smoke covered Dad, two fire trucks and several firemen. The only person missing was Norman Rockwell to paint this scene of Americana at its best. After all, the show must go on!! Since I was in the building business, I was able to call some of my crew and subcontractors for help, and we were back in the house by late the next day. Oh yes, the girls made it to the rehearsal and they performed beautifully in the next night's performance.

⚜

The journey through the building and real estate business has come with many ups and downs. One of my biggest regrets occurred before I actually got started in the business. It is amazing how good hindsight can be. While in college, I remember Mom and Dad coming down to Duke one beautiful sunny Saturday afternoon for a football game. They met me in front of Cathy's dorm. I could tell there was something on their minds as soon as they got out of the car. Mom said that Dad had something important to tell me. Dad was not a touchy feely kind of guy and emotional presentations were not his long suit. As a result, I was unable to grasp the importance of the moment. My mind was focusing on meeting Cathy and getting to the football game on time. I was always excited when Mom and Dad came to campus and joined us for a game. In other words, I was pumped up and did not see what was coming.

Dad told me that he had bought out his partner of 25 years that week. Now, he said, there was room for me in the family business if I wanted to come back and join him. I remember saying something like that was great, but we were going to be late for the football game. This was truly a life changing and career changing moment and I was too distracted to recognize it. If I could only get that moment in time back, I would give it the respect it deserved. As a parent, I now know how much that meant to him, and how long he had planned the moment. I simply blew it. Dan Fogleberg said it best in a song titled *The Leader of the Band*, when he says, "Papa I don't think I said I love you near enough."

The building and real estate business has an unlimited supply of funny stories and some not-so funny. Some of the stories fall on the bright side and some on the dark side. They all have one thing in common. The stories star men and women who use their talents, knowledge, muscles and sweat to build our houses. They also star the men and women who sell those houses while working strictly on commission, with no guarantees, in order to help all of us achieve that prized goal of home ownership. The stories also feature buyers and sellers who care about their homes, deal fairly with each other, nurture families and participate enthusiastically in the American Dreams of home ownership and building of community. Despite the economic conditions that are stressing housing in the second decade of the 21st century, I still believe that the long-term future of housing will be bright. In the meantime, I am glad my son went to law school.

Made in the USA
Charleston, SC
09 December 2011